Creating Poetry

Creating Poetry

JOHN DRURY

Cincinnati, Ohio

Creating Poetry. Copyright © 1991 by John Drury. Printed and bound in the United States of America. All rights reserved. No part of this book may be reproduced in any form or by any electronic or mechanical means including information storage and retrieval systems without permission in writing from the publisher, except by a reviewer, who may quote brief passages in a review. Published by Writer's Digest Books, an imprint of F&W Publications, Inc., 1507 Dana Avenue, Cincinnati, Ohio 45207. First edition.

95   94   93   5   4   3

Library of Congress Cataloging in Publication Data

Drury, John.
   Creating poetry / John Drury. — 1st ed.
         p.   cm.
   Includes bibliographical references and index.
   ISBN 0-89879-443-9
   1. Poetry—Authorship.   2. Poetics.   I. Title.
PN1059.A9D78   1991   90-48504
808.1 — dc20   CIP

The following pages constitute an extension of this copyright page.

Permissions

"On the Day of His Death by an Armed Hand" by Rafael Alberti. Reprinted with permission of Atheneum Publishers, an imprint of Macmillan Publishing Company, from *The Owl's Insomnia*, translated by Mark Strand. Translation Copyright © 1972, 1973 by Mark Strand.

"Details" by Judith Baumel. Copyright © 1988 by Judith Baumel. Reprinted from *The Weight of Numbers* by permission of University Press of New England.

"A silent Perry remembered how it used to be: look" from *The Whole Truth* (part 9) copyright © by James Cummins. Reprinted by permission.

"Crumbling is not an instant's Act" from *The Complete Poems of Emily Dickinson* by Emily Dickinson. Reprinted by permission of the publishers and the Trustees of Amherst College from *The Poems of Emily Dickinson*, Thomas A. Johnson, ed., Cambridge, Mass.: The Belknap Press of Harvard University Press, copyright 1951, © 1955, 1979, 1983 by the President and Fellows of Harvard College.

"The Horse in the Drugstore" from *Instructions to the Double*. Copyright © 1976 by Tess Gallagher. Reprinted by permission of Graywolf Press.

"Ruptured Friendships, or, The High Cost of Keys" by Marilyn Hacker from *Presentation Piece*. Copyright © 1974 by Marilyn Hacker. Reprinted by permission of Frances Collin, Literary Agent.

"On the Night of the Departure by Bus" by Donald Justice. Reprinted with permission of Atheneum Publishers, an imprint of Macmillan Publishing Company, from *Departures*, by Donald Justice. Copyright © 1969, 1970, 1971, 1972, 1973 by Donald Justice.

Paris Review interview with Jack Kerouac. From *The Paris Review Interviews Writers at Work*, Fourth Series. Copyright © 1974, 1976 by The Paris Review Inc. Reprinted by permission of Viking Penguin, a division of Penguin Books USA Inc.

"Haiku" (ninth part) by Etheridge Knight. Reprinted from *The Essential Etheridge Knight*, by Etheridge Knight, by permission of the University of Pittsburgh Press. Copyright © 1986 by Etheridge Knight.

For Laurie and Eric

Acknowledgments

No one can assemble a book like this one without also compiling a heavy debt of gratitude. When I first began to write poems seriously, I wrote in secret, sharing my poems with no one. To learn how to do it, I read whatever I chanced upon, often starting with anthologies and moving on to individual books of anthologized poets who interested me. I also took voluminous notes from the critical writings of certain poets who seemed generous with advice: Ezra Pound, W.H. Auden, Robert Graves, Edith Sitwell, Theodore Roethke, Robert Lowell, Marianne Moore, Karl Shapiro, T.S. Eliot, Wallace Stevens, and Robert Frost. Many of the quotations in this book were culled from these poets. All of them were represented in the once popular anthologies by Louis Untermeyer, *Modern American Poetry* and *Modern British Poetry*. Later Mark Strand's *The Contemporary American Poets* led me to more recent poets. Especially when you're starting out, it's a good idea to listen for poetic names being dropped. Try to seek out the poems that go along with the names.

Eventually, in my late twenties, I got up the nerve to show my poems to others and began taking poetry workshops. I think it helped to wait for that kind of exchange, to spend time isolated and fumbling on my own. I owe plenty to my teachers: Louis Simpson and Harvey Gross at SUNY/Stony Brook; Richard Howard, Cynthia Macdonald, and David St. John at Johns Hopkins University; Donald Justice, Marvin Bell, Sandra McPherson, and Henry Carlile at the University of Iowa.

I also owe a lot to my classmates and friends, in and out of various universities, and to my colleagues and students at the University of Cincinnati. In particular I want to thank Jim Cummins of the Elliston Poetry Room for logistical help. My wife, Laurie Henry, first encouraged me to write this book and has cheered me on and corrected me when I needed it.

Although most of the exercises here arise from the particular subject at hand, many are—in one form or another—in wide use, and some (which I've tried to indicate and acknowledge) come from particular poet-teachers and friends. This book is essentially a compilation, something I've gathered. One of the sections is in fact called "Borrowings," and it represents an excellent way to get started in any kind of writing, whether a book of poetic advice or actual poems.

Contents

Introduction

CAVEAT SCRIPTOR: LET THE WRITER BEWARE

It's hard to write poems to order. Most of us can't impose our will on the muse like that. If we do, the results often seem forced or dead on the page. The best reason to write regularly, to keep working over drafts, and to experiment with exercises like the ones that make up this book is that they give the breath of inspiration more of a chance to slip into our lungs.

Randall Jarrell says that a poet is one who spends a lifetime standing out in thunderstorms, waiting to be hit by lightning. A willingness to get drenched and most of the time *not* get struck is equivalent to the poet sitting down regularly to write drafts that may come to nothing. Trying out exercises is one way to chance the storm — although Donald Hall has pointed out that they can be merely a "parlor game," adding that games "are repellent." Robert Frost noted that when his poems didn't work out, he called them exercises. If the word bothers you, if it makes you think of workouts and make-work and brain teasers, think of exercises as *provocations*, or *goads*, or *triggers*, or *ignition keys*.

There is, of course, an obvious danger in poetry exercises: if unaccompanied by imagination, the results will be nothing *but* exercises, not genuine poems. But there are some uses that should be noted: (1) exercises can function as musical études, five-finger drills, training in poetic craft and tradition, an education in meter and form (even if the poet breaks away from them later); (2) the poet can bend the exercises, work against them, treat them as fuel or fodder or scaffolding in the process of making real poems; (3) these self-assignments can lead to realizations and insights, to a more profound education.

In a class on poetic form at the University of Iowa, Donald Justice urged students *not* to treat the exercises he assigned as poems-in-the-making, *not* to invest too much in them, but to learn the lessons of syllabic meter or song form or rhetorical devices and to discount, or at least devalue, the written results. In a similar class, David St. John urged students to strive *beyond* the limits of a particular exercise, even if it meant discarding the original rules, the initiating lesson. Ear and eye training, on the one hand, versus prods to real writing. Either approach can pay off, as long as the poet is attentive, resourceful, actively engaged in the process. Passive compliance or "going through the paces" helps little (although one can never tell what might sneak in along the way, what might stick like burrs, what might register unconsciously).

HOW TO PROCEED

This book is organized sequentially, according to the process of writing—or rather the process of *learning* to write, which amounts to the same thing—beginning with "Preparing" and ending with "Finishing." So you could, if you like, follow that order, hunting for the poems I mention, trying out any exercises that interest you, excite you, and incite you to make a poem. Remember, though, Robert Frost's remark that "dogged determination can result in nothing but doggerel." In a sense, it doesn't matter where you start, as long as you eventually go full-circle. It might be useful to open the book at random and start reading, start writing, plunging in anywhere. This is especially true if you feel constricted, timid about beginning. Jump around. Follow your instincts, your fancies, your whims. Let your mood dictate, maybe, instead of plodding through the book relentlessly—and humorlessly. Start at the back, if you like, with the section on "Endings," and then move forward. Start with something that's new (maybe "Syllabics") or something you think you already know (maybe "Love" or "Photographs"). When you have particular questions about an aspect of poetic craft ("Image," for example), glance through the table of contents or index and look it up. If you feel intimidated by a topic (like "Accentual Meter"), you *could* skip over it, but you might do better to tackle the fear head-on. One of the book's exercises, in fact, is to attempt in a poem what you fear the most (in the "Failure" section).

COMPILING YOUR OWN ANTHOLOGY

The nature of this book precludes anything close to an anthology within its covers, so you'll have to make an effort to seek out the poems and poets I mention. All in all, that's a good thing, since if you're serious about poetry you'll have to do that anyway—and at least you have some clues. Begin with the poetry anthologies listed in the "Reading" section of Chapter I. When you find poems you especially like, seek out the poet's full-length books. Become a regular at your nearest library. Buy books of poems! If you're not near any decent bookstores, there's a wonderful mail-order poetry service, Spring Church Book Company, P.O. Box 127, Spring Church, PA 15686. They sell contemporary poetry at a discount, and they offer regular catalogs.

Poetry volumes tend to be slim, maybe fifty to eighty pages, except for selected and collected editions of a poet's work. You can often finish one of those collections in a single sitting, although you may want to dawdle and muse over individual poems. Copy poems you enjoy into a journal or notebook. Type one out and send it to a friend. If you really like it, learn it by heart, so you can repeat it to yourself whenever the mood strikes. Poems — unlike novels, in which we seem to dwell as we read them, inhabiting a different world — can be ingested and absorbed. Word for word, they can become a part of you forever.

Important Notice: I have compiled lists of "Further Readings" for most of the sections in this book. Unfortunately, there wasn't room to include them. If you would like a copy of these lists (which I plan to update regularly), please send a self-addressed 9 × 12 envelope (with priority mail postage) to Prof. John Drury, Department of English, University of Cincinnati, Cincinnati, OH 45221.

OPENING TO POETRY

If you want to write poetry, you have to *read* plenty of poems, but the way you read them may be very different from the way of the critic or the literature class. First of all, don't be deterred or put off if you don't understand a poem right away — or even after repeated readings. Rejecting something we claim not to understand is a cop-out. It's the easy way off the proverbial hook. Try, instead, to experience what's in the poem, even if that experience eludes your understanding. Let the poem startle and perplex you. Learn to go with it, to accept it on its own terms, without quailing at the first difficulty. The key to reading poems is openness. You need to be receptive, to take things as they come, to be alert enough to notice things but relaxed enough to let them drift together as they will. T.S. Eliot thought a poem could be appreciated and enjoyed before it was understood. One of the pleasures of reading poetry is mulling over a poem and its reverberations, perhaps for a lifetime.

IMITATION

The greatest single means of learning how to do something is *imitation*. In regard to painting, William Blake says "Copying Correctly . . . is the only School to the Language of Art." One way or another, we learn to write poetry by modeling our work on what we've read and admired, perhaps even envied. W.H. Auden notes in *The Dyer's Hand* that "In imitating his Master, the apprentice acquires a Censor, for he learns that, no matter how he finds it, by inspiration, by potluck, or after hours of laborious search, there is only one word or rhythm or form that is the *right* one. The right one is still not yet the *real* one, for the apprentice is ventriloquizing, but he has got away from poetry-in-general; he is learning how *a* poem is written." (His first Master, incidentally, was Thomas Hardy.) Perhaps the best way to begin writing poetry is to "latch on" to a model poet, perhaps several, and to write poems under that influence, in similar forms, on similar subjects, in response and reaction. If nothing else, it will force you to read poems attentively in order to pull off the masquerade.

WHAT IS POETRY?

Samuel Taylor Coleridge defines poetry as "that species of composition, which is opposed to works of science, by proposing for its immediate object pleasure, not truth; and from all other species . . . it is discriminated by proposing to itself such delight from the whole, as is compatible with a distinct gratification from each component part." That may sound complicated, but it's the best, truest definition of poetry I know. In other words, poetry gives pleasure first, then truth, and its language is charged, intensified, concentrated. William Wordsworth defines poetry as "the spontaneous overflow of powerful feelings: it takes its origin from emotion recollected in tranquillity. . . . "

Some poets prefer to apply practical, subjective "tests" to determine if a text is poetry or not. A.E. Housman tested a poem by repeating it to himself while shaving; if his razor ceased to move, he knew it was poetry. Interestingly, Robert Graves recounts this story by saying that "the hairs of one's chin would bristle." And Robert Lowell reports that the shaver would "cut himself."

Emily Dickinson says "If I read a book, and it makes my whole body so cold no fire ever can warm me, I know that is poetry. If I feel physically as if the top of my head were taken off, I know that is poetry."

Dylan Thomas writes "If you want a definition of poetry, say, 'Poetry is what makes me laugh or cry or yawn, what makes my toenails twinkle, what makes me want to do this or that or nothing,' and let it go at that."

NOTE: Some of the most essential poetic terms are illustrated here by self-descriptive examples; others are labeled and identified.

PROSE

VERSE
(Written in lines)

Metrical Verse

Rhymed Verse

Iambic Tetrameter

Iambic Dimeter

Blank Verse — Iambic Pentameter

Syllabics

Accentual Verse
(Anglo-Saxon strong-stress meter)

Unmetrical Verse

Free Verse

Long-lined Free Verse

A MAP OF POETIC TERMS

This is a sample of prose. See how it reaches the right-hand margin and keeps on going through the magic of word-wrap (if you're using a computer, that is). Well, this is prose. Think of short stories, essays, magazine articles, book reviews, editorials, letters and reports; they are (nearly always) prose.

Rhyme Scheme

But these lines here, in fact, are verse,	*A*
Each ending where the poet says	*B*
They end. A poet may be fierce	*A*
About her line-breaks nowadays,	*B*
Cutting a line	*C*
Against the grain; — *slant rhyme*	*C*
The words remain — *true rhyme*	*C*
Whole, nonetheless. Enjambment pays.	*B*

Thĕ lĭnes ăbóve, ŏf coúrse, ĕxemplĭfý
Metrical verse—and these lines do the same,
Counting the syllables in every line
And measuring the stresses (some say "accents"),
Yet varying the steady to-and-fro
That otherwise might sound monotonous.
(The poet is a hypnotist who pinches.) ◄——— *Metaphor*

——— *Assonance*
(vowel repetition)

We can count the syllables
for a new meter: seven,
for example, in these lines.

——— *Caesura (pause)*

We can coúnt the aćcents ↙ in a cláshing líne
Borrowed from *Beowulf,*   measuring the beats
And letting the language   alliterate strongly

——— *Alliteration*
(consonant repetition)

That which is verse
(meaning set down in lines, like the furrows ◄— *Simile*
of a plowed field) but
avoids
following a regular pattern, a steady ◄——— *enjambed*
backbeat, we call   *(run-on line)*
"free verse"—free of meter, that is.

end-stopped

And when the free verse line swells out in Biblical cadences,
    filling like sails,
As in the *Leaves of Grass* of Whitman, brawling and practically
    nude
Compared to the fine haberdashery of expert iambic pentameter, ◄
Notice how the ends of the long lines are "tucked under,"
    indicating they belong to the line above.

EXERCISE: Find other examples of assonance, alliteration, enjambment, end-stopping, caesura, simile and metaphor.

˘ = unstressed syllable
´ = stressed syllable

I. Preparing

The good news is, you've been doing it all along. Your experiences — things you've done, people you've known, memories that flash back to you, dreams that perplex or astonish you, books you've read, places you've visited — give you rich deposits of the raw material a poem refines and shapes into something valuable. Of course, this mother lode has to be mined. And before that, you've got to prospect to find out where to dig. And you never know, when you start looking, if your particular kind of wealth is subterranean and glittering, a vein of gold, or something right under your nose, as simple and wonderful as the leaves of grass Walt Whitman loved.

There is no one right place to start, but if you don't learn to enjoy *reading* poems you're denying yourself the most essential tools for digging — as well as the riches our predecessors have given us. Read, notice things, be curious, pay attention to what your senses tell you, and you've made a good start to transforming the everyday stuff you ignore and forget — your passing fancies — into poems.

BEGINNINGS

For the poet, there are at least two kinds of beginnings: when the poet starts to write and when the poem itself commences. The two occasions don't always coincide. Often when the poet sits down to begin a new poem, nothing comes — or the words that do come are disappointing. It may take time to warm up or to get in tune. And when a draft is completed, the poet may discover that the *real* opening is not the actual first line. He or she may have to cut many lines, shuffle stanzas, reword a line or come up with a whole new line to get the right beginning. A good first line may be the last thing that actually occurs to the poet.

Getting Started

Many poets would say that the poet needs to induce a trance before the *real* writing comes through. There is no "right" way to get into this frame of mind; whatever works for you, however idiosyncratic, is fine. The German poet Schiller liked to have a basket of rotting apples under his desk. Some poets drink coffee or tea. Some poets follow a set routine that might involve physical exercise, maybe jogging or a walk. Some poets read to get in the mood to write (as some composers play Bach preludes and fugues before they begin composing). Some poets sift through a box of old drafts and notes. Some poets record entries in a journal. Traditionally, the poet invokes the muse, asking for inspiration and guidance — even for the words themselves, as if the poet were merely a conductor of electricity, rather than the dynamo itself. The poet might also begin with a prayer, or by meditating, or by writing a letter, or by a spell of intentional silence.

What frightens writers, at this stage, is "writer's block," a supposed inability to do anything with the blank page. William Stafford, in "A Way of Writing," has a marvelous solution to this blockage: simply lower your standards and write *anything*. "To get started," he says, "I will accept anything that occurs to me. . . . If I let the process go on, things will occur to me that were not at all in my mind when I started. These things, odd or trivial as they may be, are somehow connected. And if I let them string out, surprising things will happen." I recommend Stafford's essay — and the book that contains it, *Writing the Australian Crawl* — as a tonic for the faint-hearted.

Another fruitful approach might be to set aside a regular time for writing, but *not* require yourself to produce anything. You might spend the time looking over old poems, searching through rough drafts for salvageable fragments, or simply looking out the window or staring at the wall. (Michelangelo urged his pupils to seek inspiration in the cracks and stains on their ceilings.)

Surrealists like André Breton pioneered "automatic writing," in which the writer starts writing and keeps going no matter what, no matter where the words lead. The pen has to keep moving; the typist has to keep typing; the speaking voice has to keep babbling, spouting anything, engaging in a kind of filibuster. The idea, for the surrealists, was to unlock the barriers of inhibition in order to let the irrational in. Much silliness and boredom will sneak in too, but they can be edited out — or possibly used for some effect.

Some poets *do* depend on a flash of inspiration, maybe a good first line, before they sit down to work (or stand up or lie down, as the case may be). Waiting is their discipline. Like all poets, they are constantly preparing for the poems they will write. This preparation may be conscious and intentional or not — Emerson speaks of the "long foreground" that must have preceded Whitman's *Leaves of Grass*. A smart poet will recognize that thinking too hard about some idea or concept may be the surest way to scare it off. Just as you sometimes remember what you've been struggling to recall when you loosen up and stop fretting about it, you can often gain more by letting up, by easing your scrutiny, by relaxing enough so that images start to connect and crackle with energy. Forcing the issue is like the pitcher in a tight baseball game who begins "aiming" his pitches, a sure sign of trouble when the smooth, easy-going, natural delivery is disrupted.

How a Poem Opens

The first line of any poem is a kind of door, an entrance into the "rooms" of the stanzas, an opening. There are many kinds of doors, some plain, some ornate, some (like Walt Whitman's) "unscrewed from their jambs," some camouflaged by sliding bookshelves or shrubbery. But there must be some sort of reasonable access so that the reader can get in. A bad opening puts off the reader, offering nothing but a barrier.

There is no formula for making a good first line, but it must have a certain freshness and allure. You don't need to shout or to shock the reader, but you have to do something enticing or interesting. Here are some sample openings:

A sudden blow. The great wings beating still,
   —*W.B. Yeats, "Leda and the Swan"*

The night sky is only a sort of carbon paper,
   —*Sylvia Plath, "Insomniac"*

Here is a coast; here is a harbor;
   —*Elizabeth Bishop, "Arrival at Santos"*

Night Music Slanted
   —*Etheridge Knight, "Cell Song"*

I play pool. I aim toward the faces
   —*Sandra McPherson, "Games"*

Runs falls rises stumbles on from darkness into darkness
   —*Robert Hayden, "Runagate Runagate"*

Is friendship with men like friendship with birds?
   —*Molly Peacock, "Friendship with Men"*

These openings range from the lyric to the conversational, from explanation to fragmentation, from action to stillness. In all cases, they are interesting and they lead on to something further. An opening should make the reader curious about "What's next?"

But a good first line does not need to be flashy. Often it will simply set the scene, giving a place name or showing a landscape. Poems can begin with descriptions, statements, questions, quotations, fragments, exclamations, off-hand remarks, images, odd or plain words. Is there a scene to describe, a character to introduce, an idea to propose, a mood to create? If your poem tells a story, can you begin *in medias res* (in the middle of things) by recounting some action? You can always use a *flashback* to explain what came earlier. Many good openings push immediately *beyond* the first line — they get things going and let them continue, like the key that turns on the ignition of a car. (Notice how most of the sample first lines end with a comma or no punctuation at all, inviting the reader to keep going.) You don't exactly have to "grab" the reader but you must usher (or hustle) the reader into the poem. You don't need to expend all your verbal fireworks before the second line. It's usually wiser to withhold them, to start at a lower pitch and then work up (although it depends on you and what the poem requires).

Many poets feel that their first line must be a *donnée*, something "given," as if by the muse — or out of thin air. This may sound like superstition, but it may simply be receptiveness, a knack for recognizing lucky ideas and felicitous phrases.

1. As William Stafford suggests, get up early, "before others are awake," pick up a pen, have a sheet of paper ready, and see what words and thoughts occur to you. Fish until you get a nibble, and then start reeling in whatever's out there — or in there. Like Stafford, be "receptive, careless of failure" as you "spin out things on the page."

2. Try automatic writing. Using a pen or a typewriter, begin writing and don't stop for anything, not even to sneeze or shake your aching hand, just keep the words coming, whatever you think of, maybe last night's dream of the helicopter in your kitchen, don't worry about what blurts out as long as the steady flow continues — get the picture?

3. Try out a series of different beginnings on the same topic. You can write about anything, but if you're at a loss, describe a place you knew in childhood and now find evocative (maybe a garage, or a soda fountain, or a vacant lot). Write a set of opening lines in the form of: a setting, a time, a statement, a question, an exclamation, an image, a metaphor or some comparison, a bit of conversation. Choose the best one and continue into the poem itself, incorporating as many of the other lines as you like along the way.

4. Look through a book of poems. Do the beginnings welcome in the reader, or are they forbidding? If they don't seem to open effectively, how could you rephrase them? If they do, how could you emulate the

effect? Use one of the substitute lines you come up with to begin a new poem of your own.

5. The poets of epics such as *The Iliad* and *The Aeneid* begin with an *invocation to the muse*, asking for divine assistance in composing their poems. The muse was supposed to speak *through* the poet, much like a ventriloquist. Write a short poem that somehow invokes the muse. Make it as modern and unaffected as possible. If it seems too artificial, don't mention the muse at all, but simply call upon the things of this world — and of the imagination — to enter your poem. Put out a welcome mat and see what turns up.

READING

If you want to write poems, you have to read. We wouldn't think much of a songwriter who didn't enjoy music. We surely wouldn't bother with a "poet" so narcissistic that he or she can't bear to open up the work of other poets. But even that puts the whole matter backwards. Presumably we want to write poems because we've been moved by reading poems. We want to do the same, either in emulation or in competition — as James Dickey remarks that he has "the temperament that won't let me be really, deeply interested in a thing without trying to do it myself." Many people, however, do begin writing "poems," usually in sing-song rhyme or in limp free verse, for "self expression" and to proclaim their feelings. But poetry does *not* come out of this self-absorbed vacuum. Poetry is not self-expression, though it may be self-discovery.

"Know how to read? You *must*/ Before you can write," Ezra Pound has translated from an air by Marie-Françoise-Catherine de Beauveau, la Marquise de Boufflers. One of the best ways to go about learning how to write poems is to read a lot of poetry — and not just poetry, but other texts that spark an interest: novels, essays, biographies, science books, travel books, whatever. Randall Jarrell advises *"Read at whim! read at whim!"*

If you're new to poetry, where do you start? Anthologies are helpful, as long as you use them as *starting-points*, guides to what's available. They can give you a fairly broad view, but it's based on the anthologist's necessary narrowing down of poets and chosen poems. And many anthologies are like ammunition depots for the editor's critical outlook. Beware of that kind of bias. Other starting points are poetry magazines, poetry readings, or simply browsing around the shelves devoted to poetry in the public library. It helps to read through a historical anthology of English and American poetry from *Beowulf* or Chaucer to the twentieth century, to get some bearings. And it helps to read some of the essential longer works of poetry: Homer's *Iliad* and *Odyssey*, Dante's *Divine Comedy*, Shakespeare's plays, Milton's *Paradise Lost*, Wordsworth's *Prelude*.

There are two kinds of reading: (1) fast, wide-ranging, touching on many subjects and kinds of writing quickly, like a scouting expedition; (2) slow, close, focused, savoring the words, probing deeply into the poem. You'll want to do both. (Marvin Bell discusses how to read poems in "The 'Technique' of Re-Reading," reprinted in *Poetics: Essays on the Art of Poetry*, edited by Mariani and Murphy, Tendril Magazine, 1984.)

There's also the choice of escapist versus involved reading. There's nothing wrong with what Graham Greene calls "entertainments," but you want a balanced diet. That doesn't mean poetry can't be entertaining. It *must* be. But you have to be alert, all ears, to receive those transmissions. Good readers will read practically anything. Indifferent readers never tax themselves or reach beyond their easy favorites.

It can be summed up simply: Read widely, read closely, and respond to what you read.

6. Read a contemporary book of poems. Respond by marking the text, copying favorite passages, jotting notes in your journal; or by writing an account of your immediate impressions of the book, by writing a review, by thinking and mulling over poems that stick with you and bother you; or by imitating the poet's style and habits and tricks to see how close you can get (a parody, in other words); or by writing a real poem of your own in reaction to something in the book—a particular form or freeness, maybe, or a tone of voice, or a kind of subterranean movement you can feel but can't explain.

7. Read and reread a single poem (maybe one mentioned in this book). Each time you read it, look or listen for something in particular: rhythm, images, metaphor, sound effects, tone, word choices, line lengths and how the lines break, the way sentences snake through the lines and are varied, what's "unsaid" in the poem, how the pacing changes or keeps steady, how the poem flows. Say the poem aloud. If you like it enough, learn it by heart. Write a brief comment on the poem in your journal (if you keep one) or in a letter to a friend who may not usually read poetry. (Remember to be specific in your comments.)

8. Go to a poetry reading. Or listen to a tape of a poet reading. (Catalogs are available from Watershed Tapes [6925 Willow St. NW, # 201, Washington, DC 20012] and Spoken Arts P.O. Box 289, New Rochelle, NY 10802]; Caedmon Records offers many recordings of twentieth century poets reading their own work.) Write some kind of response: a list, a few sentences, a letter, a full-blown essay, a poem—Galway Kinnell has early poems responding to readings by William Carlos Williams and Robert Frost.

9. Read something *not* literary. You can read it in search of new mate-

rial, or to try out a different perspective, or simply for refreshment.

10. Immerse yourself in a very long book. Don't rush through it. See what kinds of poems you write while you're involved in this other world.

11. Instead of beginning a writing session by actually writing, begin by reading—preferably something other than a newspaper or magazine. Then write.

12. Read something that seems impossibly difficult.

SOME ANTHOLOGIES

Ezra Pound and Marcella Spann, *Confucius to Cummings* (New Directions, 1964)

W.H. Auden and Norman Holmes Pearson, *The Viking Portable Poets of the English Language*, 5 volumes (Viking, 1950)

Robert Bly, *The Sea and the Honeycomb: A Book of Tiny Poems* (Beacon Press, 1971)

Robert Bly, *News of the Universe: Poems of Twofold Consciousness* (Sierra Club Books, 1980)

Hayden Carruth, *The Voice That Is Great Within Us* (Bantam, 1970)

Mark Strand, *The Contemporary American Poets* (Mentor, 1969)

Daniel Halpern, *The American Poetry Anthology* (Avon, 1975)

John Frederick Nims, *Sappho to Valery: Poems in Translation* (Princeton Univ., 1971)

John Frederick Nims, *Western Wind: An Introduction to Poetry* (Random House, 1974) —A textbook, not an anthology, but it's excellent and contains a wealth of poems and other interesting material.

Louis Simpson, *An Introduction to Poetry* (St. Martin's, 1972) —The "Glossary" of Simpson's anthology is especially good.

Ted Kooser, *The Windflower Home Almanac of Poetry* (Windflower Press, P.O. Box 82213, Lincoln, Nebraska 68501, 1980)

A. Poulin, Jr., *Contemporary American Poetry* (Houghton Mifflin, 1985)

Walter de la Mare, *Come Hither* (Knopf, 1928, 1957)

Stephen Berg and Robert Mezey, *Naked Poetry* and *The New Naked Poetry* (Bobbs-Merrill, 1969 and 1976)

Edward Field, *A Geography of Poets* (Bantam, 1979)

Jack Myers and Roger Weingarten, *New American Poets of the 80's* (Wampeter Press, 1984)

Andrei Codrescu, *American Poetry Since 1970: Up Late* (Four Walls Eight Windows, 1987)

Dave Smith and David Bottoms, *The Morrow Anthology of Younger American Poets* (Morrow, 1985)

Dudley Randall, *The Black Poets* (Bantam, 1971)

Ronald Wallace, *Vital Signs: Contemporary American Poetry from the University Presses* (Univ. of Wisconsin, 1989)

Stuart Friebert and David Young, *The Longman Anthology of Contemporary American Poetry: 1950-1980* (Longman, 1983)

Nicholas Christopher, *Under 35: The New Generation of American Poets* (Anchor, 1989)

Marie Harris and Kathleen Aguero, *An Ear to the Ground: An Anthology of Contemporary American Poetry* (Univ. of Georgia, 1989)

Jerome Rothenburg, *Technicians of the Sacred: A Range of Poetries from Africa, America, Asia, Europe, & Oceania* (Univ. of California, 1968, rev. 1985) and *Shaking the Pumpkin: Traditional Poetry of the Indian North Americas* (Doubleday, 1972)

(Note: All of the anthologies listed above were edited by *poets* — my own bias in their favor. You might also look into the textbook anthologies published by Norton, *The Harvard Anthology of Contemporary Poetry*, edited by critic Helen Vendler, and so on. There are also anthologies containing poems published in magazines like *The New Yorker* and *Poetry*, anthologies with a regional focus like *New York Poems*, and specialized anthologies, some of which I mention in later sections of the book.)

REFERENCE BOOKS

Jack Myers and Michael Simms, *The Longman Dictionary of Poetic Terms* (Longman, 1989) — A wonderful, venturesome collection of terms. Its discussions of analogous terms from movies, art, music, and dance are especially helpful and suggestive.

William Packard, *The Poet's Dictionary: A Handbook of Prosody and Poetic Devices* (Harper & Row, 1989) — Briefer than the Myers & Simms dictionary, this one seems neat and handy.

Preminger, Warnke, and Hardison, *Princeton Encyclopedia of Poetry and Poetics* (Princeton University Press, 1965) — Massive and engrossing. William Carlos Williams contributed the fascinating (and biased) entry on free verse.

Robert Peters, *Hunting the Snark: A Compendium of New Poetic Terminology* (Paragon House, 1989) — A new set of categories (such as "Dazzle Poems," "Gab Poems," "Home-Cooked Poems," "Nuclear Poems," and "Stodge") and a lot of fun to read.

HANDBOOKS ON METER AND FORM

John Hollander, *Rhyme's Reason: A Guide to English Verse* (Yale University Press, 1981, revised edition 1989) — Hollander presents and explains forms by writing *in* the particular form. Packed into 52 pages, his "self-descriptive verses" are both practical and a pleasure.

Lewis Turco, *The New Book of Forms* (University Press of New England, 1986) — Poetic forms listed in algebraic fashion, giving the essential patterns with x's, accents, and slashes. A good quick reference — and the new edition has a welcome wealth of examples, along with a "Handbook of Poetics."

Karl Shapiro and Robert Beum, *A Prosody Handbook* (Harper & Row, 1965) — *Prosody* is the "systematic, technical study of versification, including meter, rhyme, sound effects, and stanza patterns" (as defined by Louis Simpson).

Paul Fussell, *Poetic Meter & Poetic Form* (Random House, 1979)

POETRY MAGAZINES

A good place to start browsing might be one of Robert Peters's *Black and Blue Guides to Literary Magazines*, several wild, lively, opinionated guided tours of magazines ranging from *American Poetry Review* to *Telephone* to *Shenandoah* to *Wormwood Review*. (He likes those four in ascending order from least to most). Don't let him punch you silly with his opinions; try, instead, to care as much about poetry as Peters does.

Public libraries often have very little in the way of poetry journals, but you can usually read a handful of poems in *The New Yorker* or *The Atlantic Monthly*. University libraries usually offer a wider range of periodicals. If you can find a good literary bookstore, you may have better luck. You can also use reference books such as Judson Jerome's *Poet's Market* (Writer's Digest Books) and Len Fulton's *International Directory of Little Magazines* (Dustbooks) — both updated annually — to locate magazines you might find interesting. When you find a magazine you enjoy, subscribe.

Finally, you should invest in the best dictionary you can afford, preferably unabridged, preferably *The Oxford English Dictionary*, with its wealth of historical examples. (There's a two-volume set that comes with a magnifying glass — the print is tiny. You can probably get it at a discount by joining a book club.) At the very least, get a good hardbound dictionary (not a paperback, which will leave out too many words). Good ones available include the *American Heritage*, *Webster's Collegiate*, and *Webster's New World*.

SENSES

W.H. Auden calls our five senses — sight, hearing, touch, taste, and smell — the "precious five." Poetry without them is unthinkable, pointless, no fun at all. Pleasing the senses of the reader is the surest strategy for reaching the mind and the soul. As Theodore Roethke says, "The flesh can make the spirit visible."

Here are some examples of sense words:

SIGHT: shimmering, blotchy, hulking, spindly, mauve
SOUND: blare, tinkle, screech, rumble
TASTE: tart, sugary, piquant, peppery, bitter
TOUCH: rough, sticky, slick, gritty, plump
SMELL: reek, aroma, odor, stink, stench

Sight and sound predominate for the poet, but seldom in equal measure. Some poets are known for their word music, others for their powers of observation. Theodore Roethke faulted Robert Lowell for his "ear," while Lowell quibbled with Roethke's "eye." (It's a terrible insult to accuse a poet of having a "tin ear.")

Sometimes *synaesthesia*, the mixing of senses, is especially powerful, as in Blake's "London":

And the hapless Soldiers sigh
Runs in blood down Palace walls

The danger is in confusing the reader (or in making a critic gleeful that you've "mixed your metaphors"), but sometimes you want a swirling, confused effect, an intensity that makes the senses go a little haywire. The French poet and visionary Arthur Rimbaud spoke in favor of a "systematic derangement of the senses," finding color in vowels, for example, but he was soon disillusioned and renounced poetry in his early twenties. A poem can encompass only so much psychedelia.

Texture, in a poem, comes from words we can almost feel with our fingertips, taste in our mouths. Donald Hall has named the urge to make interesting sounds "milk tongue," pointing out that we first hear the joy of sound-making in a baby's babbling. Dante referred to words as being either "shaggy" or "combed." Robert Graves said that the words of a poem should rise from the page "as if in relief," a wonderful image of the poem's necessary three-dimensionality.

13. Write a poem that highlights (puts in relief, like braille) a particular texture: gritty or smooth, rubbery or sharp, slimy or dry. Do whatever you can with language and imagery to achieve this sensory effect, but DON'T cue the reader by saying "This is gritty" or "This is slimy." Make the reader *feel* it, almost physically, without being told what to feel.

14. Write a poem that's all sound, a babble of word music, letting vowels echo and consonants repeat, not worrying much about what it means. Savor the sounds. If this seems hard to begin, try listing as many delicious words as you can, words you can taste (and proper names too), like "crush" and "deliquescent" and "Susquehanna."

15. Write a poem that's about a color.

16. Use your sixth sense, your intuition, in writing a poem about something hidden or mysterious or unspoken or hard to comprehend.

17. Write a poem that mixes the senses (synaesthesia).

18. Write a poem as if you were blind or deaf — or both. To do this, you might spend time with your eyes closed, or your ears covered, perceiving what's around you by smell and touch, reaching out and fumbling for the nearest object, then reacquainting yourself with its texture, its shape, its mystery.

KNOWING AND NOT KNOWING

We tend to undervalue many of the things we know. We take them for granted. They seem unimportant. Yet this knowledge (which may or may not be book learning) underpins all our writing. Without a sense of authority, the writer can't coax the reader into belief — or at least a waiver of distrust. You know many more things than you give yourself credit for. If you have worked in a diner, you know about steam tables and monkey dishes, getting stuck and being stiffed, and how to balance a table's worth of dirty plates along your arms. If you've been a bank teller, or a graphic designer, or a lifeguard, or a mechanic, or a stamp collector, or an Army recruit, or any number of other things, you have knowledge and experiences that transfer readily into poetry, either as raw materials or as analogous processes.

But, for the writer, it also helps *not* to know things, or to know just a smattering. Henry James said that a writer could develop a whole novel based on a single glimpse into a room of people dining. The poem that is too "knowing" doesn't lead the writer anywhere but down a familiar rut. The poet has to plunge, somehow, into the unknown, the new. He or she can't simply translate preconceived ideas into poetic form. Writing poems is really a process for getting *beyond* knowledge. But it does help to start with what you know, even if you have to "unlearn" it as you go.

One way to pass on what you know is in a set of instructions, a "how to" poem that guides the reader through a process. Normally this is explained in a series of imperatives or commands: First do this, then do that. It's a form that works especially well in poetry, probably because it's economical, forceful, and usefully repetitive. You can flesh out the individual steps quite a bit. And the final poem may not be so much a practical guide as the directions for a journey, or quest, into new territory, a kind of treasure map: turn at the sassafras tree and walk twenty paces to the boulder of quartz.

19. Make a list of the things you know about and know how to do. Leave room to add words later. Consider work experience, performing skills, household abilities, mechanical flair, hobbies and pastimes and sports and arts you've mastered, languages you know, physical and mental aptitudes. Then try to zero in on a possible poem you could write about each one, jotting down a phrase or so for each kind of knowledge. Then launch into a poem based on one of these things you know. (Jobs and work places make surprisingly good subjects for poetry. Read some of Philip Levine's poems about work in his *Selected Poems*.)

20. Write a how-to poem, giving instructions on how to do something, or directions about how to find something. Write it in lines, either free or metrical, and use plenty of specific details and images. Give it flavor, as a good recipe should stimulate the taste buds.

21. Write a poem about what you *don't* know.

PHYSICAL EDUCATION

The interviews with writers in *Paris Review* usually begin with a question about where the poet or novelist writes, what hours he or she devotes to work, and what kind of writing implement is used. It's as though the secret of writing is in the tools, or the workplace, or the routine of the writer. And though the question may seem comically superficial, there *is* something to it. One could rephrase a familiar bumper sticker — "Pens don't write poems; poets do" — but the pen or pencil or typewriter may have a larger role than just recording the writer's inspirations; it may foster, encourage, or stimulate creativity by its feel or its familiarity.

If you visit the Maison Victor Hugo in Paris, you will see the writing desk at which Hugo *stood* to write; Ernest Hemingway and Thomas Wolfe (so tall he used the top of a refrigerator for a surface) also stood to do their writing. Hemingway felt that the slight discomfort helped focus his energies. Robert Lowell, on the other hand, wrote his poems and worked on his numerous revisions while lying down in bed. William Butler Yeats paced while composing his poems. Robert Frost had a special writing board he placed over his legs as he sat in a favorite chair. It is likely that certain physical conditions (and habits) put the writer into a receptive and active mental state. Exactly what that physical set-up may be depends on the whim and preference of the individual writer.

In the chapter "Nuts and Bolts" from his useful book on writing poetry, *The Triggering Town*, Richard Hugo suggests writing with a No. 2

pencil and crossing out deletions vigorously rather than erasing. He thinks highly enough of his own practice to offer it as a prescription to others. (We, of course, are entitled to choose our own weapons.) It may be superstition, but that too has a place in our habits and methods of operating.

Our bodies, of course, affect the agility and quickness of our minds. In *Design and Form: the Basic Course at the Bauhaus*, Johannes Itten explains how he brought his art students "to mental and physical readiness for intensive work through relaxing, breathing, and concentrating exercises." He adds, "The training of the body as an instrument of the mind is of the greatest importance for creative man."

22. Try writing in a different place than usual—a kitchen, a porch, an attic or basement, a diner, an airport, a library, a vacant stadium. Either (a) let the place suggest your subject, or (b) move as far from the immediate place as possible, writing about something as distant as the Amazon basin, 18th Century Venice, or everyday life in another galaxy.

23. Try writing in a different position. If you normally sit at a desk, try standing and placing your paper on a surface at a comfortable height, maybe the top of an upright piano. Or try reclining on your bed or on a sofa. Or, while a fan is blowing to create white noise (and incidentally to cool you off), try closing your eyes and composing the poem in your head. Any subject will do, but if you're stuck try beginning with a description of your actual position ("As I stand by the fire escape," "Lounging in bed all morning") and switch to a topic as far away and distant as possible—based, perhaps, on your current reading.

24. Perform some repetitive physical action that will leave your mind free to wander—washing the dishes, crocheting, swimming, walking, even showering. Concentrate on gathering material for a poem—memories, imagined conversations, words you especially like, dreams that trouble you, scenes that flash into your mind. *Don't* interrupt your activity to fetch a pen and begin jotting down notes. Finish the business at hand and *then* start writing, either rough notes or an actual poem. Even if the material you dredge up seems pale, at least you will have finished some useful task.

SPIRITUAL EXERCISES

Near the beginning of his *Spiritual Exercises*, St. Ignatius Loyola writes: "The first prelude is a composition, seeing the place. Here it is observed that in contemplation, or visible meditation, . . . the composition will be to see, with the eye of the imagination, the actual place where the object which I want to contemplate may be found." The idea that the soul must be educated through imaginative venturing, that the spirit must be inspired, correlates perfectly with the writer's quest. This "visible meditation" is a splendid way to open the gates rusted shut by routine and inattention.

Zen Buddhism makes use of another kind of "spiritual exercise" in the form of *koans*: puzzles meant to frustrate the intellect and (in Philip Kapleau's words) "liberate the mind from the snare of language." Here's a well-known example: "What is the sound of one hand clapping?" Here are some others:

"In the trees fish play, in the deep sea birds are flying."

"The flag doesn't move . . . only your mind moves."

"From where you are, stop the distant boat moving across the water."

"Today is the eighth of the month. Tomorrow is the thirteenth."

"Even though you can say something about it,/ I will give you thirty blows of the stick./ And if you can't say anything about it,/ I will also give you thirty blows of the stick."

(The last one sounds a little like the familiar trick question "When are you going to stop beating your wife?") Puzzling over koans might be a good way to short-circuit the brain—and its rationalizations—at least temporarily. Meditating, on the other hand, begins with an emptying of the mind, aided perhaps by counting breaths or repeating a "mantra" (a special word, such as "om"). This in itself can be useful to a writer. But many poets try to use language to get *beyond* language. In any case, just about all poets want their words to reverberate and resonate beyond the limits of mere definition. How far this goes, and to what end, depends on the poet.

Looking inward is an obvious way to discover the spirit. But putting yourself in the place of something *apart* from you, something *outside* the self, often gives you a new insight, a new outlook. In a letter John Keats remarks, "If a sparrow come before my window I take part in its existence and pick about the gravel." Walt Whitman says, "I do not ask the wounded person how he feels, I myself become the wounded person." The ability or knack or inclination to put yourself in the position of someone else is called *empathy*. It is literally "feeling into" another consciousness.

Empathy comes from imagination, a bodily sense of understanding how another person, or animal, or plant, or even an inanimate object really feels. The German poet Rainer Maria Rilke spent hours at a zoo in Paris, looking at a caged panther until he *felt* what its existence must be like—and then wrote a marvelous twelve-line poem, "The Panther."

Silence can be useful and rewarding in itself. Waiting patiently may help quiet the turbulent brain enough so that new work can begin. Just as intelligent farmers let fields lie fallow to rejuvenate the soil, you're conserving and gathering energy, not just frittering it away. Too many poets seem to feel they have a quota to fulfill, that their cottage industries will never boom unless they maintain a production schedule. If you don't have to write, don't write. But try not to think of this quiet time as wasted. It may make your best poems come out of hiding.

25. Spend twenty minutes or so meditating. If you have never done this before, sit down in a quiet spot, relax your muscles, loosen up, and try to clear your mind—empty it. Often it helps to concentrate on a mantra, a word you can choose for yourself (something simple and euphonious, such as a name or a favorite word, will do), and "chant" it mentally, gradually letting it recede, fade out to silence. After twenty minutes (roughly—you don't need to set a timer) reach for a pen and paper and start writing. Be receptive to any and all images that flash in your mind. Don't strain after material, but coax up whatever may be submerged within you: childhood memories, last night's dream, something you've noticed before but never mentioned (or thought worth mentioning).

26. Try to see what you can't see, in particular the inner life of a human being or another creature. Try to envision what it would be like to exist as a blade of grass, or an agate, or a weathervane. Discard the easy, clichéd associations and try to get "into" the thing or being itself. Close your eyes if it helps to sharpen the focus. Once you've spent a good fifteen minutes, at least, immersed in this otherness, write a poem about it—or just notes for a later poem, if you like.

27. Like St. Ignatius, imagine your way into a place you've heard or read about but have never visited. Call on all your senses to populate the scene, erect the buildings, make a breeze flow through the marketplace. Once you've got the scene fully in mind, write a poem about it—or about something taking place there.

28. Write a fresh response to a familiar Biblical passage. How did Naomi really feel, for example? What would it be like to see Jesus the carpenter at work? If you need hints on how to proceed, look at what painters like Rembrandt and Tintoretto have done with Biblical subjects.

29. Write a poem about a Zen *koan*. You can try to answer the puzzle, but you might do better simply to react, respond, let go.

30. Think of something you dislike: a person, place, thing, or activity. Try to see it freshly, with an open mind, from a more sympathetic point of view. What are its merits? How is it surprisingly beautiful? In what unexpected ways is it interesting? Why is it noteworthy? You might think of something you'd normally shun or exterminate, like a roach or a snake or a weed. Write a poem about it, full of images and exact detail.

You've got to look closely if you want to find your own empathy.

31. Speak up for something too weak or powerless to speak for itself. Don't allow yourself to lapse into sentimentality (an easy overstating of predictable feelings). Be hard-nosed and tough, so that your empathy packs a punch. You're speaking as a kind of advocate, presenting the case of a refugee who can't speak the language, or the plight of a still unclassified spider perishing as the rain forest burns. This is not intended as a political poem, although the voiceless are necessarily those without a real say in the business of running the world. But try to put your empathy ahead of your political convictions and party affiliations. (They represent the same, all-too-easy stock response that makes sentimentality so dispiriting.)

32. Make a special effort to cultivate solitude. Insist on being by yourself. As Richard Howard points out, "The cure for loneliness is solitude." If your urge is to escape, do it instead through language. Write a poem about loneliness, perhaps centering on a time when you never felt lonelier. Or write about a time when it was wonderful to be by yourself, when you felt inundated by a happiness no one could share — but which you could relate in words. Think of Andrew Marvell's lines: "Two paradises 'twere in one/ To live in paradise alone."

33. Write about being quiet in an otherwise noisy scene: diving underwater from a crowded party by a pool; sitting beneath a shelter as a thunderstorm roars; waking up early in a jail cell.

34. Spend an hour *not* writing. (This may be the hardest exercise in the book.) Be silent for the whole time; let your thoughts jump around freely — don't try to lead them anywhere in particular. It doesn't matter where you spend this hour — in a kitchen, in a park, in a library, anywhere indoors or out. At the end of this hour, go on to do anything — reading, talking long-distance, sewing, fixing a lamp, dashing off a postcard. You might even find that you have to write a poem, but that's not the point here, so don't push it at all. There's such a thing as trying too hard. Ease up.

II. Language

Words to the poet are like pigment to the painter, pitch to the composer, the necessary materials of the art. But it's more complicated than that, since *everyone* uses language and since words *refer* to things. In poetry, it's often a matter of those who want language to be transparent, revealing a scene or a story, versus those who want language to be opaque, itself the story. On one extreme, poets of content; on the other, poets of language. In writing, however, it's always a question of *how* we say it, which words we choose, which we omit, how we string them together. We can't have poems without words. It just depends on the way we use language — and why.

WORDS

We usually think of words as a means to an end. If I say "tree," you recognize the kind of plant I'm referring to, more or less. The word, in this case, is merely a signifier that allows us to communicate. Yet it's really not that simple. I may be thinking of a shade tree, a maple, and you may imagine a royal palm or a breadfruit tree. Even with a general word like "tree," there are many possible shades of meaning. Plato would say that there is an ideal tree, an abstraction, from which all real trees are imperfect copies. This notion is helpful to a philosopher, in that it makes the term a steadier element in the periodic chart of language. But most poetry depends on language being unbound, volatile.

The dictionary definition of a word is its *denotation*. The associations clustered around the word represent its *connotations*. A general word like "attorney" has a relatively positive connotation in most quarters, but "counselor" and "advocate" sound more flattering. "Lawyer," on the other hand, is a bit iffy, more likely to be spoken with a sneer, but it's still the most common term, both in praise and in censure, so it's usually neutral. "Shyster," "pettifogger," and "mouthpiece" all have negative connotations — and all suggest different qualities of legal shenanigans. The poet must be alert to such connotations. Some appear in dictionaries, but most do not, so the poet must learn them by example, by paying attention, by noticing those shades of meaning, that emotional weight, that flavor. Such choices are necessarily artistic.

Even the idea that words merely represent things must be questioned. While a poet like Louis Simpson, interested in the clarity of narrative, calls for poetry that "makes words disappear," words are usually highlighted, rather than de-emphasized, in a poem. Think of words as physical materials you can handle and manipulate to create a piece of art. They are important *in themselves*.

1. WORD-LIST POEM. Make a list of eight or nine words you find interesting. They need not be polysyllabic! Good, flavorful words like *mulch, cringe, daub, tweeze* work perfectly well. Try to choose nouns and verbs first, then adjectives, preferably not adverbs. If you like, have someone else suggest words to you, or draw them from whatever you're currently reading. *Then*, write a short poem using all of those words. Don't think of your subject beforehand. Concentrate on the list first, then plunge right into the poem, making connections as you go. Tess Gallagher wrote the following poem based on a word list supplied by a teacher; the exercise determined who got into a crowded poetry workshop—and Gallagher did. The word list contained: *bruise, horse, milk, reason,* and *bride.*

The Horse in the Drugstore

wants to be admired.
He no longer thinks of what he has given up
to stand here, the milk-white reason
of chickens over his head in the night, the grass
spilling on through the day. No, it is enough
to stand so with his polished chest among the nipples
and bibs, the cotton, and multiple sprays, with his black lips
parted just slightly and the forehooves doubled back
in the lavender air. He has learned when maligned to snort
dimes and to carry the inscrutable bruise like a bride.
   — *Tess Gallagher*

2. WORD-SUBSTITUTION POEM. Choose a poem that interests you. Using a fresh sheet of paper, write down new words to replace each word of your model. Substitute your *own* words for those of the other poem, making sure you keep the same arrangement of parts of speech. That is, substitute nouns for nouns, verbs for verbs, and so on. You can write down *opposites* or *antonyms* if you like ("hot" for "cold"), but don't feel restricted by that possibility. The idea is to keep the other poet's *syntax* (or arrangement of words) while providing your own building materials, your own vocabulary. For example, if the original begins "When in disgrace with fortune and men's eyes" (Shakespeare), you might sub-

stitute "Near Santa Fe with passports and Joe's lunch." Notice that it's OK to leave minor words (articles, conjunctions, some prepositions) unchanged. Even so, the transformation is nearly absolute, although Shakespeare's "sugared sonnets" still lurk behind the rhythms and the syntax. Through this word-substitution exercise, you can (1) learn how another writer operates from word to word, (2) add to your own tool chest of techniques, thereby expanding your poetic range, (3) get a "head start" on a new poem by using a handy blueprint, (4) stimulate fresh word choices by the need to puzzle out nouns and verbs that fit the syntax. The writer may acknowledge the debt by saluting the other poet in a headnote, "after Shakespeare," but often, once the process of revision has run its course, the trail will have disappeared and no one will ever detect the borrowing. And it's not stealing or plagiarizing. The real invention, finally, is all your own responsibility — the choice of each word, the creation of the effect you desire. At worst, it's a kind of parody, but the exercise can be much more ambitious than that.

On the following pages are a poem by Rafael Alberti and the word substitution made by Donald Justice, who also modeled his "Variations on a Text by Vallejo" (which begins "I will die in Miami in the sun") on Cesar Vallejo's "Black Stone Lying on a White Stone" ("I will die in Paris, on a rainy day"). This practice resembles that of a musician composing variations on another composer's theme.

On the Day of His Death by an Armed Hand

Come right out and tell me if those weren't the good old days.
5 × 5 was not yet 25
nor had the dawn considered the pointless existence of knives gone
    dull.

I swear to you by the moon I won't be a cook,
you swear to me by the moon you won't be a cook,
he swears to us by the moon he won't even be smoke in such a sad
    kitchen.

Who died?

The goose is sorry for being a duck,
the sparrow for being a professor of Chinese,
the rooster for being a man,
and I for having talent and marveling at how miserable
the sole of a shoe usually is in winter.

A queen has lost her crown,
a president of a republic his hat,
and I . . .

> I believe that I have lost nothing,
> that I have never lost anything,
> that I . . .

> What does buenos dias mean?
> —*Rafael Alberti*

On the Night of the Departure by Bus

Tell me if you were not happy in those days.
You were not yet twenty-five
And you had not yet abandoned the guitar.

I swore to you by your nakedness that you were a guitar,
You swore to me by your nakedness that you were a guitar,
The moon swore to us both by your nakedness that you had
    abandoned yourself completely.

Who would not go on living?

The typewriter will be glad to have become the poem,
The guitar to have been your body,
I to have had the luck to envy the sole of your shoe in the dead of
    winter.

A passenger has lost his claim-check
The brunette her barrette,
And I—I think that there are moths eating holes in my pockets,
That my place in line is evaporating,
That the moon is not the moon and the bus is not the bus.

What is the word for goodbye?
    —*Donald Justice*

3. Think of a particular mood (happy, sad, wild, morose, lethargic, intoxicated, amorous, angry). Jot down words, phrases, and images that would be appropriate to the scene. Ask yourself what kind of tree? animal? terrain, weather? building? room? furniture? season? would suit the mood. Be as specific as possible. Don't choose the obvious—a bedroom

for an amorous mood, for example. Once you've made lists for various moods, see if you have the setting or scene for a poem. Try to use those words, but change them if the actual poem needs something else.

4. Try to find *le mot juste*, the "exactly right word" for what you mean to say. Gustave Flaubert urged Guy de Maupassant to describe a tree so it couldn't be mistaken for any other tree. Mark Twain said that the difference between the right word and the almost right word was the difference between "lightning" and the "lightning-bug." Try to find *le mot juste* in every line. Specify general words. What *kind* of tree, flower, bird, coat, tool, weapon, fruit, or automobile do you want to evoke? How will brand names change the mood of your poem? Are any words *too* specific? Sometimes the "just right" word is general: stone, cloud, leaf. Those words often have an "emblematic" quality; they're definite, but not *too* definite. The poet's choice of words is called *diction*.

5. Use nomenclature from a specific area: nautical, culinary, botanical, occult, judicial, athletic, architectural. Either write about a subject you know well or do some research. Write a poem using some of those particular terms. When you revise, make sure you haven't overloaded the poem with technicalities. They can spice up a poem and give it an air of authority, but they can also sink it if they're overused.

6. Try some "plain speaking," saying directly what you have in mind, using simple words and no embellishment: "Fool, look in thy heart and write." The muse delivers this command, but she was careful to direct it to Sir Philip Sidney, no fool when it came to writing. Don't fall into the trap of considering the heart as something mushy and saccharine. Think of the muscle that pumps blood through the circulatory system, and think of Dylan Thomas's "force that through the green fuse drives the flower." Write a short poem that says something as plainly and as directly as possible. Read John Keats's "This Living Hand."

7. Try to use ornate, fancy language—what Wallace Stevens calls "the essential gaudiness of poetry."

8. According to Robert Graves, Walter de la Mare compiled "lists of mellifluous words, such as *bergamot, chrysoprase, cresset, foredone, besprent*." Start your own word list in a notebook, jotting down interesting words you stumble across, including definitions and their etymology or origins, perhaps on a facing page. When you've done this for about a week, study the list and look for a word catchy enough to trigger a poem. Let the word suggest your subject.

9. A poet needs to pay attention to the ambiguities—multiple or overlapping meanings—of words. Since ambiguity is a common fault in shoddy writing, the poet should usually aim for exactness in his or her diction. But there are ways to revel in ambiguity as well, to let words suggest other possibilities, unexpected connections between things.

The most familiar use of this ambiguity is the *pun*, as when Benjamin Franklin remarked to his fellow signers of the Declaration of Independence that they'd better hang together, or they would assuredly hang separately. List about twenty words that have multiple meanings. (Look up *run*, for example, in your dictionary to see the wealth of possibilities a word may offer.) Then make a poem based on one or more of these puns. Your poem can actually be quite serious!

CONCRETENESS AND ABSTRACTION

The most basic advice for a beginning poet is usually "Show, don't tell." In other words, use particular images to convey a feeling or idea, instead of simply stating it. Present an action instead of summing it up. Rather than state "she felt angry," the poet might say "she kicked stones along the path." Rather than sum up "he was hoping for love," the poet might say "as he looked up, the moon overflowed like a chalice." Instead of glossing over an action ("he tore apart the room"), the poet will choose particular details that *show* this violence: "he tugged at the drawers, splintering the rough pine as it banged on the floor, as her underwear poured out."

Poets should depend primarily on their senses, handling words as a potter handles clay, hefting the wet lumps and shaping them with fingers as they spin. Words that refer to things we can touch are called *concrete* (Latin for "grown together, hardened"). Concrete words give the reader an almost physical experience, instead of just a rough idea or a vague sense of emotion. When we see a movie, we don't want to be told "the woman's car ran off a pier." We want to *see* it happen, as we do in Truffaut's *Jules and Jim*. The same thing is true for poetry (or fiction, for that matter): we want to see it for ourselves, and then draw our *own* conclusions.

Sometimes, however, the poet has a compelling reason to be more general: perhaps to give the reader an overall sense of what's going on, or to explain something that isn't very obvious, or to present an insight into the nature of things. Words that deal with ideas, concepts, and things we *can't* touch are called *abstract* (Latin for "removed from," meaning removed from concrete reality). Concrete words include *cat, umbrella, skyscraper, wool, festoon, stomp, dribble*. Abstract words include *peace, emotion, rational, hyperactive, relegate*. The concrete words appeal to the senses and have more flavor. Yet far too many beginners choose abstract words in their poems. Perhaps we are taught too relentlessly in school that summarizing matters most in our education, when in fact it's the knack for *noticing* specific things that enlarges our awareness of the world.

Ezra Pound advises the beginning poet to "Go in fear of abstractions."

Theodore Roethke suggests that we try to "anger the abstraction." This view of *diction*, or word choice, predominates today. It supplies an effective tonic (and purgative) for the student who speaks in generalities, mouths clichés, or passes off mere sentiments as ideas. Be specific, not general. Be concrete, not abstract.

But there is still a place for abstraction. John Ashbery aims to imitate the abstract quality of music (like a symphony, for example, which has no connection with anything but the sounds themselves and their arrangement) and of nonrepresentational painting (the abstract art that might be splashes of paint on a canvas or a swatch of pure color in the hands of Jackson Pollack or Mark Rothko). Ashbery wants to cut words loose from their usual moorings of meaning, so that concrete nouns and verbs swirl into a pattern we've never seen before. In his "Notes Toward a Supreme Fiction," Wallace Stevens goes so far as to assert of poetry that "It Must Be Abstract":

Begin, ephebe, by perceiving the idea
Of this invention, this invented world . . .

The key word here is *perceiving*, the habit of grasping an idea by noticing the particular thing, the "invented world." Often it's those uncertain, nebulous things that have no other reality that compel the poet to write, "to give to airy nothing," as Shakespeare says, "A local habitation and a name." The words themselves can furnish an equivalent for some feeling or state of mind. The poet can actually use words to get *beyond* words.

How *does* a writer deal with ideas poetically? He or she can write an essay in verse, as Alexander Pope did in his essays on "Man" and "Criticism"; or use metaphor to bring in something real that can clarify and vivify the abstractions; or shape the ideas into a story, a narrative that illustrates the concepts, makes them visible and alive; or play with sounds and phrases and repetitions in a way that imitates music. In other words, the poet can draw on the same strategies that work in a poem of images.

William Carlos Williams says "No ideas but in things," meaning that ideas have a place in poetry, but only if they present themselves in the guise of specific details and concrete images. Samuel Taylor Coleridge talks about "the danger of thinking without images." And William Blake declares "To Generalize is to be an Idiot."

Keep in mind that a poem is literally a "made thing." It can be more than a copy of nature, or a portrait of a friend, or a declaration of emotion, or a statement about truth. It can be something palpable in itself, an object with a life of its own.

10.   Think of an abstraction (such as love, peace, hope, mortality) and write a poem that is entirely concrete, full of sensory details, specific images (a parachute hanging from a sycamore, a burst piñata, a sunrise over the marsh). You may use the abstraction as a title, but do *not* use it, or any other abstraction, in the poem itself. A free verse poem of 10-30 lines might be a good set-up, so you won't be distracted by the demands of meter or rhyme, but any form will do. If you chose to write on mortality, for example, you might describe an incident when, as a child, you found a dying cardinal beside a tool shed. Every time you feel tempted to generalize or philosophize, remind yourself "Get specific, give examples!"

11.   Think about an idea that interests you. Then transfer—or translate—your ruminations into a poem, adding concrete details to bring your abstractions alive. Blend the original ideas into a flow of images and metaphors. If, for example, you are mulling over stoicism (the view that one should endure pain without complaining), give examples of how a stoic might act in a particular situation. William Stafford's poem "Bess" describes a woman dying of cancer who listens patiently to the people around her as they whine about petty things: "At her job at the library/ she arranged better and better flowers, and when/ students asked for books her hand went out/ to help."

12.   Write a poem the way an abstract painter uses pigment: splashes of color arranged in some pattern as you go. Jackson Pollack stood above a canvas laid flat on the floor and dribbled, flicked, flung, or poured paint across the surface. His "action painting" depended on energy and on paying keen attention as he transformed a mess, a series of accidents, into a work of art. Try to "splash" images from line to line, keeping each image clear and sharp and vivid but *not* trying to connect them in any logical way. You'll find it difficult to keep the poem flowing unless you use some transitions, but try to make them "positional" (left, next to, after, across the street, then) rather than logical. You might start by listing images, but that's a kind of cheating. Try to make things up as you go.

13.   Read a poem of images and try to formulate an idea that those images suggest. For instance, a poem describing a desert scene might suggest emptiness, or human extremity, or despair, or resourcefulness, depending on how the poet develops that imagery. Once you've singled out an idea (which may very well be the *theme* of the poem), write a poem on that idea using *different* images. The process, in short, can be formulated as *image ▶ idea ▶ image*. Feel free to imitate the original poem's manner or meter, as well as its theme, but make sure your range of imagery is completely different.

14.   Write an essay in verse. Alexander Pope used *heroic couplets* (iam-

bic pentameter rhymed AABBCC, etc.) in writing his "Essay on Man" and "Essay on Criticism," but you can use any meter you like — or free verse. Remember that it will strengthen your essay if you keep the imagery coming. Your topic should be some issue or question that interests you: destruction of the environment, civil rights, the nature of freedom or justice or beauty. If you feel stumped, take a look at the essays of Michel de Montaigne. He pioneered the form — and influenced Shakespeare through the still available translation by John Florio. Even a glance at his topics may help. More recent essays by Lewis Thomas, Steven J. Gould, Joan Didion, and others should give you further ideas on how to proceed. Remember that an *essay* is literally an "attempt," a kind of experiment in understanding.

NAMING

When Adam "gave names to all cattle, and to the fowl of the air, and to every beast of the field," he acted as the first poet, giving each creature another reality, distinguishing *antelope* from *zebu*, making them live in language and music, ready to be invoked even in their absence and brought to mind through human speech. If you know the name of something, it gives you power. Think of the story of Rumpelstiltskin. Think of how the name of the Hebrew God was sacred, a secret, powerful in itself.

Names are sometimes called "handles" — and the nickname makes a handy metaphor, suggesting something you can grasp and carry. A name not only lets you refer quickly to something complicated; it also has a music and specificity of its own: Caligula, Thor, Guinevere, Oshkosh, Vladivostok, Pike's Peak, Mekong, Caribbean. Most of us feel strongly about names for people, perhaps loving "Heather" but abhorring "Hortense." Partly it's the sound of the name, partly the personal and cultural associations, partly the familiarity or strangeness. In any case, a poem can take on a good deal of color and character by using names (of all sorts of things) effectively.

How specific should the naming be? Sometimes the generic noun ("dog," for example) is enough. Sometimes you need to specify "whippet." And sometimes you need to single out a particular whippet, "Esmeralda." If the name isn't enough, you have to describe and define, taking up more room — and more of your reader's patience. Names are a short-cut. Chosen well, each particular name "rings a bell" for the listener.

15. Write a poem that uses plenty of different names: first names, surnames, places, titles, brand-names, and so on. Be very specific. It may

help to use a third person point of view and to call the "he" or "she" by name. When you're through, do there seem to be *too many* proper names? If so, you can always change them to their common nouns, so that "Chesapeake" becomes "the bay." Use the names as you would use imagery: to make the experience of the poem more vivid.

16. Write a poem that sticks with generic words for things: the river, the tree, the bird, the house. This kind of noun may be relatively unspecific (compared to the Rio Grande, the shagbark hickory, the oriole, and the pink split-level with flaking paint), but if it's concrete it can have enormous power, the magic of a talisman, the psychic force of a mantra repeated over and over in meditation. Start by making a list of nouns that have this quality of strong and simple virtue. Don't use abstractions like "peace" or "love" or even "home." Make sure the nouns refer to things that are palpably real.

17. Write a poem in which you "name" things that have no names.

18. Write a poem that "defines" a proper name. You can do this by describing the appearance, or noting the habits, or by showing some action of the person, place, or thing that's named. You might look into a field guide (to birds or trees, for example) to see how different species are differentiated and made memorable.

ETYMOLOGY

According to most definitions, poetry is intensified, charged, concentrated language. Every word counts. In prose, the language is usually fast-moving and transparent, but we slow down to read and savor poems, paying attention to the texture, feel, taste, sound, and suggestiveness of the words. One way a poet makes words more suggestive, more three-dimensional, and more resonant is by making use of a word's history: how it came to English, what it originally meant, and how its meanings overlap.

A dictionary will list a word's roots, its derivation, its *etymology*. Like thoroughbreds, words have "bloodlines," and it makes a poem richer if the poet is aware of these. The best place to examine an English word's lineage and observe where it originated and how it has changed through the centuries is the Oxford English Dictionary (or O.E.D.), which gives quotations to illustrate a word's various uses. There are also many books specifically on etymology, from scholarly to popular. Browsing in these word books is fun—and pays dividends very quickly.

English is essentially a by-product of the Norman Conquest of 1066, combining Anglo-Saxon with French, the first a Germanic language and the second a Romance language. (Both of these belong to the immense Indo-European family of languages.) This hybrid quality gives English variety, strength, and a large vocabulary with many shades of meaning. English also absorbs words easily from other tongues, especially Latin, Greek, and Scandinavian languages, but also from Arabic ("algebra"), Hebrew ("amen"), Chinese ("silk"), Turkish ("coffee"), Hindi ("shampoo"), American-Indian languages ("toboggan"), and many others.

Macbeth's great lines "No, this hand would rather/ The multitudinous seas incarnadine,/ Making the green one red" offer a practical lesson in how to apply this word history. Shakespeare mixes his Latinate and Anglo-Saxon words with much virtuosity: "multitudinous" and "incarnadine" are long, loud, rumbling words. Any more of them would sink the passage. But notice how effective they are when surrounded — buoyed, even — by the monosyllables "hand," "seas," "green," and "red," all stout Germanic words. (The tag "Latinate" refers to French and other Romance-language words derived from Latin.) Generally, the Anglo-Saxon words impart a down-to-earth quality; the Latinate words sound fancier and often more abstract.

19. With a good dictionary close by, write a poem that consciously mixes Anglo-Saxon words with Latinate words (those derived from Latin and French). Notice what happens to a line when you add one kind of word. See what happens to lines predominated by either. Try substituting Latinate for Anglo-Saxon words, and vice versa. You can also apply this exercise to old poems you want to revise. Think of it as similar to a musician's "ear training."

20. Write a poem that's based on a word's etymology. (Sometimes these histories are in dispute; in a poem, that hardly matters.) Feel free to branch off, letting the word's associations steer you in unexpected directions. The etymology is only the starting point, the springboard. If you like, begin with a phrase and explore its history.

GRAMMAR AND PUNCTUATION

Grammar may seem like a tedious subject, but the word is related to *glamour*; originally grammar was seen as a kind of magic, or rather as the means of handling the magic of language.

Knowing something about grammar will help your poems in several ways: first of all, you can be your own best proofreader, avoiding errors that might make a literate reader scoff; second, you will have more tools at your disposal, more ways to bend and shape language; third, you will be in a better position to *break* the rules of grammar successfully if you know what they are.

The bones, blood, and muscle of language are the nouns (persons, places, and things) and verbs (which show action or a state of being). Adjectives and adverbs modify nouns and verbs respectively. Adjectives tell us "which one," "what kind," and "how many." Adverbs tell us "when," "where," "how," and "how much." These modifiers can weaken a poem if they appear too frequently; they can seem like mere decoration, inessential, and can often be profitably omitted. Pronouns (like "she" and "whoever") stand in for nouns; they are fairly invisible, so they make good substitutions if you want to keep things moving or avoid repeating the same noun. The verb "to be" is also relatively invisible, linking what precedes it and what follows it, like an equal sign. It is also the weakest of verbs, showing no motion or action whatsoever. Overused, it can disable an entire poem, like a car that runs out of gas. Prepositions (such as "for," "by," "of," and "among") link lesser nouns to more important ones — "a basket *of* raspberries" or "raspberries *in* a basket" — but prepositional phrases function as modifiers. Conjunctions (such as "and" and "or," "if" and "because") connect parts of a sentence. If the parts they connect are equal, the conjunctions are "coordinate"; if one part is subservient to and dependent upon another, they are "subordinate":

| Coordinate: | The dog barks, *and* the cat meows. |
| | Dogs *and* cats delight us. |

| Subordinate: | *Because* the dog barks, the cat meows. |
| | Cats delight us, *if* we let them. |

The last "part of speech" is the interjection, an exclamation like "Wow!" or "Oh!" or "Ouch!"

The poet should populate the poem mainly with nouns and verbs, minimizing the number of adjectives and adverbs, avoiding clusters of boring, insignificant, prosy words (such as "it is to be said that, in accordance with the above"), using *active* verbs (such as "The boxer *punched* the wall") rather than weak and wordy *passive* verbs ("The wall *was punched by* the boxer").

Some poets discard punctuation altogether, omitting commas and periods (though not always the question mark), letting the poem seem to float off the page. Punctuation nails it down, keeps it earthbound. Remember that an unpunctuated poem is harder to control (because you've removed all the traffic signs) and harder to pace. It will seem ghostlier, less conversational, stranger, more distant. Sometimes it does gain in music. For some poets, the line unit is punctuation enough.

Whether or not to capitalize the first letter of each line is entirely up to the poet. You'd think that free verse poets would tend *not* to capitalize automatically, and that formal or metrical poets would insist on punctuation, but that's not always the case. Each line of Norman Dubie's free verse begins with a capital, while only letters that begin sentences or form proper names are capitalized in Mary Jo Salter's metrical verse. Some poets, such as Edward Hirsch, switch protocols as the mood strikes. Go by what you like, or follow the example of your favorite poets.

Some poets dislike subordinate clauses, or words that end in "-y" or "-ing," or semicolons, or exclamation points, or comma splices, or poems *without* sentence fragments, or any number of other peeves. This is personal. How simple do you want your poems to sound? How complicated or sophisticated? Would you like them to wind and meander, or jab and punch? Do you want them airy or earthy, elevated or artless? These are the real poetic questions that can animate the dry bones of grammar and punctuation.

21. Write a poem that doesn't use punctuation. (Try it in free verse.) Is it hard to enjamb (letting the sense of one line run over to the next)? Does it sound unnatural? Try to emphasize the song-like qualities of the language. Try to open up some mysteries.

22. Write a poem that uses a wild array of punctuation.

23. Write a poem with nothing but simple sentences. Then rewrite, combining as many sentences as possible. You can do that by using conjunctions and by turning some sentences into dependent clauses. Rephrasing and relining the poem will often help. Which version do you prefer? Can you say why?

24. Write a poem that uses sentence fragments freely.

25. Write a poem in "bad grammar"—yet make it a real poem. You might try to capture a particular dialect, or the talk of a nonnative speaker. Think of a situation that justifies divergence from proper English, and imagine your way from there.

(Note: You may find a handbook of grammar and usage helpful.)

ALLUSIONS

No matter how casual its manner may appear, poetry is language that has been condensed, compacted, tightened, and trimmed. It's weakened by extra words—which might, in prose, help the reader understand something complicated more gradually, step by step. Because poetry is "charged language," it depends on the spark of sudden perception, the lightning flash of insight. One of the ways in which poetry compresses language is through *allusion*, reference to other literary works or outside knowledge the reader is expected to know or at least to recognize.

What, though, should the poet expect the reader to know? In *The Waste Land*, T.S. Eliot alludes so widely, and so arcanely at times, that he had to add a section of lengthy notes to the poem. Traditionally, poets have alluded most abundantly to the Bible and to Greek and Roman myths. To decide how far you can go in alluding to outside material, you must first envision your reader. Are you writing poems for an elite audience that will pick up your veiled references to literature and culture? Are you writing for a solitary reader who has a reasonable, though not scholarly, background in reading? Are you writing for the average woman or man who holds a job, raises a family, and might enjoy a poem that seems unpretentious and down to earth? Are you writing for a hip crowd of jazz musicians who will get any musical references but maybe not too many others? Either consciously or unconsciously (by the way you write) you will necessarily sort out this dilemma for yourself.

Some writers dislike allusions on principle. Walt Whitman wanted them out of his poems, just as he wanted the muse "install'd amid the kitchenware," so that his poems could encompass the real America of his day, without the encumbrances of the past. When you allude to something, you're generally casting a backward glance at an old world, not striking out for a new one. Too many allusions can clutter up a poem. Allusions that are too obscure can make a poem needlessly difficult and make the reader give up. Sometimes allusions seem pretentious, the writer showing off. But they have a time-honored place in poetry. After all, we can't read a poem at all if we don't know what the words signify. Allusions are simply other kinds of words or phrases. Some are everyday expressions: the patience of Job, casting your bread on the water, an Achilles heel. Use allusions when they vivify the poem and make it quicker, clearer, richer, deeper. You may not want to confine yourself to the reader with a grade school education.

26. Write a poem to the person you imagine as your ideal or typical reader. You might describe this person, or talk to him or her directly, or speak from that person's point of view. Good model poems include Ted Kooser's "Selecting a Reader" and Linda Pastan's "To My Reader." The most famous of such poems is Charles Baudelaire's "To the Reader," which concludes, in Richard Howard's translation: "—hypocrite reader,—my alias,—my twin!"

27. Write a poem that begins with an allusion to the Bible or to Greek myth (Noah's Ark, for example, or Orpheus descending into the underworld), but bring the rest of the poem up to date so that it is about something more than just the reference. An allusion is really a remark *in passing*, not a full-blown treatment of the subject. In Andrew Hudgins' "The Yellow Steeple," the speaker describes a walk through a graveyard;

yellow paint overturned on a steeple, spatters all over him and recalls the myth of Zeus appearing as a golden rain to impregnate Danae. The allusion makes an accident seem like a blessing.

28. Look through your old poems in search of places where an allusion might clarify, strengthen, or condense a passage of lines. In "Sway," Louis Simpson describes a mother supervising a boyfriend's visit to her daughter, "pretending to sew, and keeping an eye on them/ like Fate." One of the three Greek Fates spun the thread of life, one measured it, and one cut it, so the reference is compact and witty, suggesting something comically portentous in the distrustful mother. Look for resemblances to scenes and situations in the Bible, in mythology, in famous novels, in Shakespeare's plays, in the history of science, in well-known biographies. A reference to Napoleon's retreat from Russia, as in Richard Wilbur's "After the Last Bulletins," makes sense; a reference to an obscure skirmish does not — and will annoy the reader. (Of course, you can always deal with that skirmish by describing the action so vividly that the reader feels transported to the scene, but then it's not an allusion.)

PURE AND IMPURE POEMS

Robert Penn Warren has remarked, "poetry aspires to purity; poems do not." This distinction is useful. The beauty of a poem need not come from beautiful things; it will probably come from the overall pattern, the vividness of the images, the experience it gives the reader. Of course, it's all relative. The purest, most perfect poem would teeter on the edge of absolute silence. Make a poem *too* impure and you've got a case of indecent exposure — or prose. How much a poet allows into a poem depends on the poet and the particular needs of a poem. The world can be largely excluded or included in a poem, depending on the poet's vision, artistic views, and willingness to let the poem itself lead the way.

After the elegant metrics of the fifties, both Louis Simpson and Karl Shapiro announced that they wanted to write "bad poems" — not bad in quality, but bad in the sense of rebellious, undercutting the good manners that had come to seem stifling. It helps to be dissatisfied. If you are, you free yourself to try something new, to break through the confinements of smugness and familiarity.

Marianne Moore thought any material should be possible in a poem, "nor is it valid/ to discriminate against 'business documents and/ schoolbooks.'" We tend to censor ourselves about what is suitably "poetic." But many poets of the past hundred years have sought to open the doors wider — or, in Whitman's terms, to "Unscrew the locks from the doors!/ Unscrew the doors themselves from their jambs!" Ezra Pound conceived his voluminous *Cantos* as a kind of "grab bag." He quoted whole letters and long passages in foreign languages, refusing to exclude them since he couldn't deny that these things existed.

In his essay "Toward an Impure Poetry," Pablo Neruda calls for a poetry "impure as the clothing we wear, or our bodies, soup-stained, soiled with our shameful behavior, our wrinkles and vigils and dreams, observations and prophecies, declarations of loathing and love, idyls and beasts, the shocks of encounter, political loyalties, denials and doubts, affirmations and taxes."

We can welcome things in, letting them flood the poem; or we can filter things out, erecting a kind of dike around the poem. It's a matter of preference, taste—and maybe a sign of how adventurous we choose to be.

29. Make a list of things, subjects, objects, feelings, and images that you don't think belong in a poem. Then write a poem about one of them. (You can keep going until you exhaust the list—and you can keep adding to the list.) *Anything* should be possible material for a poem, depending on how it's treated.

30. "Decorum" deals with what is "fitting" in a poem. What would be appropriate for a meditation on mortality might not be right for a poem about hard times in a ghetto (although you might get a stronger poem by blending the two approaches). Write a poem that observes the proper decorum (as you imagine it) for a particular subject. Then write an answer by a disgruntled bystander or injured party who objects to your niceties. Which poem is more gripping, more interesting? Combine the two versions, or parts of them, if you like. The goal is an interesting poem, however it comes into being.

31. Write an impure poem. Feel free to bring in the things of this world, references to names and places, unpoetic vocabulary, bizarre metaphors, wide-ranging and detailed imagery. Vary your tone of voice—don't be hushed or melodious all the time. Be witty, or sly, or wry, or ironic, or angry, or rambunctious. Don't be the stereotypical poet with flower in one hand, quill in the other, and an aversion to the real world and its intricacies.

32. If you still think poems need to be pretty and about beautiful things, try writing an *anti-poem*: one that rejects the conventionally beautiful (and often, therefore, the trite) in favor of gritty realism or down-to-earth slang. Instead of writing about tulips or sunsets, write about electric can openers or acid rain. Choose words that are as *un*poetic as possible. This is poetry in the raw, without its makeup. It can borrow from the vocabulary of the newspaper, the supermarket tabloid, the baseball color commentator, the disk-jockey, the commercial. If your results sound like a conventional poem, you're doing it wrong.

33. Try to write a pure poem that's interesting. You'll have to purify it by filtering out all sorts of things: harsh noises, irony, ugly images, maybe images altogether. How would you write a pure poem in free verse? Does rhyme purify or merely decorate? Remember that puritans are often iconoclasts, smashing graven images. You can use images in a pure poem, but they need to be stripped down, simplified. The main problem with most "pure poems" is blandness. Because there's not much there, they can seem empty, fake, poeticized. But purity can also elevate the mood to something spiritual and metaphysical, quieting the mind, letting it drift — or holding it very steady. Think of Shaker furniture, Bach's partitas for solo violin, a calm clear afternoon.

III. *Sight*

Much contemporary poetry is written primarily for the eye. The reader takes in the poem, usually, in silence. That may be a good reason—if only to practice contrariness—to cultivate the sound and rhythm in a poem, to emphasize its music. Nevertheless, the visual predominates. Sight is the sense most entrusted with discovery—and invention. And this means the poem "gets to us" by the vividness and freshness of its imagery, the surprising rightness of its metaphors.

IMAGE

In poetry, an *image* is a mental picture. Although sight may be the main sense invoked by an image, all the senses can take part. A good image puts the reader right in the scene itself, making him see, hear, smell, taste, and touch what's there.

Imagery has always mattered in poetry, but many twentieth century poets have elevated it to primary importance. Instead of spelling out their ideas, they let the image *suggest* ideas by its vividness, emotional depth, psychological overtones, strangeness or familiarity, and connections to other images in the poem. There are many good ways to come up with good, fresh images: observing and taking notes, reconstructing memories, picturing how a scene might look, combining unrelated elements in a new situation, recalling dreams, meditating to see what rises into view, scaring up flashes of imagery by "automatic writing," letting words suggest mental pictures, fleshing out a brief glimpse, expanding on a story, free-associating, studying a photograph or painting. Hunting for imagery can be a valuable exercise in itself—but so can waiting, attentively, for whatever comes to you.

Here is a little anthology of images:

In stinking swamps I have seen great hulks:
A Leviathan that rotted in the reeds!
   —*Arthur Rimbaud, "The Drunken Boat" (tr. Paul Schmidt)*

Spits of glitter in lowgrade ore,
precious stones too poorly surrounded for harvest
   —*A.R. Ammons, "Conserving the Magnitude of Uselessness"*

The sprinkling can
Slumbered on the dock
    —John Ashbery, "Canzone"

Her wings torn shawls, her long body
Rubbed of its plush—
    —Sylvia Plath, "Stings" (referring to a queen bee)

A virtuoso dog at midnight—high wavering howl
resolved in three staccato low barks.
    —Denise Levertov, "Strange Song"

the utter waste of pollen, a scum
of it on every pond and puddle.
    —Andrew Hudgins, "The Persistence of Nature in Our Lives"

White daisies against the burnt orange of the windowframe,
lusterless redwood in the nickel grey of winter
    —Robert Hass, "Natural Theology"

spiders had wrapped up
the crystal chandelier
    —Mary Oliver, "An Old Whorehouse"

A latch lifting, an edged den of light
Opens across the yard.
    —Seamus Heaney, "Good-Night"

A revolver lying next to a camera,
violins hanging in the air like hams. . . .
    —Louis Simpson, "The Pawnshop"

I remember how she rose with nothing on
but water, as the pool's aqua mirror lapsed
    —Mark Irwin, "Domnica"

Beulah gazes through the pale speckled linoleum
to the webbed loam with its salt and worms.
    —Rita Dove, "Pomade"

I saw the dusty little threshing ground
that makes us ravenous for our mad sins,

saw it from mountain crest to lowest shore.
    — *Dante,* Paradiso *XXII (tr. John Ciardi)*

There are stone breakers in straw hats
Drinking from jars under a shade tree.
    — *Norman Dubie, "About Infinity"*

It takes more than description — usually — to make a good image. Concrete, specific, interesting words help. (Notice the palpable words like "swamps," "hulks," "dock," "shawls," "plush," "scum," "pond," "chandelier," "latch," "violins," "hams," "loam," "jars," and "stone breakers" in the sample lines.) Sound effects help: the repeated vowels of "spits of glitter" and "Rubbed of its plush" and "edged den"; the repeated consonants of "pollen," "pond," and "puddle" and of "hanging" and "hams." Senses other than sight can also contribute, as in the "high wavering howl" and "staccato low barks" of the musical dog. And things that you really couldn't see can be visualized: Beulah staring right through the floor into the loam of the earth. The image can be simple or elaborate, fleeting or sustained, clear or mysterious.

One of the most common and powerful forms of imagery is the *metaphor* (called a *simile* if "like" or "as" or another linking word explains the connection), in which one thing is compared to another. Try to see how many of the images I've listed make use of it. Metaphor can alter the poem's mood by making us see something particular in a new light, a new context. It colors both the image and the reader's emotional response.

1. Browse through an anthology of poems, circling or copying images that give you a vivid mental picture. Mark an X through any images that fizzle and fail to project anything striking. What do you like about the images that work? How many of the five senses do they conjure up? What interesting words do they contain? What sound effects do they use? If they are metaphors, how similar or dissimilar are the two things that are compared?

2. Start hunting for images. Jot down sensory details you observe at home or work or school or in the streets; try to record your dreams; try to remember scenes and people from years past; try to notice resemblances between different things you see. Drawing from this stockpile of images, write a poem that (1) expands upon a key image or (2) combines and connects differing images.

3. Sitting at a desk, without referring to notes or journals, without observing anything in the room or out the window, make a quick list of images. Jump from one thing to another, ranging as widely as you can.

Don't try to connect the images in a poem; just see what comes up when you give your imagination free rein. If you start with, say, a parachute caught in a railroad trestle, move far from that scene, maybe to a young girl in a wheelchair, reading on a porch. Be specific. Be concrete. When you have a sizable list, begin selecting, arranging, connecting, and expanding some of the images into a poem.

4. Write a poem that revolves around a single image.

5. Using nothing but specific images, write a poem that you can't explain and don't understand. Forge ahead into the darkness; let the poem be odd, unresolved — as long as the images are vivid, specific, and striking. The recipe: clear images, mysterious connections.

6. Sometimes images need filling out, but sometimes they should be less cluttered. Go through a list of images or a journal or an old poem you're not happy with and try to pare down some of the overly elaborate images. Our scientific principle here is the law of conservation of energy: the more economically you can suggest an image, the more powerfully it will surge in the reader's mind. Remember, however, that if you cut too much, your image may sound unnatural or impenetrable.

METAPHOR AND SIMILE

Aristotle thought that having a command of metaphor was the "mark of genius" in a poet, "for to make good metaphors implies an eye for resemblances" (in S.H. Butcher's translation). The knack for making metaphors may be, as Aristotle believed, unteachable, but that doesn't mean a poet can't discover or develop it. Most learning amounts to a kind of prospecting; we don't really know what riches or fool's gold our claim holds until we've mined it — and even then we might make something of what seems paltry at first, if we're resourceful enough.

Metaphor comes from a Greek word meaning to "transfer" or to "bear or convey change." (The prefix *meta-* deals with change, as in "metamorphosis.") In a true metaphor, we say A = B, as in Sylvia Plath's "The air is a mill of hooks" (from her poem "Mystic"). In a *simile*, on the other hand, A is *similar to* B, as in Elizabeth Bishop's "The turtles lumbered by, high-domed,/ hissing like teakettles" (from "Crusoe in England"). The difference is important. A metaphor, which fuses together two separate things, packs a wallop and can shock us by its equations; it offers no comfortable distance between objects. A simile, which points out a likeness *between* different things, is more easygoing, off-handed, relaxed; it lets us superimpose one object over another temporarily. You'd think that, because of its greater intensity, metaphor would be "better" than simile, but that's not the case. It all depends on what the poem needs. Generally, the "glue" of a metaphor holds longer. A simile lets us keep going and refer in passing to other similes as they come up. A simile sounds more casual, and perhaps more natural. A metaphor shifts the language of the poem into a higher gear, intensifying it.

Both metaphors and similes are prone to particular dangers. Unless you want to disrupt the poem or disorient the reader, you shouldn't "mix" your metaphors by shifting the basis of comparison in midsentence. *The New Yorker* often prints funny mixed metaphors under the heading "Block That Metaphor!": "POLITICIANS' TUNNEL VISION FALLS ON DEAF EARS IN NEWSROOM." Many clichés, such as "light as a feather," are cast in the form of similes; make sure your comparisons haven't gone stale. Also make sure you don't pile up too many similes in a row. The connecting words or phrases necessary to a simile ("like," "as," "as if," "similar to," and so on) will begin to sound obtrusive and irritating—unless they are intentionally part of a repetitive pattern. But if you avoid mixed metaphors and awkward repetitions, there's no reason why you can't *switch* metaphors or similes quickly and frequently. That can be a good source of energy.

Some other terms may help. An *analogy* is a comparison, usually drawn out, equating something known with something unknown, used in an argument or persuasive essay. It often compares situations or ideas rather than things. A *parable* is a story told to illustrate a point, like the parable of the sowers told by Jesus (who spoke in metaphors so that everyone would understand his teachings). A *conceit* presents a striking, involved parallel. An *extended metaphor* is a comparison that's elaborated at some length, perhaps through an entire poem. John Donne offers many wonderful examples, as in "The Bait" and "The Flea."

Sandra McPherson once related a rule of thumb she learned from Elizabeth Bishop: "in a good comparison, you should be able to say one thing is *exactly* like another." But the two things you compare shouldn't be *too* similar. The power of metaphor comes from the distance bridged and the pleasurable shock we get from that electrical connection between two seemingly different entities. Quickness matters too. We don't want our metaphors, any more than our jokes, explained to us. We want to get them immediately. The writer needs to be as economical as possible, recognizing that comparisons may require some space in the name of clarity. We want both exactitude and a flight of fancy.

Metaphor, however, shouldn't be strange for its own sake. A good comparison can be psychological, or mysterious, or fantastic, but it shouldn't be forced or arbitrary. It has to hit the target, however distant; it has to make imaginative sense, however surreal or weird it may be.

The whole poem can be thought of as a kind of grand metaphor. When people have trouble with poetry, it's usually because they can't see the metaphorical connections. But most poetry is *figurative*, not just *literal*. If an archaeological site is described at length (as in Lynn Emanuel's "The Dig"), we might suppose that some sort of inner digging or mining of the self is being suggested. Good literal description will often (maybe always) have figurative resonance. We should be able to "pick up" figurative connections with our reader's antennae — not just coldly analyze and rationally pick apart the poem. We should try to hear the echoes while listening to the sounds themselves.

Some writers dispense with "local" metaphors and similes, presenting their poems as direct, plain-speaking. At their worst, metaphor and simile can be mere decoration and ornamentation. They can be trite, cliché, obvious, uninteresting. To work well, comparisons should have a point, however shrouded, however dimly understood by the poet.

There are two good ways to go about making metaphors and similes: (1) jot down resemblances you have noticed during the day in a journal or notebook; (2) discover resemblances in the process of writing a poem. In either case, you'll want to be on the lookout, ready to spot the almost hidden links between things.

Imagery often becomes clearer, more sharply focused, more strikingly *visible* when it's presented in the guise of metaphor. As Richard Wilbur points out, "Odd that a thing is most itself when likened."

Here are some examples of similes and metaphors:

Similes

I spend my life sitting, like an angel in a barber's chair
 — *Arthur Rimbaud, "Evening Prayer" (tr. Paul Schmidt)*

A fine fume of rain driving in from the sea,
Riddling the sand, like a wide spray of buckshot
 — *Theodore Roethke, "The Storm"*

In the barn's huge gloom
light falls through cracks
the way swordblades
pierce a magician's box.
 — *Gregory Orr, "Morning Song"*

These peninsulas take the water between thumb and finger
like women feeling for the smoothness of yard-goods.
 — *Elizabeth Bishop, "The Map"*

and through the streets the blood of the children
flowed simply like the blood of children
> — *Pablo Neruda, "Explanation of a Few Things"*
> *(an approximation of his Spanish)*

Metaphors

The alphabet of
the trees
> — *William Carlos Williams, "The Botticellian Trees"*

The lamplight falls on all fours on the grass.
> — *Robert Bly, "Driving Toward the Lac Qui Parle River"*

Vowels of delicious clarity
For the little red schoolhouse of our mouths.
> — *Charles Simic, "Breasts"*

... and the full-breasted tulips
open their pink blouses
> — *Brigit Pegeen Kelly, "Doing Laundry on Sunday"*

Sleep kept snowing down while she was talking,
and when she left I slept. The snow came ...
> — *Laura Jensen, "Poem" (from* Memory)

Far off the logging birds saw into heartwood
with rusty blades, and the grouse cranks up
his eternally unstartable Model T
and the oilcan bird comes with his liquid pock pock
> — *Maxine Kumin, "The Hermit Wakes to Bird Sounds"*

7. Take a field trip somewhere, indoors or out. Look for resemblances and put any you discover in a notebook. Remember that it's not just a matter of noticing; you also have to *articulate* your comparison in just the right words. Be as exact as you can, without being too wordy. Once you're home (or on the spot, if you can't stand the wait), begin a poem using some or all of the comparisons.

8. Write a poem that uses metaphors and/or similes. Describe something (a day at the zoo, for example) that gives you an opportunity to discover vivid likenesses — someplace rich in things to see and experience.

9. A useful exercise for gathering material is to make two lists of

nouns, one made up of things you observe, the other made up of random, flavorful words that don't refer consciously to the scene you've just been observing. Aim for at least a dozen nouns on each list: things you've just seen, things you haven't seen. Then mix and match nouns from the two lists, jumping around from image to image. Even if connections don't magically appear (although they very well might!), some of the "near misses" might suggest a pairing that has the sudden electric force of a good metaphor. Try approaching this exercise with a keen sense of playfulness. If the list-making doesn't seem productive, you can try another method: write lively, concrete words on slips of paper; then mix and split them randomly into pairs and see if any of the combinations ("dog" and "sofa cushion," for example) make sense as likenesses. Although some of these pairings will be nonsensical, some may be surprisingly apt—and surprise is the real trick of metaphor.

10. Try to write a poem of one metaphor after another. Write as many lines as you can, then cut the ones that don't seem striking enough.

11. Take an old poem of yours and examine its metaphors and similes—or lack of them. Where could you omit the comparisons? Where could they be sharpened, improved? Where do you need to rephrase? Where do you need to insert new metaphors?

12. Look through a book or anthology of poems and hunt for metaphors and similes. Mark or copy the ones that jump out at you. What do you like about them? Can you imitate the effect they create by substituting different words? Do they express their comparisons in new ways?

SYMBOLS, ETC.

So many beginning poets—and readers of poetry—react bizarrely to the word *symbol* that it's tempting to pretend the term doesn't exist. Some people take it to heart—imagining "At last! Here is the key!"—and deposit symbols everywhere, even if they overload the poor poem. Other people become fearful that symbols lurk in every shadow, ready to assault them when they're not paying attention. Think of a symbol as any image that resonates with meaning and recurs throughout a poem.

Usually, that meaning cannot be adequately defined *except* in terms of the image itself; it can't be summed up easily. If an image does have that A = B simplicity, we're really dealing with *allegory*, in which a particular image represents a specific, assigned concept or abstraction.

It's hard, especially for a newcomer, to write poems while concentrating on symbolism. A hatchet might very well symbolize animosity, but if we *write* that way, concentrating on getting the sense of animosity across, we're heading straight toward abstraction; we're reducing the hatchet to a signpost. It might be better to cultivate a *feel* for the suggestiveness and reverberations and resonances of the words we use. It might be better to make the words palpable, so that we can almost run our thumbs along the cracked pine handle or the nicked blade of the hatchet.

There are other ways to use imagery as a means of naming something. *Synecdoche* means "a part for the whole," as when we refer to a car as a "set of wheels." I'm not sure how practical and useful the term may be to the poet dreaming up poems. I'd rather stress the use of suggestion, the imaginative shuttling between large and small, part and whole, general and specific, visible and invisible. Oddly enough, a modern effect of synecdoche is not to signal a whole entity but to suggest a kind of dismemberment, as in T.S. Eliot's "pair of ragged claws/ Scuttling across the floors of silent seas" in "The Love Song of J. Alfred Prufrock."

Metonymy is a related term, but refers to things simply *associated* with the main thing, as when we say "the crown" to indicate the Queen of England.

13.   Take a familiar symbol (like a red rose, or an anchor, or a crucifix) and write a poem that restores the object to something tangible, something you can see, hear, smell, taste, and touch. Place it in some context, some seemingly real place.

14.   Write a poem in which you refer not to things themselves, but to parts of them: the antler rather than the buck, the telescopic sight rather than the rifle, the bouffant rather than the barmaid, the fire escape rather than the building. Jump from image to image, using free association, asking yourself "what does this remind me of?" When you come to a halt, see what all the images and shifts and "parts for the whole" suggest, what they add up to.

VISION

One way or another, vision is crucial to poetry. Of the five senses, the sense of sight is responsible for most imagery and most metaphor. Some poets, such as Robert Frost, would argue that hearing is the crucial sense for poems, but really it supplements rather than supplants clear vision and close observation.

But seeing things may not be as important to the poet as seeing *beyond* or *into* things. Sight must lead to insight. The teenaged Rimbaud wanted to become a seer, a visionary, and considered that the poet's true mission. Here we're on slippery ground. It's absurd and pretentious to set up shop as a visionary, and yet that kind of seeing can make the difference between poetry that's middling and poetry that matters. But that visionary quality need not be embodied in the stereotypically wide-eyed, long-bearded prophet. There's no reason a visionary poet can't be quiet, introspective, realistic—even humorous.

It doesn't hurt to attempt the opposite of what you do well, to see if you can stretch and expand your range. If your poetry is modest and unassuming, try to be more ambitious; rouse the tone. If your poetry is bombastic and grandiose, try to observe more closely and to use more precise imagery; calm the tone. We could construct a "vision scale" based on how visual or visionary a poem (or poet) might be. The visionary depends on what's indefinable and mysterious and hard to see.

15. Wherever you are, close your eyes and try to reconstruct the scene around you in your head, in your "mind's eye." When you've completed the picture, open your eyes and check the results. Jot it down in a notebook or journal, if you like. Repeat this exercise frequently, in different places. If a poem comes out of this, fine, but that's not the immediate point. Learning to see is.

16. Practice close observation the way Sherlock Holmes would. Try to notice everything about a person or a place. Then try to "deduce" what's behind that person or place: the dirty fingers of the bank teller, the crushed, greasy thumbnail of the mechanic, the door-shaped discoloration on the wallpaper. Be a detective. Then write a poem about what you've observed, perhaps in the voice of the crimebuster or mystery solver.

17. Imagine you've been blindfolded and taken to some strange location. Visualize what the place might look like. Is it indoors or out? cold or hot or mild? dark or light? What colors do you see? What sounds can you hear? What actions are taking place around you, if any? What plants do you see? what animals? what objects? what other people? Write a poem about what you do next when stranded in that place.

18. Look at something for a long time, longer than you think necessary. An animal, a scene, a picture, a person, the night sky, a field. Then describe what's invisible but nevertheless there. Make what you don't see as real as what you see. Write a poem that moves back and forth between the seen and the unseen.

19. Picture what a place will look like in a hundred years—or what it looked like a century ago. Don't allow yourself the clichés of science fiction. Don't assume an apocalypse or a nothingness. Imagine as fully as you can. Start by trying to figure out where the scene now is headed, then set out from the trail of logic into the wilderness of fantasy.

IV. Sound

Although the sense of sight may dominate contemporary poetry, the astute poet will want to engage the sense of hearing as well. Poets have long been judged by their "ears," their knack for verbal music, the orchestration of language. A hundred years ago, most critics would have said that poetry depended primarily on sound. But despite the current popularity of poetry readings, most of us get our poems in silence, from the page itself. What that leads to, more often than not, is a poetry that's muffled, droning, offering little to the ears. Don't impoverish your poems by ignoring how they sound. Use your eyes *and* your ears — along with your other senses. And when you're reading, remember that Robert Frost said it's OK to move your lips when you read poems.

ALLITERATION

The repetition of initial consonants is called alliteration. If the consonants aren't at the beginnings of words, we call that *consonance*, but the distinction may be more useful academically than creatively. If we allow alliteration, as a term, to cover more ground, perhaps we can treat it more flexibly in our own writing, since we'll be less encumbered with technical jargon.

Since alliteration has a memorable quality, it comes up often, not just in poetry but in political speeches, advertising campaigns, mottoes and sayings. It's an easy device to use, but hard to use well.

Lord Tennyson found it difficult *not* to alliterate in his poems; he had to make a conscious effort to suppress the urge to echo his consonant sounds. But the poet whom W.H. Auden credited with "the best ear in English poetry" *did* suppress the urge when necessary.

One problem with alliteration is its place in tongue-twisters: "Peter Piper picked a peck of pickled peppers." There is often something absurd about it. It's just so *noticeable*! Although it may be great for clanging effects, we don't necessarily want a trumpet fanfare in every line.

Anglo-Saxon poetry was *based* on alliteration, but most English poetry since has used it irregularly, for expressive or musical purposes. (See the section on "Accentual Meter," in the "Movement" chapter, for examples.)

The pacing of alliterating sounds is important. How quickly does one follow another? At what point has the ear forgotten the sound? When, in other words, does the alliteration switch off or fade out? You should also consider how many times the alliteration should occur. Oddly enough, three times often sounds more natural than two. Certainly it sounds more intentional. Four times seems like overdoing it. Five or more is simply ludicrous. Even an Anglo-Saxon bard (called a *scop*) might cringe at chanting so many.

1. Make a list of alliterating words, grouping them in threes. (Go through the alphabet to trigger ideas.) The words can be nouns, verbs, or adjectives: *bridle, breathe, brimming*. Notice that the alliterating sound can be a combination (such as "br"), as well as a single letter. The more sounds you cluster, however, the more slowed-down, or even clogged, your rhythm will become. (Think of how "skr" sounds would affect a line!) When you have a list of about ten trios, begin a poem that uses them sparingly (maybe one group every four lines). Don't feel you have to use all the groups, and don't go in alphabetical order. Jump around, fiddle with the words (*breathe* could become *breathless* or *breed* or *beard*). Let the words you've listed lead you to the poem you write.

2. Write a poem that *hides* its alliteration—by delaying it or embedding it. For instance, instead of a phrase like "the towers and traffic of the town," try delaying those emphatic "t" sounds: "the towers presided over the town's uproarious traffic." (You don't necessarily have to be wordier.) Or try embedding the "t" sound: "The towers and antennae on the routes and short-cuts." (Technically, remember, this embedding of repeated consonants is called *consonance*.) If you need a subject, try describing your own town or city.

3. Revise a poem by adding (or removing) alliteration. If you have a line like "the forest spread for miles along the road," try spicing it up with some alliteration: "the maples reddened by the muddy road." Notice how the "m" and "r" sounds "cross over" to link up and alliterate, a good way to make the sound richer, more intertwined.

ASSONANCE

Assonance is the repetition of vowel sounds. In the nineteenth century, poets preferred alliteration and generally aimed to vary their vowel sounds. Today, poets often find alliteration too noticeable and prefer the echo of vowel sounds. In any case, the repetition, variation, and arrangement of vowel sounds makes an enormous difference in the musicality of a poem.

A singer will practice vowels by chanting, on the same note, "ma, may, mi, mo, moo," and then raising it pitch by pitch. The exercise might be a good one for poets to perform in *their* "singing schools." We tend to pay little conscious attention to where the vowel sounds fall and in what order, counting on our "ears" to guide us. But even talented singers need ear training. We want to know what we're doing so thoroughly that in the actual process of writing we don't have to think about it.

The French poet Arthur Rimbaud saw color in vowels: "Black A, white E, red I, green U, blue O." Edith Sitwell considered consonants the "physical identity" but vowels the "spirit" of a word. In fact, they are the breathy part of any syllable, fleshed out by the consonants. If you remove the vowels from a sentence, it's usually easy to read the sentence:

D-gs r-n thr—gh th- str—ts -f N-w H-v-n.

But the vowels supply most of the melody:

aw uh ōō uh ēē uh ōō ā uh

Ezra Pound urged poets to concentrate on vowel sequence as a means of poetic melody. Robert Graves urged restraint in the use of assonance and advised withholding it until important moments the poet wanted to emphasize.

Vowels can be long (the "o" in "phone") or short (the "u" in "fun"). We mark long vowels with a macron (ˉ), short ones with a breve (˘). Consulting a dictionary is helpful in resolving difficulties about what's long and what's short. We also have plenty of *diphthongs* in English, combinations of vowels like "oi" and "ia" ("boy" and "dial," for example). Actually, many of our vowels are technically diphthongs, since we don't use many of the pure vowels found in German or Italian.

In his excellent textbook *Western Wind: An Introduction to Poetry* (Random House, 1974), John Frederick Nims presents a useful "Frequency Scale of English Vowel Sounds":

ōō	ō	oo	aw		oi	ow		ah	u	u(r)	a	e	i	ī	ā
boo	bone	book	bought		boy	bough		bar	bud	bird	bat	bet	bit	buy	bay
ēē
bee

If you speak the words in order, you can hear the pitch rise from low (the "oo" sound that can boom and moo) to high (the "ee" sound that can shriek and squeal). Remember that it's not just the five vowels (a, e, i, o, u), but the vowel *sounds* (which may be spelled oddly, like the long "a" sound in "reign") and the combination of sounds (like "cho*i*ce"), that matter.

4. Rearrange this list into a vowel scale of low to high pitch:

dance dean dune dine dun don't deign den don din dawn

Read the new list aloud. Do you hear the pitch rising? Then read the original list. Do you hear the pitch jump around? Try to become more attuned to the differences between vowel sounds so that, in your own poems, you can vary the vowel sequences as well as use assonance for repetitive effects. Go on to make your own list, starting with a consonant other than "b" or "d" and trying out the different vowel sounds. You can extend the words beyond monosyllables if you like — the list above could then include "ordain," "dented," "diner," or "dunces." Finally, if you want to keep going, choose a few words from one of these lists to begin a poem, paying special attention to the dance of vowels and the shifting spectrum of word sounds.

5. Write a short poem that uses assonance in each line (or from one line to another). Try to use as many *different* vowels as possible. (If you need a subject, write about wading through a crowd in an open-air market.) Examine your results and circle the most audible and obvious examples of assonance; then underline the examples of assonance that aren't so apparent, that almost elude your notice. (You may find that some vowel repetition has slipped in without your even trying to include it!) It helps this exercise if you wait a day or two before hunting for the assonance (so you can forget some of your original combinations); it also helps to exchange exercises with another writer (so you won't have any idea beforehand where the assonance may be planted).

6. Write a song that's two stanzas long. In the first one, use any meter or rhyme scheme you like. Feel free to make it regular (lines the same length) or irregular (lines of different lengths). Use from four to eight lines in building this unit. If you have no preference, try an iambic tetrameter quatrain rhymed ABAB, like this:

> They rowed until they reached the cove
> > Where flooded, leafless trees turned white
> And high tide swelled and swirled above
> > A sunken tugboat, just in sight.

In the second stanza, not only follow the same pattern of stressed and unstressed syllables, but also use the same *vowel sounds* in exactly the same positions. Basil Bunting thought this the minimal requirement of a poet composing any song: to keep the vowel sequence constant throughout, but it's fiendishly difficult. Think of the vowel sequence as a melody. If your first stanza begins "Bring in the wash that sags the line," your second stanza must retain the vowel sequence, for example: "Quick with the saw, Dad stacks a pile." Do you hear the vowel repetition?

7. Revise a poem by inserting or removing assonance. Where would a vowel echo strengthen a line? Where is the repetition annoying or intrusive or monotonous?

RHYME

As children, we respond gleefully to any kind of chime or echo in nursery rhymes; as adults, we expect popular songs to rhyme, and we feel disappointed if they don't. But poets have been quarreling about rhyme for centuries, both attacking and defending it. Ancient Greek and Latin poetry did *not* rhyme (though late Latin hymns did). Ancient Chinese poetry, on the other hand, usually rhymed according to a pattern of tones. In the West, the Troubadours made rhyme popular in the Middle Ages in their elaborate poems about courtly love. For us, the issue is moot: we're free to rhyme, but we don't have to.

Ezra Pound remarks in "A Retrospect" that a rhyme must have "some slight element of surprise if it is to give pleasure; it need not be bizarre or curious, but it must be well used if used at all." You don't win points for the simple feat of rhyming any old words, no matter how trite or dull. Your rhymes must be well chosen, and they must fit their context naturally—unless you're after some wrenching, violent effect.

A rhymed poem should sound contemporary, not like a throwback to an earlier style. This is really a matter of diction, your choice of words, but it's important to keep in mind. We may not like the time we live in, but we can't escape it by wishful thinking or anachronisms, only by imagination. This is not to say, however, that a poem can't focus on earlier times, or speak in the voice of an historical character.

Rhymes (often monosyllabic words) that end on a stressed syllable are called *masculine* (train/grain, complain/terrain). Rhymes (usually polysyllabic words) that end on an unstressed syllable (stinging/clinging, vibration/consternation) are called *feminine*. If this terminology bothers you because of its gender typing, feel free to call the first a *rising* rhyme and the second a *falling* rhyme. Three-syllable rhymes often sound comic, as in Lord Byron's *Don Juan*: "eligible"/"unintelligible," "And rash enthusiasm in good society/ Were nothing but a moral inebriety."

Many poems follow a *rhyme scheme*. To mark the pattern, we use the letters of the alphabet in a kind of literary algebra:

Had we but World enough, and Time,   A
This coyness Lady were no crime.   A
We would sit down, and think which way   B
To walk, and pass our long Loves Day   B
   — *Andrew Marvell, "To His Coy Mistress" (1-4)*

Familiar schemes include rhyming in couplets (AABBCC, as in Marvell's poem), cross-rhyming (ABAB, as in the quatrains of Shakespeare's sonnets), enclosed rhyming (ABBA, as in Tennyson's "In Memoriam") and *terza rima* (ABA BCB CDC etc., as used by Dante in his *Divine Comedy*). Improvised patterns crop up frequently, depending on the poet's purposes and ingenuity. (There's a list at the end of the "Patterns" chapter.) But poems need not rhyme according to a regular pattern or scheme at all. Randall Jarrell says that he prefers rhyme that comes at irregular intervals. If, however, you *establish* a rhyme scheme you should usually adhere to it, unless you intend to break it off for some good reason.

Sometimes it's effective to rhyme the last two lines of a passage, to "clinch" the poem. Shakespeare often does this in his blank verse soliloquies. Even in free verse, rhyme can come in handy at the end, as in Louis Simpson's poem "Working Late." Rhymed poems need not be in meter, though they usually are.

Many contemporary poets prefer *slant rhymes*. (Other terms include "off rhyme" and "approximate rhyme.") Instead of chiming the sound exactly (*sun*, *run*), the poet intentionally makes it imperfect (*sun*, *ban*). This usually involves altering the vowel or the consonant. Of course, if the divergence is too great, there won't be any sense of rhyme left. Here are some slant rhymes:

boat/beat	bone/thin	shore/char
rabble/Bible	waken/thicken	house/whose
crime/scram	mirror/bare	day/dough ·

Poets usually prefer, in their slant rhymes, to alter the vowels and preserve the consonants; songwriters usually do just the opposite. The reason, I believe, is that the vowel change is subtler, more pleasing to the silent reader or even to the reciter of the poem. But listening to a song, we want to hear the clear echo of the vowel, even if the consonants scatter wildly; we want to hear the assonance.

Emily Dickinson was a pioneer of slant rhyme. One of her first editors remarked that "in many cases . . . she intentionally avoided the smoother and more usual rhymes." Dickinson pairs "wake" and "crack," "Pearl" and "School," "Score" and "Her." Wilfred Owen used slant rhyme to great effect in his harrowing poems of the First World War. In "Strange Meeting," the story of two enemy soldiers meeting in the underworld, Owen rhymes "escaped" and "scooped," "groaned" and "groined." William Butler Yeats allowed himself the liberty of using slant rhymes for expressive purposes. Of course, since English is a "rhyme-poor" language (compared to Italian, for example, where it is relatively easy), the poet lightens his task by allowing this freedom. To our modern ears, these "off rhymes" offer more surprise, more pleasure in the unexpected.

In "That Night When Joy Began," W.H. Auden uses a kind of "double" rhyme scheme. Here are the rhyme words that appear in his first stanza:

(1) *began*
(2) *flush*
(3) *flash*
(4) *gun*

You immediately notice the slant rhymes based on consonance: the "g-n" that links *began* and *gun*, the "fl-sh" that links *flush* and *flash*. So the rhyme scheme is ABBA. But listen to the vowels. There is assonance between *began* and *flash* (the short "a" sound) and between *flush* and *gun* (the short "u" sound). So it also rhymes ABAB. Ingenious. It's not surprising that the poem is just three stanzas long.

The presence of rhyme does *not* excuse the absence of imagery, specific words, and a hard, clean edge in the language. Rhyme does not compensate for slackness, abstractness, or excessive softness. Rhyme does not justify sentimentality. It's true that poems on abstract subjects often work better in rhyme or meter, but overuse of abstractions is always a problem. Who wants to seek his reading pleasure in a sensory deprivation tank?

Rhyme is invaluable as (a) an audible echo or resonance; (b) an organizing device, for "zoning" your poems; (c) a technique for discovering fresh, surprising words that might not occur to you without the pressure of rhyming; (d) a link to poetic tradition. In their *Prosody Handbook*, Karl Shapiro and Robert Beum point out that rhyme can be attention-getting, musical, architectural, emphatic (making a word conspicuous), heuristic (helping "directly in the birth and growth of a poem"), formal, mnemonic, and distancing ("moving the original experience just far enough to the rear of the immediate feelings involved"). They point out the "power of rhyme to drive its way into the memory."

In *Out of Africa*, Isak Dinesen describes how the East Africans working in her maize-field loved the sound of rhyme, "laughed at it when it came," and begged her: "Speak again. Speak like rain." Good rhyme (as

well as good metaphor) often affects us with hilarity; we laugh because
we are surprised and pleased — we *get* it.

8. Write a poem that uses one of the following rhyme schemes: AABB,
ABAB, ABBA, ABA BCB CDC etc. Use the scheme as a stanza unit, and
compose several stanzas. If you need a subject, write about what's outside your window. When you're through, apply this test, as honestly as
possible: are any of the rhyme words forced by the rhyme? could someone
tell which rhyme word occurred to you first? If the rhymes do seem
forced, or if any seem predictable, find better, fresher, more surprising
rhymes — and revise the context to make the new choice fit naturally!
Harder than the first way, isn't it? But better. Richard Wilbur says that
if you can't make certain lines work with the rhymes you've chosen, you
have to give up the rhymes. It sounds logical, but how often do we insist
on our rhymes over our reason?

9. Make a list of slant rhymes. Try to be a good matchmaker, pairing
interesting words whose connectedness might not be obvious. Make
sure that each word on your list has gusto. But don't feel you need to
link noun with noun, verb with verb. You can do that, of course, but
mixing them up will lead to a more fluid poem, because you'll be enjambing more (using more lines that run over into the next lines). Concentrate on monosyllables, but include a good number of two-syllable words.
Then write a poem using those slant rhymes.

10. If you have a rhyming dictionary, get rid of it. Instead, try searching for rhymes in your head by going through the alphabet, starting with
any word (*drip*, for example) and listing all words that sound interesting:
*blip, chip, clip, dip, flip, grip, gyp, hip, lip, nip, pip, quip, rip, sip, slip, strip,
tip, trip, whip*. Then look for slant rhymes: *ape, bop, cap, cup, gripe* — they
will certainly be more numerous than the true rhymes. The reasons for
eschewing the rhyming dictionary? It's too much of a crutch; you might
feel lost when it isn't around; you don't call upon your own resourcefulness and inventiveness; you won't find slant rhymes there. It's better to
rely on your own mind and memory. So you forget a few? Well, that can
actually help channel what you want to say. Robert Graves carried this
prohibition a step further by refusing to consult a thesaurus when composing a poem.

11. Matching a monosyllable with a three-syllable word often makes
a good, subtle rhyme, especially if the punchy monosyllable comes first.
Examples: *bread/forfeited, sting/hollering*. Write a poem that uses this kind
of rhyme, in as many lines as possible. (You won't always care to be so
relentless, but it's good training.)

12. In James Merrill's "The Octopus," the rhymes are *apocopated*:
"*sur*face"/"sini*ster*" and "*sei*zure"/"*freeze*," for example. It's one way of

hiding the rhyme a little, making it more elusive. Another way to disguise rhyme is to have an *internal* rhyme (somewhere within a line) match an end rhyme:

> She rode her *horse* along a stony ridge
> And down a dry creek bed to the golf *course*.

Write a poem that uses rhyme but disguises it.

SOUND EFFECTS

Onomatopoeia refers to words that sound like what they mean: buzz, whine, clatter, crash, ping, splat. We usually think of it as a decoration, but Ezra Pound asserted that onomatopoeia was essential to poetry. If we think of it in a broad sense—that the sound of words can effectively imitate *anything*, even an emotional state or something visual—he has a point.

Some theorists agree that onomatopoeia is important to poetry, finding that vowels and consonants often, in a good poem, imitate the action or mood being described. But skeptics point out that the sound effects depend mostly on the meaning of the words and the power of suggestion.

Here are some examples of imitative sound effects:

> Madame Sosostris, famous clairvoyante,
> Had a bad cold.
> > —*T.S. Eliot, The Waste Land*

> Beat, beat, whirr, thud, in the soft turf
> under the apple trees
> > —*Ezra Pound, "Canto IV"*

> The moan of doves in immemorial elms,
> And murmuring of innumerable bees.
> > —*Alfred Tennyson*

> Through the precarious crack of light
> Quacking Wake Wake
> > —*Ted Hughes, "The Wild Duck"*

> and the Kyrie of a chain saw . . .
> > —*Galway Kinnell, "Getting the Mail"*

The lobbed ball plops, then dribbles to the cup. . . .
— *Robert Lowell, "Ford Madox Ford"*

These effects depend on both vowels (as in Eliot's lines imitating someone with a cold) and consonants (the nasal "m" and "n" sounds Tennyson uses to suggest doves and bees). But do certain letters always suggest the same things? Or do the effects depend on context? In Karl Shapiro and Robert Beum's *Prosody Handbook*, several kinds of "sound color" are listed:

Resonance: n, m, ng, z, zh (for "lingering, droning, vibrant effects").
Harshness: k, g, hard c (throaty sounds, for dissonance and cacophony).
Plosiveness. b, p, t, d, g, k (percussive sounds).
Breathiness: h (breathlessness); f, th, s, sh, ch (hissing and whispering).
Liquidity: l, r, w (for resonant musical lines).

If these pointers help you pay closer attention to the sound of your poems, fine. But don't use them as a set of recipes, sprinkling in a pinch of plosives and a dash of liquids. Be sensitive to them.

Robert Graves remarked "When I come to my death bed, I have a . . . message to deliver: 'The art of poetry consists in knowing exactly how to manipulate the letter S.' " Edith Sitwell found that "Sibilants [the S sound] slow the line." If you speak the letter out loud — and hold the sound — everyone will recognize the snake-like hissing. Although you may want to imitate hissing in certain situations (repeat the last four words to hear the effect), the letter S can sound annoying if it comes up too often. (Recording engineers use "de-essers," in fact, to minimize the "S" noises made by a singer.)

Meter can be onomatopoeic, as in "I sprang to the stirrup, and Joris and he;/ I galloped, Dirck galloped, we galloped all three" — not Robert Browning at his best, but it does sound like galloping, or at least like the radio sound effect of halved coconuts clopped on a table. It is usually the *combination* of sounds that creates an effect or suggests a mood. As Alexander Pope points out in Part II of his "Essay on Criticism" (which contains wonderful examples of sound effects), "The sound must seem an Echo to the sense."

13. Write several lines imitating different sounds. Develop any or all of them into a poem. If possible, don't mention what you're imitating. Just try to capture the sound of chalk on a blackboard, or a lawn mower,

or wind chimes, or a basketball dribbled on blacktop.

14. Write a short poem without using the letter S. It *can* be done! For example:

> The children dawdle through the afternoon,
> their football lolling in a birdbath, wind
> flickering in the yard, the empty pool.

Once you've finished your draft, go back and re-phrase (using "s" sounds where necessary) to make the lines sound natural.

15. Write a short poem, trying to capture the onomatopoeia of a mood. Let your rhythms suggest the right pacing. Let your vowels and consonants suggest the musical "colors" of the mood. For instance, if you want to capture a sense of elation, speed up the poem by enjambing many of the lines (letting the sense run over to the next line instead of stopping the motion with a period), by extending sentences, by using plenty of "l" sounds and the humming of "m" and "n." But even that sounds like a prescription. Experiment with sounds and rhythms. Find out by trial and error how to suggest depression, or tranquility, or commotion, or irritation. (Appropriate images will help immensely!) Let the sound and sense reinforce each other.

V. Movement

Poetry, like music, is a temporal art; it moves in time — unlike painting and sculpture, which are spatial arts. Although the poem on the page may seem like a visual object, its meaning depends on reading, on the passing and keeping of time. And time in a poem depends on the duration of words, the movement of lines, the rise and fall of sentences, the flow of stanzas. Whether it uses metrical verse or free verse or even prose, the movement of a poem is its *rhythm*. And that rhythm may be smooth or choppy, fast or slow, measured or free.

METER

A piece of music that's four beats to the bar, each beat a quarter-note, is in 4/4 time. That's its *meter*. The term works similarly for poetry. Anything used to measure the lines of a poem in a regular, recurring fashion is called a meter. Poetry written in measured lines is metrical.

Rhythm is something quite different. Prose has rhythm but is usually not measured (although passages of Melville's *Moby Dick* are written in hidden iambic pentameter). Rhythm is the rise and fall and surge and abatement of words — the melody. It can be in prose, in free verse, or in meter.

There are four principal ways in which we count a poem's meter:

1. *Number of syllables*. French and Japanese poems are measured in syllables, as is much twentieth-century English and American poetry.

2. *Number of accents* (also called stresses or beats). Anglo-Saxon strong stress meter, nursery rhymes, and some contemporary poems are accentual.

3. *Number of syllables* and *accents*. Syllable-stress meter, such as iambic pentameter and trochaic tetrameter, is the most common type in English.

4. *Length of syllables*. Quantitative meter, used in ancient Greek and most Latin poetry, is based on the duration of vowels and consonants. "Range" would be a long syllable; "cat" would be short. But even with short vowels, the consonants around them make a huge difference. Compare "stretch" and "bet." The second one is much shorter, though the vowel is identical.

Refer to the sections on "Accentual Meter," "Iambics," and "Syllabics" for more detailed treatment of those familiar measures.

Any method of counting a regular pattern in the lines of a poem qualifies as meter. Here are some meters that poets have invented:

1. *Word count.* The poet counts the number of words, regardless of their accents or syllables, in each line. (Robert Francis used this meter.) Notice the difference in the number of syllables in the following example that counts four words in each line:

Collaring perpetrators, investigating stick-ups,   (14)
A cop jots notes.   (4)

2. *Typewriter spacing.* James Laughlin, in typing his poems, follows a rule that "in a couplet any second line has to be within two typewriter spaces of the line preceding it."

3. *Graph paper.* W.D. Snodgrass, in his *Fuehrer Bunker* poems spoken in the voice of Heinrich Himmler, assigns a letter to each square of graph paper, dots to the empty spaces, and keeps the margins straight up and down on both sides, making each stanza a perfect rectangle.

Our standard terminology for meter comes from the Greek. T.S. Eliot claimed not to know these terms, but he certainly was a master of meter. If the terms help you write better, or understand how poems work, use them. They are, in fact, a shortcut. Eliot's way must have been to read so widely and deeply that he absorbed the practice, rather than the theory—if we believe his extraordinary claim. The best way to begin understanding iambic pentameter, for example, is by reading (and listening to) the plays of Shakespeare. But until then, here are the most essential terms for syllable-stress meter:

Feet

ˇ ´   iamb (iambic)
´ ˇ   trochee (trochaic)
ˇ ˇ ´   anapest (anapestic)
´ ˇ ˇ   dactyl (dactylic)
´ ´   spondee (spondaic)
ˇ ˇ   pyrrhic
´ ˇ ´   amphimacer or cretic
ˇ ´ ˇ   amphibrach
ˇ ˇ ´ ´   minor ionic (pyrrhic + spondee)
´ ´ ˇ ˇ   major ionic (spondee + pyrrhic)

´ = accent or stress   ˇ = unstressed syllable

Line Length

monometer = 1 foot
dimeter = 2 feet
trimeter = 3 feet
tetrameter = 4 feet
pentameter = 5 feet
hexameter = 6 feet
heptameter = 7 feet
octameter = 8 feet

1. Write a poem in trochaic tetrameter. Rhyme if you like. If you leave off the final unstressed syllable (as Percy Bysshe Shelley does in the first two lines of the following stanza), the line is called catalectic:

Music, when soft voices die,
Vibrates in the memory;
Odours, when sweet violets sicken,
Live within the sense they quicken.

Trochaic meter often sounds relentless and hammering, an effect captured memorably in William Blake's "The Tyger." ("Tyger, Tyger, burning bright,/ In the forests of the night.") You might capitalize on this quality by describing a parade or a fireworks display in your poem. Or you might try to undercut it, work against it, by presenting something very quiet, like an evening by a lake.

2. Although we don't normally measure the lengths of syllables as in quantitative meter, we *can* be aware of long sounds and short ones. They do affect the pacing of a line. For example, listen to this song by Ben Jonson:

Slow, slow, fresh fount, keep time with my salt tears;
Yet slower, yet; O faintly, gentle springs;
List to the heavy part the music bears,
Woe weeps out her division when she sings.
Droop, herbs and flowers;
Fall, grief, in showers,
Our beauties are not ours;
O, I could still,

Like melting snow upon some craggy hill,
     Drop, drop, drop, drop,
          Since nature's pride is now a withered daffodil.

The first line moves with great slowness, mainly because of all the long vowels: "slow," "fount," "keep," "time," "my," and "tears." The "t" sounds also slow down the line, as does the word "fresh," with its "fr" and "sh" sounds. Ezra Pound uses "quantities" in much of his *Cantos*: "Great mass, huge bulk, thesaurus," for example. Write a poem that uses long sounds and moves slowly. It will help to pick a *subject* that involves slow motion. Think of how a movie director slows down the action of important parts of a film.

3. Then write a poem that uses short vowels ("map," "spin," "ramble," "run") and moves quickly.

4. Write a poem in which each line has the same number of *words*. From line to line in this word-count poem, vary the number of syllables and accents while adhering to the same number of words—five might be a good number. Possible subject: performing a chore.

FREE VERSE

Free verse is simply free of meter, not measured in syllables or accents or anything else. It is irregular, yet it is still divided into lines. It is not the same as prose, although some detractors claim it is. It serves as a kind of intermediate ground between prose and metrical verse (such as iambic pentameter), using the line, not the metrical foot or the sentence, as its main controlling unit. (Don't confuse it with blank verse, which is unrhymed iambic pentameter.)

The poetry of the Old Testament is a kind of free verse, as is most of Walt Whitman's *Leaves of Grass* and occasional poems by otherwise metrical writers, such as Goethe ("Prometheus"). Ezra Pound and T.S. Eliot did much to make free verse (originally called *vers libre* because of French precursors like Arthur Rimbaud), popular and notorious. Pound's notion was to "break the pentameter," to loosen a metrical stranglehold he felt was stifling the music of poetry. T.S. Eliot came to feel that "no *vers* is *libre* for the man who wants to do a good job." Free verse was not intended as a labor-saving device.

In writing free verse, the main concern is how to move from line to line. Where does one end and another begin? In iambic pentameter, the question doesn't come up: you end after five iambic feet. But in free verse, you're really on your own when it comes to *line breaks*, the points where lines end. You can end-stop (where there's a definite halt, like a period) or enjamb (where the sense of one line runs over into the next). There are precedents, but no rules. Louis Simpson points out that poets break their lines according to personal impulse. Allen Ginsberg speaks of breath as the main factor in where a poet's lines break. There are several ways a poet can break lines:

1. where natural pauses occur, between phrases, after punctuation;
2. in the middle of a natural phrase, cutting "across the grain," disrupting the syntax;
3. at a point of suspense, leaving the matter hanging until the next line picks it up and satisfies the reader's curiosity, providing suspense, a musical suspension.

Even though a poet is free to break lines as he or she pleases, the results may be good or bad, nimble or clumsy, apt or ridiculous. For instance, you achieve no suspense if you break before the obvious continuation:

The pitcher hurled the base
ball to home
plate.

Marvin Bell has criticized "enjambing out of anxiety." Make sure your line breaks make some kind of sense: musical, suspenseful, contributing to the flow or overall rhythm.

Charles Wright talks about scanning his free verse lines, marking the unstressed and stressed syllables, to make sure no adjacent lines have the same count of syllables or accents. It's an interesting practice that makes the poet more conscious of words, phrases, lines, and rhythms. A free verse poem should be rhythmic and musical, not dull and flat. The danger in giving up meter is losing the music, becoming prosaic. Too much free verse sounds like a drone, or a mumble, or a computerized voice. Make a special effort to let the lines sing a little. You can do that by paying attention to vowels and consonants, deleting the extra verbiage, and attending to the ebb and flow of rhythm, breaking lines to highlight the music. Even if you try to capture the voice of everyday speech, don't lose the music of talk.

Donald Justice reports that Mark Strand, in his early free verse poems, tried to make the lines come out fairly even on the page, more or less the same length; later on, Strand was trying to vary the line lengths more, making the shape on the page more ragged. That kind of visual prosody is one way free verse can be composed.

Although there aren't any real rules for free verse, we can distinguish several types:

1. *Long-lined*, the rolling cadences of *Psalms* and Walt Whitman, usually end-stopped, often kept going by rhetorical devices such as initial repetition (called *anaphora*), as in these lines which begin with "With":

> With the pomp of inloop'd flags, with the cities draped
>   in black,
> With the show of the States themselves as of crape-veil'd
>   women standing,
> With processions long and winding and the flambeaus of the
>   night
>   — *Whitman, "When Lilacs Last in the Dooryard Bloom'd"*

Notice that when a line is too long for the right-hand margin, it must be "tucked under" as it continues, indented to show that it's not a new line. If the margins of the page were wide enough, the line could stretch out to its full length — but might be very hard to take in visually.

2. *Short-lined* (as in many poems by William Carlos Williams, Denise Levertov, and Robert Creeley), often song-like, often heavily enjambed:

> The vaulter's
> fiberglass pole teeters
> in the wind, in
> the loose wood chips
> like a compass
> needle.

3. *Varied length*, moving from short to long to in-between, but not in any regular, measurable fashion:

> When the gate springs open, the crowd
> detonates, the whole
> rodeo blasted into a beer-spilling yippee
> for eight
> seconds of bucking, clutched reins, a bronco's
> bared teeth seething, the dust swirling as a cowboy hat
> floats and catches in the fence.

4. *Open field composition*, the term coined and the style practiced by Robert Duncan (and similar to Charles Olson's "projective verse"),

which is free to have short, medium, and long lines, to indent freely, to include blocks of prose, to use blank space expressively, to spread and sprawl all over the page—open in form and composed "organically."

5. *Triadic lines*, the three-step arrangement invented by William Carlos Williams to embody his "variable foot" (each step equalling one foot, one pulse, no matter how many words it might contain):

> Here is the clinic
>> glistening
>>> with aluminum and antiseptic,
> glaring in the white sun
>> as interns return, twirling
>>> their stethoscopes.

To compensate for its lack of meter, free verse makes abundant use of word music (especially assonance and consonance), internal rhyme, surprising and inventive line breaks, rhetorical devices (such as repeating a word at the beginning or end of a succession of lines), phrases of different lengths, sudden exclamations or questions, ruptured syntax (syntax being the arrangement of words in a sentence), and the visual design of words and lines on the page.

Free verse can have an open quality, a refreshing airiness, a swinging motion, a rhapsodic explosiveness. Or it can be clipped and clinical, scrupulously exact. Or it can be packed solid with details. On the other hand, free verse poems are often shoddy, haphazard, so unstructured and simple-minded that they have become the clichéd popular style of the present (as rhymed doggerel once was). Yet they may be harder to write well than formal verse, since you don't have the technical props of meter and rhyme to supply a structure and keep you going. You're flying solo, dependent on your own inventiveness in the absence of most navigational landmarks.

5. Write a poem in short-lined free verse. Be sure to enjamb (let the lines spill over to the next ones) frequently.

6. Write a poem in long-lined free verse. Use anaphora (initial repetition)—either a single triggering word ("When," "And," "Despite") or perhaps a short phrase ("When I die," "Near the town").

7. Take a poem in short free verse lines (either one of your own or one you've read) and revise it into long lines, adding details as you go. Both poems should have roughly the same total number of lines, so you'll have to flesh out a great deal that's compact or sketchy in the short-lined version.

8. Take a long-lined poem (your own or someone else's) and trim it

into short-lined free verse. Retain the most vivid details, but cut out most of the modifiers. Make the new version lean, wiry, taut.

9. Write a description of a place in lines of constantly changing length. Let the lines shift as your description shifts from left to right, top to bottom, inside to outside, from colors to shapes, from large to small to medium-sized. But don't let the lines become mechanical and stiff; they should be fluid, subtle, suggestive.

10. Write a poem using open-field composition. Bring in facts from an outside source like an encyclopedia or a textbook. Mix those facts with sensory details, descriptions, maybe an emotional outburst or a snatch of song. Quote if you like. Use the full page, letting the words scatter and jump: a stanza clumped on the left, a series of step-like indented lines, a single word isolated in the middle of white space. Try to compose it on the typewriter.

11. Write a poem in triadic lines. Describe a person performing some kind of action. Consult the Williams poems "A Negro Woman" and "The Artist" if you'd like models to work from.

12. Take any poem (yours, a friend's, one by a famous poet) and rebreak the lines. Put them into some sort of free verse, according to your own instincts and sense of rhythm. Although you could simply indicate new breaks by inserting virgules (/), it's better to write out the whole poem (or type it), so you really become involved in the line-breaking process. How is the new version different? What is its rhythmic effect? Try to explain what that difference is (faster, slower, choppier, smoother, denser, looser, etc.) in a short note.

13. Change something you've written in prose into free verse. Omit unnecessary words and phrases. Notice how much altering it takes, and notice the kinds of phrases that make the prose prosy. For example, "I know that they are there because I've seen them" could be shortened to "I know. I've seen them."

Poets To Consult

Short-lined free verse: H.D., Robert Creeley, Denise Levertov, A.R. Ammons, Louis Zukofsky, William Carlos Williams (also for the triadic line), Lucille Clifton

Long-lined free verse: Walt Whitman, Robinson Jeffers, D.H. Lawrence, Allen Ginsberg, Gregory Corso, Gerald Stern, C.K. Williams, Rodney Jones, Lynn Emanuel

Free verse by poets who began more formally: W.S. Merwin,

Galway Kinnell, Theodore Roethke, Robert Lowell, Adrienne
Rich, Louis Simpson, James Wright, Louise Glück, Donald Hall

Many free verse poets write in both long and short lines. James
Schuyler, for example, has poems in short lines (such as "June 30, 1974"
and "En Route to Southampton") and poems in long lines (such as "The
Crystal Lithium" and "Hymn to Life") gathered in *Selected Poems* (FSG,
1988). Frank O'Hara is another poet who moves easily in both short and
long lines.

In C.K. Williams's *Flesh and Blood*, his long lines (always so long they
bump into the right margin and have to be tucked under in order to
continue) often sound like two lines of iambic pentameter jammed together, each containing about ten stresses and twenty or more syllables—a kind of double blank verse.

PROSE

Richard Howard likes to remark that "prose proceeds, verse reverses."
The way prose "proceeds" is by flowing within margins down the page.
If the margins are narrow, the lines of each paragraph will be narrow; wide
margins mean wide lines. In prose, the "line" is simply a typographical
necessity; the prose writer ignores it totally. If you use a word processor,
you may recognize this as "word wrap," the way you type out a paragraph
without pressing a carriage return. In prose, it doesn't matter where the
lines are divided—as long as the right margin is straight (flush or justi-
fied, in other words). Verse is *defined* by the lines and where they are
broken; the typesetter *must* respect those line-breaks.

Most poems are written in verse, but the *prose poem* is an obvious
exception to that. We often talk of flowery or rhapsodic passages in a
novel as "poetic" or "purple patches." But the poem in prose comes to
us from nineteenth-century French poets such as Charles Baudelaire
(*Paris Spleen* or *Little Poems in Prose*) and Arthur Rimbaud (*Illuminations*).
In the twentieth century, some French poets are known mainly for their
prose poems: St. John Perse, Francis Ponge. The form took a while to
gain acceptance in English, but it is now fairly common.

What makes a prose poem different from a short short story? Sometimes nothing. The prose poem can be, as David Young remarks, "a
distilling and mimicking of the normal ways of prose ... life histories
reduced to paragraphs, essays the size of postcards, novels in nutshells,
maps on postage stamps, mind-bending laundry lists, theologies scrib-
bled on napkins." If calling them "poems" troubles you, call them
"sketches." They are concentrated paragraphs, poems because of their
vivid imagery, compelling prose rhythms, or stunning ideas. They may

seem like stories, or essays, or descriptions, but some quality of radiance or charged language qualifies them as poems. As you might guess, the question of what makes something a poem (in prose or in verse) is still open to debate and disagreement.

Another possibility for the poet involves mixing prose and verse in the same poem. Japanese *haibun* alternates verse and prose. It's a good way to introduce variety, a formal back-and-forth motion, into poems. It can be a wonderful musical device, marking clearly—and audibly—the shifting rhythms.

14. Write a prose poem. Keep it under a full page. Try to use many of the usual resources of a lined poem (images, metaphors, vowel repetition, rhythm and cadence). Rhyme may be a problem, as it usually is something to avoid in prose. (Robert Graves points this out in *The Reader Over Your Shoulder*.) Your prose poem can be arranged as a single block, or as stanza-like units separated by spaces, or as indented paragraphs.

15. At what point does a long line become a prose paragraph? Try writing a long-lined free verse poem (like Walt Whitman's "Song of Myself"), gradually lengthening the long lines as much as you can. At what point do you feel you are no longer writing in verse, but in prose sentences? Any subject will do, but it might help to have a large topic ("work" or "war" or "wilderness") you can treat in numerous, detailed images.

16. Write a poem mixing verse and prose. There are many ways to do this. A two-part structure might begin with prose and end with verse, imitating an opera's recitative and aria. Or it might begin with the verse and then relax into prose. In either case, the verse will probably seem more intense and formal than the prose. A three-part structure resembles a sandwich: verse surrounded by prose or vice versa. Returning to the original form is usually a pleasing strategy that satisfies our expectation of recurrence. It also "frames" the part in the middle, thereby emphasizing it, like a diamond in a setting of pearls. Four parts and beyond give the sense of alternating, switching back and forth as need dictates. You might begin by thinking of subjects suitable for this kind of "mixed" treatment.

IAMBICS

Robert Frost said that there are only two kinds of meter: "strict" and "loose" iambics. The *iamb* is a combination of an unstressed syllable followed by a stressed or accented syllable, marked ˘ ´. Single-word examples include "accost," "relief," "delay," "complete," "begrudge." Like a measure in musical notation, each iamb is called a *foot*. String five of these feet together, and you have a line of iambic pentameter: "The land was ours before we were the land's" ("The Gift Outright" by Robert Frost).

The basic pattern is a simple seesawing of unstressed and stressed syllables: ti-DUM ti-DUM ti-DUM ti-DUM ti-DUM. In his essay on the origins of meter, "Harp, Anvil, Oar," Robert Graves says that iambic meter originated in the blacksmith's hammering on an anvil. In any case, you need to imagine the basic, mechanical pattern as a kind of drum beat you can hear only through headphones; the words of the poem should be the audible melody.

The most common length of iambic meter is the *pentameter* line, like the opening of Shakespeare's *Sonnets*: "From fairest creatures, we desire increase. . . . " The next most common is *tetrameter*, as in this line by William Butler Yeats: "I went out to a hazel wood" ("Song of Wandering Aengus"). *Trimeter* is occasionally used, as in Theodore Roethke's "My heart keeps open house" ("Open House"). Two-foot (*dimeter*) and one-foot (*monometer*) lines are possible but rare, as in Robert Herrick's monometer:

Thus I
Passe by,
And die:
As One,
Unknown,
And gon:
I'm made
A shade,
And laid
I'th grave,
There have
My Cave.
Where tell
I dwell,
Farewell.

The *hexameter* (six-foot) line, also called the *alexandrine*, crops up occasionally, usually providing contrast in poems that are predominantly iambic pentameter, as in the elongated last lines of both the Spenserian stanza and John Berryman's stanza in "Homage to Mistress Bradstreet." Before blank verse established itself, the *fourteener* (seven-foot line) was popular, but long lines tend to break down into smaller units, so that the fourteener is really four + three.

Two kinds of iambic pentameter deserve special mention: *blank verse* (unrhymed iambic pentameter) and *heroic couplets* (iambic pentameter rhymed AABBCCDD and so on). Much of Shakespeare's drama exemplifies blank verse (though he wrote plenty of couplets as well); Alexander Pope perfected the heroic couplet (though Chaucer was our first master of the form).

In writing iambic poems, it's crucial to vary the rhythms of each line. T.S. Eliot spoke of "fixity" and "flux" as the two opposing poles of rhythm. The poet should be neither too regular nor too free. There's room in between to navigate. We want variations from the norm, but remember that if there's *too* much variety the norm disappears.

There are really two kinds of accent: speech stress and metrical stress. When speaking, we naturally accent certain syllables to emphasize the important parts. Usually we stress nouns and verbs, but we may emphasize minor parts of speech to make a point, as in Lincoln's "*of* the people, *by* the people, *for* the people." Metrical stress, however, recurs more frequently—every other syllable, more or less, in iambics. In this case, the speech stresses represent the "flux" Eliot pointed out, the metrical stresses his "fixity." For example:

Wálking along the ócean late at níght . . .

In speaking this line of iambic pentameter we accent "Walk," the "o" of "ocean," and "night"—three speech stresses. But in scanning the meter, we can count all five official stresses of iambic pentameter:

Wálking alóng the ócean láte at níght . . .

It's important to remember that these accents are NOT equal in emphasis; they're simply marked the same to demonstrate the underlying pattern. Many critics assign secondary stresses (marked ˋ) as in the pronunciation guides of a dictionary, when they scan a line to examine its meter. Some prosodists (specialists in poetic meter and form) assign up to four levels of relative stress to give a more accurate rendering of how a poem's rhythm actually sounds. But for our purposes that would be an exercise in pedantry. We're interested in how to synthesize poems, not just analyze them, and it helps to keep things simple.

Two basic techniques for varying the rhythm include (1) stressing what's normally unstressed and (2) leaving unstressed what's normally accented. For example, you can pack accents into a line of iambic pentameter:

Thíck, dárk bráids dámp wǐth spláshed póol wátĕr shíne.

I count eight stresses there, all of the syllables but "with" and the "er" of "water." But you may not want so much density! (Or at least not all the time.) You can loosen a line considerably by omitting stresses:

Aňd thě ăpprén̆tĭce ŏf thě táilŏr wátched.

Just three real stresses: "pren," "tail," and "watched." In fact, if we change the occupation to some three-syllable trade (and delete the verb), we're down to two stresses:

And the apprén̆tice of the cárpenter . . .

Of course, the context makes all the difference. If you have a line of iambics overstuffed with accents, or airy with unstressed syllables, or wildly irregular, surround it with lines that conform more to the pattern:

Shě wálks ŭntíl thě lóafĕrs húrt hěr féet:
Búrnĭng, thě crámped tóes númb, sóles brúised, héels blístĕred
ănd réadў fór sŏme óintmĕnt ánd ă bándăge.

The second line of that example shows some metrical variations you can use. These alterations to the basic pattern are called *substitutions*. The most common substitutions for an iambic foot are:

1. *an extra unstressed syllable* at the end of the line (the so-called feminine ending) — "blistered," for example, adding an eleventh syllable to the average iambic pentameter line;
2. *a trochee* (´ ˘), such as "Burning," an especially effective substitution at the beginning of a line, or just after a pause (often called a "trochaic inversion" since it inverts or switches around the usual iamb);
3. *an anapest* (˘ ˘ ´), giving the foot an extra unstressed syllable, thereby loosening the meter;
4. *a pyrrhic* (˘ ˘), such as "-ment and" in the third line of the example, making both syllables unstressed;
5. *a spondee* (´ ´), such as "soles bruised," making both syllables stressed;
6. *pyrrhic + spondee* (˘ ˘ ´ ´ , technically called a "minor ionic"), a very common substitution, also considered a "double foot," that occurs frequently at the beginning or the end of a line: "in a *dark time*," "when I *think back*," "and the *birds sing*." The nature of English grammar makes this phrasing common: preposition-article-adjective-noun, for example. The preponderance of monosyllables helps explain it too.

There are some tricks that can make your iambic line more flexible. Vary the number of monosyllabic and polysyllabic words. Remember that, metrically, three monosyllables may equal one three-syllable word, but they *sound* very different, usually slower. Compare "plump red fruit" with "nectarine"—the same number of syllables, but what a different sound! (Edith Sitwell calls this the principle of "equivalence.")

Letting some words cross over from one foot to another gives a more musically *legato*, or smoother, quality. Maintaining those divisions between feet sounds *staccato*, or choppy. (The musical terms are entirely appropriate here. Ezra Pound says, "Don't chop your poem into separate iambs. Behave as a musician would, a good musician.")

Don't put a pause (called a *caesura*) at the same position in every line, or even in consecutive lines if you can help it. The pentameter line is so long, you're bound to have one or more pauses, sometimes marked by punctuation, sometimes appearing where phrases meet, sometimes where a speaker might hesitate.

You should also pay attention to whether your lines are end-stopping (halted at the end by punctuation or sense) or *enjambed* (running over to the following line). For example:

We looked into the almanac for help.
It told us that October would bring showers
Melting us with their bursts of acid rain.

The first line is end-stopped; the second is enjambed.

In iambic pentameter, an occasional short line (three feet for Shakespeare, Milton, Robert Lowell; four feet, often, for Elizabeth Bishop) can be effective, another kind of variation.

It's OK to use your fingers when composing in iambic pentameter. In fact, it's especially handy having five fingers to count the accents—or both hands to count the ten syllables of each line. But try to learn how to *hear* the iambic pentameter line, first when you read a poem aloud, or hear it recited, and then right in your head. Donald Hall has recounted how he and his poet friends used to make a game of talking back and forth in a kind of iambic pentameter volleying. He found it almost too easy—and it is, once you've listened and practiced it enough.

If you're really intent on learning the meter, read as many of Shakespeare's plays as you can. Pay attention to the differences between his predominant iambic pentameter and the occasional songs, prose passages, and tetrameter lines. Memorize some of his sonnets and maybe some poems in iambic pentameter by other masters: Geoffrey Chaucer, John Milton, John Donne, Alexander Pope, William Wordsworth, John Keats, Robert Browning, Robert Frost, W.B. Yeats, Wallace Stevens.

17. For most beginners, iambic tetrameter (four feet long) seems easier to work with than pentameter. Write a dozen lines of iambic tetrameter, enjambing as much as possible. If you need a subject, write about the weather. If you want an extra challenge, rhyme the poem in couplets, as Andrew Marvell does in "To His Coy Mistress" and as Blake does in "Auguries of Innocence":

A truth that's told with bad intent
Beats all the lies you can invent.

18. Write a dozen sentences, each exactly one line of iambic pentameter. Just write normal, everyday phrases:

Remind me, if you ever get the chance.
The morning paper's late again today!
Emergency! Please send an ambulance!

Use the most interesting line you come up with as the opening of a poem. (Stick to iambic pentameter, but feel free to enjamb.)

19. Write ten lines of iambic pentameter that are all one long sentence. Possible subject: the last exciting thing you did.

20. Write a short poem in iambic trimeter about a trip home. (Theodore Roethke does that in "Night Journey," describing a train ride he can't bear to sleep through). This should be less a "sentimental journey" than a study of sensory impressions, action, imagery, the motion of your conveyance, and the scenery that's passing by.

21. Write six lines of hexameter (six-foot lines), not necessarily connected. Where does the pause fall in each line? Right in the middle? It's characteristic of the hexameter line to break down into three-three. Try to complete a poem from the lines you've created, going into fuller description of your topic.

22. Write ten lines of iambic pentameter that are as regular (and even mechanical) as possible. No variations, no substitutions. (It may be hard to do without the slack of a few pyrrhic feet, so allow yourself the liberty.) Once you know you can do that perfectly well (and atrociously), start substituting. Manipulate your word choices and parts of speech and phrases to accommodate trochaic inversions, spondees, the pyrrhic-spondee combination. Keep going until the poem starts to fall out of the metrical pattern altogether. How much variation does that take? Probably three substitutions per line will do it, but it depends on the circumstances. You can't stretch the pattern too far, unless you want a different meter—or free verse.

23. Write a dozen lines of blank verse (unrhymed iambic pentameter). If you need a subject, write a speech you could deliver to a group of insurance salesmen. Then maneuver the poem into heroic couplets (rhymed AABBCCDD, etc.), changing as much as necessary. Robert Lowell wrote many of his early rhymed poems this way.

24. Write a poem in the "loose iambics" that Frost mentions. That means including extra unstressed syllables *without* losing the basic iambic movement. Here's a "loose iambic" line: "When a storm whips up the Florida coast to Savannah." Any more unstressed syllables and the poem topples over into anapestic meter. The second and third feet ("whips up the Flor-") keep it, barely, "in line." The extra syllables impart a conversational quality, which Frost displays wonderfully in *North of Boston*.

ACCENTUAL METER

One of the ways to measure lines of poetry is to count the number of *accents* (also called *stresses* or *beats*). But this kind of mathematics is an approximate science at best. Traditionally, scanning English poetry has involved marking the stressed and unstressed syllables in a line, as in Shakespeare's Sonnet 73:

Thăt tíme ŏf yéar thŏu máyst ĭn mé běhóld.

In iambic pentameter, each line has (theoretically) five stresses or accents and ten syllables altogether; each line can be divided into five "feet" or measures. But in accentual meter, we count only the stresses.

What makes an accent? Emphasis mainly, a slight rise in pitch and loudness. We emphasize important words, often nouns and verbs, but usually not the minor parts of speech (articles, conjunctions, prepositions). In polysyllabic words, one syllable usually has the primary emphasis: um-BREL-la, for example, or prog-NOS-ti-cate. If this seems unfamiliar, spend some time browsing through a dictionary, examining how accents are marked for various words. Determining accents becomes tricky with iambics, but it's pretty straightforward with accentual meter. You have to hear it audibly. It has to land with a thump.

You can be rough in counting accentual meter as you write, listening for the heavy downbeat and skimming over lesser accents (which we would pay close attention to in iambics). Try, in fact, to vary the number of unstressed syllables. Make sure you don't fall into some regular syllable-stress meter! In adding extra syllables, it's all too easy to fall into galloping "triple meters" like anapestic (˘ ˘ ´) or dactylic (´ ˘ ˘). Avoid that regularity by cutting or adding unstressed syllables in those lulls between stresses. For example, change "In the *stores* on the *bor*der of *Wav*erly *Park*" to something like "In *store*fronts on the *edge* of *Wav*erly *Park*." Notice how the number of unstressed syllables clustered together changes in the revised line. Even if the regularity of the first version seems more pleasing and seductive, try to resist the temptation to let your verse gallop away. Rhythmic subtlety matters more—and lets you *do* more.

Traditional Anglo-Saxon meter (the "strong stress" line) contains four beats, three of them alliterating, with a *caesura* (a break or a pause) in the middle. *Beowulf* is written in this rough-hewn meter, as is William Langland's "Piers Plowman," whose first line is "In a *sum*mer *sea*son, when *soft* was the *sun*." Notice that all four accents in this line alliterate, an acceptable variation. You can also alliterate the first two stresses together and the last two together, or you can use assonance, the repetition of vowel sounds. Richard Wilbur's "Junk" and "Lilacs" are examples of contemporary use of this form. W.H. Auden used Anglo-Saxon alliterative meter in his long poem *The Age of Anxiety*.

In addition to the four accents and the alliteration of Anglo-Saxon meter, you also have to place a pause (or *caesura*) in the middle of each line, so that two accents fall on either side of the break:

Dríving home the Dódge, ‖ he dámaged the fénder.

Each half-line is called a *hemistich*. The second can be dropped to the next typed line to emphasize the caesura:

In a wórld of wíles
                        whát can amáze us?

This typographical arrangement may make it easier for the reader to follow the pattern of Anglo-Saxon meter.

Gerard Manley Hopkins coined the term *sprung rhythm* for verse measured solely by the number of accents. In his sonnet "The Windhover," Hopkins adheres to the five-stresses of iambic pentameter, but he allows many unstressed syllables into his lines (so that a single line might total as many as sixteen syllables):

I cáught this mórning mórning's mínion, kíng-
dom of dáylight's dáuphin, dápple-dawn-drawn Fálcon, in his ríding

He counts only the strongest accents in his sprung rhythm. Notice that he's also adopted the heavy alliteration of Anglo-Saxon poetry. In a letter, Hopkins says that his new rhythm "consists in scanning by accents or stresses alone, without any account of the number of syllables, so that a foot may be one strong syllable or it may be many light and one strong." He qualified the "newness" of this sprung rhythm by referring to nursery rhymes and popular jingles as his precedents.

25. Write a poem in accentual meter. Choose two, three, or four beats per line and stick to it. The result should sound a little "bumpy," with the bounce of a good nursery rhyme. For subject matter, describe a particular scene closely, using plenty of sense impressions. Try to use good, hard words derived from Anglo-Saxon (such as *weed*, *stone*, *plough*, *flint*, *blast*). There's a discussion of word derivations in the "Words" chapter of this book. You should also consult a dictionary.

26. Write a poem in Anglo-Saxon strong-stress meter. Try to change the alliterating sound with each line. If you use "b" in the first line ("In the *Bi*ble *Belt*, even *bar*tenders *preach*"), switch to a different sound ("on a *tai*lgate they *talk* about *sin* and *tith*ing") in each following line. Though the form is heroic in *Beowulf*, it can be very effective for treating the modern anti-hero or nearly any theme from popular culture, so feel free to select a lively subject.

27. If you have any poems written in strict iambics, revise them by "roughing them up," adding unstressed syllables, jamming stresses together. Replace trite words by nouns and verbs that are gritty, flashy, boisterous, gleeful. A mechanical line like "She sees the day begin with cloudy skies" can use a few jolts: "she sneers at the clouds, the wash-lines of heaven." If you begin with an anemic pentameter line, transplant it into *four* beats; likewise, if you begin with tetrameter, change it to three beats. In other words, subtract one accent when you switch from syllable-stress meter to accentual meter.

28. Write an adult nursery rhyme. Keep the bouncing quality of a real nursery rhyme ("Jack and Jill" or "Old Mother Hubbard," for example) but treat something that involves weightier issues. Draw your vocabulary from contemporary sources, the lingo of contemporary life and current affairs. Hopkins cites "One, two, buckle my shoe" to show how emphatic the beats of a nursery rhyme must be—suitable for chanting and foot-tapping.

SYLLABICS

If you want the regularity of meter but not the almost audible metronome of iambic pentameter, try syllabics. In this measure, only the number of syllables is counted, not the number of accents or stresses. To some listeners, the results sound like free verse or prose; they assert you can't actually hear the meter. But Charles Wright claims that he can "hear a seven-syllable line through a brick wall." Syllabics were not common in English or American poetry before the twentieth century, so the difficulty in recognizing them when they're read aloud may come from unfamiliarity.

French and Japanese poetry traditionally counts the number of syllables per line. In French, the standard line is the *alexandrine*, a twelve-syllable line with a caesura, or pause, in the middle. (In English, an alexandrine is a line of iambic hexameter—a syllable-stress line, *not* a syllabic line.) In Japanese, a *haiku* requires 5, 7, and 5 syllables in its three lines; a *tanka* requires 5, 7, 5, 7, 7 in its five.

But in English, accent is a crucial part of verbal rhythm. Even though the poet writing syllabics may not *count* the accents, he or she should pay attention to where they crop up and revise lines accordingly. If you measure the same number of syllables per line, it's a good idea to *vary* the number of accents.

If each line has the same number of syllables, it helps, in English, to make that an *odd* number: 5, 7, 9, 11. An even number makes it more likely that the poem will fall into an iambic swing, alternating unstressed and stressed syllables. You want to avoid that in this meter—otherwise it can lose its whole character.

Syllabics can also be organized in stanzas with lines of varying length—as long as those stanzas repeat. You might have, for example, three syllables in line one, seven in line two, and five in line three:

> At the door   3
> a man in torn gabardine 7
> scuffed at the door mat, 5
>
> his wet boots   3
> gritty with sand, a medal 7
> pinned on his lapel.   5

If you don't repeat the stanza at least once, you're *not* writing in meter. Repetition is what gives it regularity. In this stanza form, arranging the lines in an indented pattern gives the reader a clue that the poem is in meter, which might be hard to spot if the lines were all arranged flush left.

Syllabics can sound very prosy—that's their virtue and their vice. But they provide an organizing principle, an invisible regulation of language. They also tend to make the rhythms steadier, because they're more controlled, while leaving an air of freedom. A careful poet will try to balance the lines, making sure there are *enough* accents in each one. It helps here, especially, to condense the language, cut out unnecessary words, choose concrete nouns and verbs rather than abstractions, since syllabic lines can easily go slack if you write with too much laxity. The essential looseness of the form makes it good for conversational material.

29. Write a poem in lines that are five or seven syllables long—at least a dozen lines altogether. Then write a poem on the same subject with nine- or eleven-syllable lines. Keep it the same overall length as the first one. Does the first version sound cramped, unnatural in its phrasing, undeveloped? Or does it have a pleasant tightness, an economy of expression? What did you have to add to the second version to fill out the meter? Do you find extra padding, unnecessary adjectives, rhythmic looseness? (Look for an absence of audible stresses.) Or have you used the extra space to flesh out the subject with vivid, lively words?

30. Choose a subject and then a syllable count that seems appropriate, maybe short lines to suggest nervousness or mystery, longer lines for a relaxed or talkative mood. Write a poem about twenty lines long. Make sure to use fresh details and vivid imagery. Try to include at least one interesting word in every line.

31. Arrange a stanza shape with lines of varying syllabic lengths and write a letter in verse to a fictional character. Choose someone from a novel you enjoy, someone you would like to speak to. If you want to "cheat," you can write out a letter in prose and then fit in into your stanza shape, but the results might be unsatisfying. The advantage of composing *in* the meter is that you can better control the rhythm of your syllabics, tightening them by adding stresses, loosening them with, perhaps, a prepositional phrase.

32. Some writers of syllabics permit themselves the liberty of hyphenating words to make them fit the syllabic pattern:

The thermos swishing its lem-	7
onade toppled from the boat.	7

It's also common to see a syllabic line end with an article or preposition or conjunction:

Walking back from the	5
picnic, the king of	5
the hoboes doffed and	5
tossed out his disguise.	5

Although ending a line with a minor word can sometimes be effective (impelling the reader on to find the next word of interest), too many of these weak line endings sabotage the poem. Write twenty lines, with the same number of syllables in each, on the first subject that comes to mind, ending every line with either a noun, verb, or adjective. Make sure the words are concrete and give a sensory impression.

Poets To Consult

Marianne Moore, Dylan Thomas, Kenneth Rexroth, W.H. Auden, Richard Howard, Thom Gunn, Donald Justice (some of the work in *Night Light*, Wesleyan Univ., 1967), Jordan Smith (*An Apology for Loving the Old Hymns*, Princeton Univ., 1982), Eric Pankey (*Heartwood*, Atheneum, 1988)

PACING

The pacing of a poem, how it flows and moves, seems to derive from the poet's innate sense of the heartbeat's tempo. For most poets, this is *andante*, a walking pace. But some poets move noticeably (and characteristically) slower or faster.

Ezra Pound thought "slowness is beauty," and some of the best passages in his *Cantos* move very slowly, even when the subject (such as dogs attacking a stag in the woods) may not seem very slow:

Gold, gold, a sheaf of hair,
    Thick like a wheat swath

The "th" sounds in the second line thicken the texture considerably. Other poets prefer speed, like Anne Waldman in "Fast Speaking Woman" or Allen Ginsberg in "Howl."

A given poem, of course, will vary its pace, depending on what's being said and how urgent it is. Song-like poems tend to move more slowly than conversational poems.

How dense and packed should a poem be? Kenneth Rosen suggests allowing some "air" in your lines, some room between the chunks and nuggets of rich language. How "airy" can a poem afford to be? Sandra McPherson has said that she tries to put at least two interesting words in each line. Generally, denseness slows the poem down; airiness keeps it moving. A dense poem may not sound very conversational, so if you want a natural, spoken quality, don't pile on the rich words too heavily.

33. Write a poem all-in-a-rush. Start anywhere (even with the word "start") and go as fast as you can, breaking lines willy-nilly, keeping things moving. Let words suggest other words as they fly by. This is a

kind of scat singing, where the rhythm and the discoveries matter, not the occasional bloops and bleeps. Frank O'Hara wrote many fast-paced poems that simply "go on their nerves" and breeze along. He called them his "I do this, I do that" poems. If it helps you to improvise and carry on more freely, think of this onrush poem the same way: you do this, you do that.

34. Try to speed up a slow poem (either yours or someone else's) by lightening the vowels and consonants, loosening the rhythm, simplifying the language, enjambing more of the lines (letting them run over to the next line), and adding some words that suggest quickness. Then try to slow down a fast poem by adding more stresses, end-stopping more lines, placing pauses within lines, massaging out the poem's nervous edges, introducing words with a still or motionless quality.

VI. Shaping

In shaping a poem, the poet acts as designer, sculptor, composer, weaver, architect. The poet's two basic tools — or are they materials? forces? — are the line and the sentence. Like the composer, the poet can use them contrapuntally, perhaps syncopating one against the other. As the poet writes and revises — sometimes starting with a pattern in mind, a regular beat, a tradition, sometimes experimenting, venturing in the dark — the poem's form takes shape.

LINES

Not all poetry is written in lines, but most is. The line calls attention to itself and requires a pause (however slight) before going on to the next one. As in a song, each line sounds out as a unit, even though sentences may go on for several lines. The eye takes in lines differently from the way it takes in a paragraph of prose.

Some critics like to lambaste free verse by printing it out as prose and saying "See?" But it's inevitably different if you remove the lineation, no matter if the writing itself is good or bad. Certainly much poetry is weakened by excessive prosiness, but it deserves to be viewed as the poet intended: *in lines*. And the critic who can't tell the difference needs a hearing test — or at least an eye examination.

In "The Working Line," which appeared in the Spring 1973 issue of *Field*, Sandra McPherson calls the line "a unit to *work* in . . . a compositional aid." She says, "Without rhyme or strict meter the line can still help distribute the cadences and aid our response to the speed of the poem. Since variation in line length often gives pleasure, the line elicits a physical response, an inner dancing." In a responding essay, Louis Simpson says, "The line is a unit of rhythm. The poet is moved by impulses of rhythm which he expresses in lines of verse. Impulse determines where each line breaks, and the impulse of the poem as a whole determines the look of the poem on the page or its sound in the air."

Another word for line is "verse," whose Latin root comes from *vertere*, to turn, and refers specifically to the furrows of a plowed field. (The end of each verse is where the farmer *turns*.)

1. Write a poem (on any subject) in either long or short lines. Then

write a variation of that poem—an alternate version, an expansion or a condensation—in the opposite length of line. Try to use the same number of lines for each poem. Keep in mind that if your first poem is in long lines, you will have to omit details (or compress them) in order to shorten the lines. Also keep in mind the saying of the Greek philosopher Herakleitos: "You can't step into the same river twice." (In other words, you're not writing two versions of the same poem; you're writing two different poems that happen to share subject matter and wording.)

2. Work on a single line until it's as interesting as you can make it. Don't feel you have to complete the thought. You can (and probably should) leave the line incomplete, open-ended, so that the *next* line can pick up the motion. Of course, the line *can* be end-stopped (instead of enjambed, or running over). In any case, once you've shaped the line, go on to the next, and push and shove the words and images there until they pick up what the first one left up in the air. When that's done to your satisfaction, go on to the next, and the next, until you've completed a poem. Believe it or not, some poets *do* write poems exactly this way, one line at a time. They may spend hours on a single line, instead of breezing along to complete a whole draft.

3. Pick a phrase you like and use it as what Donald Justice calls a "model line," thinking of it as the "norm" or "meter" for the poem you're going to write. It can be the first line of the poem, or a line embedded later on, or the title, or maybe something you won't actually include in the finished poem. But the other lines should approximate it in some way: number of syllables or accents, number of words, use of a single polysyllabic word surrounded by several monosyllables.

SENTENCES

One of the joys of writing poems is playing off sentences against lines—a resource the prose writer sorely lacks. The line, of course, is the poet's basic unit of composition, but there are several ways of laying out sentences on that gridwork:

1. Sentence = Line

Be not disturb'd with my infirmity.

2. Sentence = Part of a line

What would my potent master? Here I am.

3. Sentence = More than one line

> We are such stuff
> As dreams are made on, and our little life
> Is rounded with a sleep.

Those lines all come from Shakespeare's *Tempest*. Here are several lines from *King Lear*, spoken by the king, that exemplify all three ways:

> Rumble thy bellyful! Spit, fire! spout, rain!
> Nor rain, wind, thunder, fire are my daughters.
> I tax not you, you elements, with unkindness.
> I never gave you kingdom, call'd you children,
> You owe me no subscription. Then let fall
> Your horrible pleasure. Here I stand your slave,
> A poor, infirm, weak, and despis'd old man.
> But yet I call you servile ministers,
> That will with two pernicious daughters join
> Your high-engender'd battles 'gainst a head
> So old and white as this! O! O! 'tis foul!

Shakespeare uses *end-stopping* (halting at the end of a line, usually aided by a period or another punctuation mark) and *enjambment* (letting one line spill over into the next). The line-break gives a slight pause, but a line that's enjambed will still push over strongly into the next. It's as if the end of a line swelled up like a wave, letting the words surf right along, flowing into the next line. Good enjambment has an exhilarating feel; it's breathless; it's an onrush. Good end-stopping takes a breath, pausing contentedly.

Think of the lines as a kind of framework on which you lay different lengths of colorful material. Sometimes you'll need short little scraps, a patchwork of quick utterances. Sometimes you'll need to wind a long sentence over the course of many lines — perhaps an entire poem consisting of a single sentence. In general, the longer the sentences, the more a poem flows. Short sentences have a choppy, bouncy, nervous, intense feel. In general, long sentences lull, short sentences rouse. It depends on whether you want the sweep of violins or the percussion of kettle drums. Of course, the poet (like a shrewd composer) will usually want to *vary* sentence lengths for emphasis, variety, a sense of melody, and surprise.

It helps to know how to keep a sentence going and how to cut it short. Take a simple declarative sentence: "The downpour flooded High Street." You can make it longer by putting extra details *before* the main sentence ("In two wet hours, the downpour flooded High Street"), *in the middle of* the main sentence ("The downpour, sudden and furious, flooded High Street"), or *after* the main sentence ("The downpour flooded High Street, tugging down stop signs, breaking through burglar-proof shop windows, carrying off sofas and nightgowns"). All three ways of expanding sentences can be used in various combinations (and all are useful), but the one most frequently used is adding material *after* the main clause, since it gives us our bearings (the main subject and verb that tell us what's *mainly* happening) before we start elaborating and spinning out variations.

To cut a sentence short, you can reword minor parts of the sentence into new sentences of their own, so that something like "In late June, driving through Death Valley, the pickup starts belching steam and the elderly driver eases to a halt beside a broken-down shack, a sandy wind scratching at his face" into something more percussive: "Late June. Death Valley. The pickup belches steam. The old man downshifts to neutral. Rolls to a halt. He looks at a broken-down shack by the road. A sandy wind scratches his face." Notice that several of the "sentences" are mere fragments: the first two contain just subjects, the fifth one just a verb.

Sometimes a writer will *delay* the main point in a long sentence. Those who have studied German will recognize the effect of waiting and waiting to get to the verb — the "pay-off": "The giraffe, lifting its head from the water and straightening its legs again, its ears perking up at the sound of laughter, turned." This kind of sentence is called *periodic*.

Reading good prose by a variety of writers will help give you a sense of how to shape sentences, how to vary the kinds of sentences you use, how to control *pacing* by sentence length. If you don't know much about phrases (groups of words lacking both subject and verb) or dependent clauses (which include both subject and verb but are *subordinated* to a more important clause and thus can't, theoretically, stand alone), you might look into a composition handbook — or you might simply pay closer attention to what writers actually *do* with their sentences. Learning by example is certainly more fun and probably more helpful in the long run.

Of course, we have the added excitement of fitting sentences into *lines* when we write any kind of poetry except the prose poem.

4. Write a whole poem that is one long sentence. Aim for at least a dozen lines, but extend it to a full page, if possible. Coordinate conjunctions (*and*, *or*, *but*) may come in handy. So might connective words (relative conjunctions or prepositions) such as *because*, *after*, and *in*. You want to modify, qualify, contradict, divert, reroute, and otherwise elaborate the sentence. Let things happen and change as the sentence progresses

over its long trackage of lines. It's a kind of train excursion through cities, farmland, and mountains, over bridges and through tunnels.

5. Write a poem that uses plenty of short, punchy sentences. Fragments and exclamations are welcome! If you need a longer sentence and some enjambment here or there, use them. Start by fixing on a subject or mood that seems appropriate for these jabbing sentences.

6. W.B. Yeats wanted his verse sentences to coincide with his stanzas, so that there would be a definite pause in the white space between them. Write a poem in regular stanzas (perhaps six lines in each, in meter and rhyme if you like), making each stanza end with a period.

STANZAS

A *stanza* is a group of lines set apart from the rest of a poem by white space above and below. It is sometimes, especially when it occurs in free verse, called a *verse paragraph*. Glance at any anthology or collection of poetry; unless the text is a solid block of lines, with no space breaks at all, the poem will contain stanzas.

In Italian, where the word originated, a stanza is a "room." (The word also means "station" or "stopping place.") It's useful to keep that derivation in mind as you write. Moving from stanza to stanza is like moving from room to room; each chamber has a different function and particular furniture, but all are somehow connected—or should be—some by elegant French doors, some by secret passageways. You might think of Edgar Allan Poe's "Masque of the Red Death," much of which describes a series of symbolically decorated chambers.

In many poems, the stanzas all have the same number of lines. Here are some terms:

couplet	2 lines
tercet	3 lines
quatrain	4 lines
cinquain	5 lines
sestet	6 lines
septet	7 lines
octave	8 lines

The first three terms are the most common, although we hear much of the octave and sestet in the sonnet (in which eight + six = fourteen lines). Stanzas of nine, ten, and more lines (especially that sonnet length of fourteen lines) occur frequently, but after a certain point it's clearer to say "eleven-line stanza" than something like "hendecastrophic."

Greek choral odes, which you'll find in the tragedies of Aeschylus and

Sophocles, began with a *strophe* (pronounced *stro*-fee), during which the chorus moved to the left, followed by an *antistrophe* (pronounced an-*tís*-tro-fee), during which the chorus moved back to the right, followed by an *epode* (pronounced *eh*-pode), with the chorus standing still: a song of three stanzas. We now use the term *strophe* specifically for stanzas that are irregular in length. But in the process of writing, it may be more helpful to lump strophes, stanzas, and verse paragraphs together as "stanzas," whether they're regular or not, rather than classify them precisely. The extra latitude may open greater possibilities than the strict observance of proper nomenclature.

Stanzas can make a poem more inviting. Their white spaces offer the reader some breathing room. Small units of lines are much easier to read than a monolith of text. Each stanza is like the verse of a song—a confusing term for us, since in poetry *verse* means either a single line or anything written in lines.

A poem that is written in a continuous flow of lines, without stanza breaks, is called "stichic" (pronounced "stick-ic")—a *stich* being a single line. Despite the advantages of stanzas, there are reasons for dispensing with them sometimes: they may seem arbitrary or unnecessary; they may impede the flow of the poem; they may ruin the pace of the story. It all depends on the poet's choice and the needs of the particular poem.

In *I Wanted to Write a Poem*, William Carlos Williams discusses how he revised a poem containing one stanza of five lines and one of four into a balanced poem of two four-line stanzas "in the normal process of concentrating the poem, getting rid of redundancies in the line—and in the attempt to go faster." He was exploring "how to divide a poem" according to his "lyrical sense." After presenting the original and revised versions of this poem, "The Nightingales," side by side, he points out "See how much better it conforms to the page, how much better it looks?" If your stanzas are only slightly irregular, you might want to revise them into orderly, regular ones; otherwise the differences might seem like mistakes. Irregularity in stanza length should probably be noticeable if it's there at all.

Stanzas can also be given a particular visual shape, either by centering them (all too easy if you use a word processor), or by indenting lines according to the meter or line-length. The odes of Wordsworth and Keats, the songs of Shakespeare, the dramatic monologues of Richard Howard, the syllabic poems of Marianne Moore, and some of the stanzaic poems of Richard Wilbur exemplify this visual patterning of stanzas.

(Note: Other sections of this book that deal with stanza shapes ("Ballad," "Ghazal," "Iambics," "Ode," "Pantoum," "Rhyme," "Sapphics," "Sestina," "Song," and "Sonnet") are gathered in the "Patterns and

Traditions" chapter, which ends with a "Summary of Forms.")

7. Write a poem in regular stanzas. Couplets, tercets, and quatrains work especially well, but try any length that seems agreeable.

8. Write a poem in which the stanzas vary in length. (Try not to let any adjacent stanzas contain the same number of lines.) This kind of poem will seem less formal (because less regulated), but you can rhyme if you like, perhaps occasionally (for special effects) or in an elaborate, irregular pattern (varying the number of lines *between* rhymes). You don't, of course, *have* to rhyme, especially if your poem is in free verse.

9. Write a poem in one solid block and then try to divide it into stanzas. Will it fit into stanzas of the same number of lines? Will it work better in irregular stanzas? Will each stanza end where a sentence ends — or will you let the thought run over (be *enjambed*) to the next stanza? Feel free to cut lines, add new ones, rearrange phrases, shorten or lengthen lines — whatever makes the poem work in stanzas.

10. Write a poem in stanzas that have a distinct (and repeated) visual shape. Use indentation to create your pattern. (Rhyme can reinforce or counterpoint the pattern, but it's optional.)

11. John Berryman discusses how he invented a stanza form for his lengthy "Homage to Mistress Bradstreet": the eight-line stanza he invented "breaks not at midpoint but after the short third line; a strange four-beat line leads to the balancing heroic couplet of lines five and six, after which seven is again short (three feet, like line three) and then the stanza widens into an alexandrine rhyming all the way back to one. I wanted something at once flexible and grave, intense and quiet, able to deal with matter both high and low." Here is the metrical pattern and rhyme scheme of the stanza he quotes in his essay, "One Answer to a Question: Changes":

Syllables	*Accents*	*Rhyme*	
10	5	A	
10	5	B	
7	3	C	
8	4	B	
10	5	D	heroic couplet
10	5	D	heroic couplet
5	3	B	
12	6	A	alexandrine

(Note: His B rhyme is actually the same word, "still," all three times; in other sections he prefers rhyming lines 2 and 4 together and lines 3 and 7 together, although he varies this and sometimes rhymes none of them.)

Write a poem either (1) using Berryman's "Mistress Bradstreet" stanza or (2) inventing your own stanza shape.

REPETITION AND VARIATION

Poetry thrives on the constant tugging between repetition and variation. Meter represents a monotonous, hypnotic regularity; metrical substitutions (placing stresses, for example, in a spot that's normally weak and unstressed) rouse us by the surprise of variety; they represent the constant and the variable, the norm and the departure, the backbeat and the syncopation, the familiar and the unexpected. Poems may highlight one or the other, but both are necessary.

Poems can repeat key words, or phrases, or whole lines (called refrains), or particular sounds (consonants or vowels or rhymes), or images. They can "echo" what's gone before, perhaps using an image that resembles an earlier one (for example, an early mention of leaves falling might later be echoed by a glass dropping to the floor and shattering). But already we're veering into the realm of variation, where we shift directions suddenly, unload a surprise, say something unexpected. We want to keep the reader entranced. Too much repetition would be monotonous. Too much variation would break the spell. We want to suspend the reader somewhere between the two extremes, at a point where the wakeful mind relaxes enough to follow a poem's hints and suggestions.

12. Write a poem that repeats words, phrases, or whole lines effectively and expressively. Don't repeat *everything*, but try to repeat frequently, as a jazz musician might return to the same notes over and over or play the same riff every so often. Think of the repeated word or phrase or line as a home base; you need to return to it whenever you stray too far afield. But try to *change* what you repeat as the poem goes on. You might also "leap-frog" different repetitions: first A, then B, then A, then B, and so on.

13. Write a poem in which each line repeats *one word* from the previous line.

14. Write a poem in which one important word comes up again and again throughout the poem, maybe once a line, maybe even more frequently. This is bound to make an obsessive poem. Make sure the hammering repetition is balanced by an array of imagery and flights of language between the repetitions of the "key word."

15. Write a poem that is constant variation, always moving farther from its starting point, changing the subject, drawing in new imagery.

16. Begin each new stanza of a poem with "I saw"—as Charles Simic does in "Note Slipped Under a Door":

I saw a high window struck blind
By the late afternoon sunlight.

Each of the following stanzas begins with the same words: "I saw. . . ." If you prefer, begin each stanza "I hear."

VISUAL SHAPE

On the printed page, many poems present themselves in a kind of uniform: the lines arranged with a straight left-hand margin. We're so used to this appearance that it seems transparent, a window through which the words and music and images of the poem can pass easily and unobtrusively. That, in fact, is the best reason for minimizing the look of a poem on the page.

But some writers choose to use the page actively, playing with shapes, both imitative and abstract, and arranging lines in visual patterns. Although the typewriter and the computer have simplified the process, visually shaped poems go way back, probably originating in inscriptions on tombstones and statues. In the seventeenth century, George Herbert wrote "emblematic poems" such as "Easter Wings," shaped like a pair of wings, and "The Altar."

In the early twentieth century, Guillaume Apollinaire wrote "calligrammes." In his poem, "It's Raining" ("*Il Pleut*"), the words drizzle down the page vertically. In *Rhyme's Reason*, John Hollander mentions "pattern poems" and "shaped verse." Hollander has in fact written a whole collection of pattern poems, *Types of Shape*, including poems shaped like a máp of New York state and like a swan and its reflection in the water.

When the visual shape overwhelms the audible text, it's called *concrete poetry*. How much poetry it contains is open to debate. If the concept interests you, you might look into the works and criticism of Richard Kostelanetz and go on from there. But I think there's a simple way to draw a line: if you can read it aloud, it's a poem. If an oral performance of it seems absurd, it's a branch of visual art. (In the twentieth century, we have seen paintings by Picasso, Larry Rivers, Jennifer Bartlett and many others that *do* include actual words and text).

Some of the most satisfying shaped verse imitates its subject loosely or impressionistically, rather than explicitly. May Swenson has written many remarkable poems that look intriguing and read beautifully; she often loads them with metaphor, so that the visual shape becomes simply another likeness. She has also used "gutters" (a space or trough running down through the center of a poem), squiggly lines worming between letters and words, and a diagonal streak made by spacing, even if it cuts words in half (in her poem, "The Lightning"). In these poems, the shape seems far more than decoration (which would qualify the poem as a kind of light verse). It's integral and powerful. Her poem, "Out of the Sea Early," for example, looks like a great circle of words rising out of a single line, like the sun emerging above the horizon. And her descriptions *within* this graphic shape add to the visual impression. The sun is likened to a "bloody/ egg yolk," a "burnt hole," a "furnace hatchway," and even more startling things.

The typewriter seems essential to this poetry—and why not? If the poet composes at the keyboard, perhaps the page can serve literally as a score, the words as notes. You can arrange the words graphically, abstractly, letting them jump around the page acrobatically, enacting a dance performance, a spatial improvisation.

Even if shaped verse seems too extreme, or too self-conscious, you might consider using more indentation, sometimes lowering the second half of a line down a level, sometimes dividing a line into a series of steps, sometimes shaping a narrow strip of lines to contrast with larger blocks made up of longer lines. The poet can use this kind of shaping to indicate shifts, to show a poem's structure, to suggest pauses, to emphasize rhythms, or simply to liven up the page. Charles Wright's poems in *The Southern Cross*, and in later volumes, do this. Historically, many songs and odes and sonnets have been indented to show the rhyme schemes or the metrical differences between lines.

17. Write a poem that's shaped like whatever you're describing. Try to choose something interesting that you can also describe with imagery and metaphor.

18. Write a poem modeled on May Swenson's work in shaped verse. Be freer with the shaping, less strictly imitative.

19. Write a poem in which you indent some of the lines, or drop down parts of lines, to give the poem some visual liveliness. Are some of the indentations effective, others not?

TITLES

The first thing we notice about a poem is usually the title. It's also the tag we use to remember a poem and refer to it. Of course, titles can draw attention to themselves or they can be matter-of-fact, virtually invisible. They can be flashy or functional, intriguing or explanatory. They can even be omitted altogether—the way Juan Ramon Jimenez, the great Spanish poet and Nobel Prize winner, often presents his "naked poetry." There are, after all, many experiences and states of being that don't fit comfortably under *any* heading.

Wallace Stevens is our greatest master of imaginative titles, many of which sound like little poems in themselves:

"The Paltry Nude Starts on a Spring Voyage"
"Hibiscus on the Sleeping Shores"
"Floral Decorations for Bananas"
"The Curtains in the House of the Metaphysician"
"Frogs Eat Butterflies. Snakes Eat Frogs. Hogs Eat Snakes. Men Eat Hogs."
"The Revolutionists Stop for Orangeade"
"The Bagatelles the Madrigals"
"The House Was Quiet and the World Was Calm"
"Mountains Covered with Cats"

These titles are pleasing in themselves; they invite us into the poems — which had better live up to their names, at least in *some* fashion.

But while a good title need not dazzle us with fireworks, it must draw us in, or at least avoid impeding our progress into the poem. In *The Longman Dictionary of Poetic Terms*, Jack Myers and Michael Simms offer twelve pages discussing various kinds of titles. They define five general categories: titles that (1) "describe the poem"; (2) "are reader-directed"; (3) "use outside references"; (4) "are dedicatory"; and (5) "are self-effacing." I recommend their discussion of titles (and their fascinating dictionary as a whole), but looking at a variety of examples, perhaps in the table of contents of a recent poetry anthology, may be more helpful than any categorization. (Myers and Simms do offer plenty of examples, but it is *their* list.) Try making your own discoveries and deciding what sorts of titles you prefer. The range of possibilities is wide open.

As lovely as Stevens's titles can be, it is a distortion to separate them from their poems. A good title is above all appropriate, of a piece with what follows. It may sum up the poem in some way, pointing inward. It may look outward by nodding to an influence, quoting a phrase, or honoring a friend.

William Stafford has a poem called "The Title Comes Later"; the last lines of the first stanza are:

(The title is "Remembering, or
Guide Your Dreams Awake.")

Frank O'Hara titles many of his poems "Poem." Emily Dickinson didn't use titles (although her first editors attached some). Where there is no title, we refer to the poem by its first line. The *real* problem with not titling a poem at all is that it looks odd on the page. It bursts in unannounced. It doesn't leave a calling card. Some poets (and editors) get around this dilemma by arranging untitled poems in numbered sequences, so that there's at least *something* on top, like a little hat.

Some poets, like Marianne Moore and William Carlos Williams, often start the poem itself with the title, as in Moore's

THE FISH
wade
through black jade . . .

Some poets like to choose a title before they write the poem, letting it trigger whatever follows. Many poets affix a title after everything else in the poem is done, almost as a necessary formality. Some poems go through numerous titles, even in print, before settling down. We have many examples and precedents, but no rules. At worst, a title shouldn't hurt a poem. At best, it should deepen and vivify the words that follow.

In particular, a title is a good place for a quick explanation or for background information you don't want to force into the poem itself. Chinese titles can be extremely long, as in Meng Hao-jan's "Spending the Night at the Hillside Lodge of Master Yeh and Waiting for My Friend Ting, Who Does Not Arrive" (taken from *Sunflower Splendor*, an anthology of Chinese poetry). Such titles have been imitated by American poets such as James Wright and Robert Bly. If you don't want a long title, you might insert a note or explanation or suitable quotation between title and poem, indented and given white space above and below. It's called an *epigraph* or *head note* and can be helpful both in informing the reader and in simplifying the poem.

20. Start with a title and let it propel you into the poem. (Don't have any of the poem written beforehand.)

21. Write a poem whose title serves as the first line. Think about how to bridge the space in between, how to move from capital letters to lower case, how to keep the poem moving and not trip it up at the starting gate.

22. Find a title for an untitled poem by a well-known poet. What do you look for? Does it merely sum up, or does it add something? If you're pleased with your title, use it as the start of one of your own poems (perhaps quoting the famous poem briefly in an epigraph).

23. Take an old poem of yours with a boring or otherwise unappealing title and find a new one.

LETTERS

Letters have long served, not only as a means of correspondence, but also as a vehicle for poems and stories. The reader has the giddy thrill of peeking into someone's private mail, without even the trouble of steaming open an envelope and gluing it back undetected. Many novels take the form of a series of letters, from the eighteenth century (Samuel Richardson's *Pamela* and Choderlos de Laclos's *Les Liaisons Dangereuses*) to the twentieth (Alice Walker's *The Color Purple* and John Barth's *Letters*). In poetry, the precedent goes back farther, including the Roman poet Horace's epistles. We might also think of the Biblical epistles.

The main advantage of the letter form is its intimacy. In most poems, the sense of an audience is hazy. (That's not true of love poetry, but how often love poems are really billets-doux!) A letter though, unless it's open and public, like a letter to the editor, speaks to a particular person, a character if you like. That rudimentary dramatic set-up seems invaluable for poetry. It's no accident that Richard Howard frames many of his dramatic monologues as letters. Another advantage of the letter is that it provides its own occasion, its own reason for the poet to write (to catch up with a friend, or to respond to another letter, or to open an exchange with a stranger). It can be loose and teasing or it can be stiffly formal, depending on the writer and the recipient — either of whom, or both, can be real or fictional.

Poems in letter form can use or ignore meter and rhyme, but they can't dally the way our personal letters might — at least not for long. Small talk makes them especially puny, and banter soon annoys rather than titillates. The poet who writes letters-in-verse needs to ease into the letter (renewing the acquaintance) and yet move quickly into the heart of the matter. "Hi, how are you" and banalities about the weather should have some ulterior motive, revealing something about the sender or the reader.

The conventions of a real letter (date, return address, salutation, complimentary close) can be used or not, according to the needs of the particular poem. They seem useful for historical verisimilitude, less so for real letters set in the present. The more fictional your letter is, the more you need suitable costumes and disguises.

Incidentally, the real letters of poets such as John Keats and Emily Dickinson make wonderful reading. Richard Howard considers them, along with the poet's poems and criticism, the third major part of a poet's lifework. Most of us have a head start in writing letters (although long distance telephoning has cut severely into the habit). But sometimes you want the directness of a real letter, not the artifice of a poem. There's no reason we can't have both.

24. In Saul Bellow's *Herzog*, the title character writes many letters to famous people. Write a letter to someone famous, living or dead. Not a fan letter! Don't gush. Air a grievance or point out something or relate an experience the person might enjoy hearing about.

25. Write a letter in verse to a friend. Use free verse unless you feel comfortable with meter. Don't rhyme unless you have to and have mastered its intricacies. Tell the friend something you've never mentioned before — not a confession, exactly, but something you've noticed or experienced that seemed untellable yet important. Try to say the unsayable.

26. Write a satirical letter about something that makes you angry. Be as venomous as you can. The heroic couplets of Alexander Pope (iambic pentameter rhymed in pairs) might be a good vehicle for venting your spleen, but so might the onrushing long-breathed wild-eyed Biblical free verse of Allen Ginsberg. Aim your barbs at a particular person.

27. Write a love letter (that billet-doux again) that doesn't mention love explicitly, that doesn't burble with amorous clichés, that doesn't resort to exclamation points. Address it to someone you really love, but remember that the love can take many forms — erotic, fraternal, filial, unrequited, admiring, grudging.

28. Read some letters by a master of the art: Keats, Dickinson, Virginia Woolf, Vincent Van Gogh, E.B. White. Try to write a real letter in prose to someone you've known all your life. Talk especially about something you've read, or a scene you observed and wanted to explain, or an idea that bugs you, or a recollection you've reconsidered.

29. Write a letter from the point of view of another person (living or dead, real or fictional) to yourself. Use some sort of meter, maybe blank verse (unrhymed iambic pentameter) or the elaborate syllabic stanzas favored by Richard Howard (in which line one of each stanza might contain three syllables; line two, eight; line three, five; line four, nine; line five, seven; each stanza can take on a similar visual shape by indenting lines according to their length). Gather whatever material you need to impersonate your speaker effectively.

FORM AND CONTENT

Robert Creeley says that "form is merely an extension of content." Ezra Pound says "I think there is a 'fluid' as well as a 'solid' content, that some poems may have form as a tree has form, some as water poured into a vase."

Some poets write in a habitual form: Emily Dickinson uses the hymn stanza or ballad stanza (see "Ballad" in the next chapter) in most of her poems. Some poets seek out a new form each time they write: Richard Wilbur might use stanzas modeled on haiku in one poem, Anglo-Saxon meter in another, and a stanza made up of varying line lengths and interlocking rhyme in another (see "Haiku" in the next chapter). It has little to do with whether the poet writes in meter or not. Many free verse poets use the same kind of free verse in nearly every poem. Denise Levertov speaks of an "organic form" which takes shape in a free verse poem as it grows. Robert Hass points out that "the music of the poem as it develops imposes its own restrictions. That is how it comes to form."

In our own poems, the choice of a form need not be conscious; we can simply write and see what form develops in the poem. On the other hand, we can also begin with a set "form," such as the villanelle, and use it as a kind of mold or blueprint. Or we can begin writing and discover, after a line or two, that we're writing in iambic tetrameter; we may also find rhymes cropping up and imposing a set scheme only *after* the poem is underway. Or we can invent forms to fit the subject matter, perhaps borrowing a kind of organization or imitating an action.

Charles Simic's "*errata*," for example, imitates the corrections that might appear in a scholarly book:

Where it says snow
read teeth-marks of a virgin

In *The Weight of Numbers*, Judith Baumel imitates the Fibonacci sequence (a mathematical progression of 1, 1, 2, 3, 5, 8, 13, 21, 34 . . . in which each number is the sum of the two previous numbers) in two poems, "Fibonacci" and "Speaking in Blizzards," by having the number of lines in her stanzas correspond to the progression. (Each of these poems begins with two one-line stanzas and ends with a thirteen-line stanza.)

Other poems may have forms that imitate what they're about. Linda Pastan's "Getting Down to Work," a poem about the poet clearing her desk to make way for new poetic ventures, consists of three free-verse stanzas. The first is nine lines long, the second is a single line, and the third is—again—nine lines long. Here is the line she isolates in the middle stanza: "In the middle now this small cleared space." The form of the poem clearly imitates the action described.

In "The Death of the Moon" (in *The POETRY Anthology: 1912-1977*,

Houghton Mifflin, 1978), David Wagoner invents a form to imitate the waning of the moon: his first stanza is five lines of iambic pentameter; his second, four lines of tetrameter; his third, three lines of trimeter; his fourth, two lines of dimeter; and his fifth, a single line of monometer: "Her darkness." Wagoner's "Song to Accompany the Bearer of Bad News" begins with an eighteen-line stanza ("Kings kill their messengers/ Sometimes, slicing wildly"), then tears the lines in half—like someone ripping up a message—putting these fragments in a new, jumbled order, and *then* drops them into a kind of pile with two or three of the torn pieces in each line. In all, there are three stanzas, each containing exactly the same words. Poor messenger. It makes an interesting— and probably unrepeatable—form.

30. Start writing a poem. After you've done a few lines, stop and see if you can sense a particular form taking hold. Maybe you've fallen into three-beat lines, or something close to iambic pentameter; maybe the lines are short, or quite long, or mixed; maybe there's actually a rhyme. Resume writing and see how this awareness of what you've unconsciously been doing helps shape the rest of your poem.

31. Invent a form and write a poem in it. Imitating an action or type of organization may offer the richest possibilities.

VII. Patterns and Traditions

Resist the idea that this chapter consists of a set of recipes — although, in a way, that's true. Be wary about referring to them blithely as "forms" — although that's what most people call them. Think of them as patterns, traditional guidelines and sets of restrictions. Remember that, as Robert Hass points out, no two sonnets, even if they share the same meter and rhyme scheme, ever have the same form. And remember that you can work *in* a tradition or *against* a tradition.

ANTHOLOGY

Philip Dacey and David Jauss, *Strong Measures: Contemporary American Poetry in Traditional Forms* (Harper & Row, 1986) — a wonderful collection of poems in most of the "forms" covered here (ballad, haiku, pantoum, sapphics, sestina, sonnet, villanelle), as well as others such as the canzone, glose, kyrielle, rimas dissolutas, rondeau, rondel, and triolet.

BALLAD

A traditional ballad is essentially a song that tells a story. Its usual form, the ballad stanza, consists of a quatrain with four beats in the first and third lines, three beats in the second and fourth (which also rhyme):

> There *lived* a *wife* at *Ush*er's *Well*,
>> And a *weal*thy *wife* was *she*;   A
> She *had* three *stout* and *stal*wart *sons*
>> And *sent* them *o'er* the *sea*.   A

The second and fourth lines are sometimes stretched out to four beats (to match lines one and three), making an iambic tetrameter quatrain. And sometimes the first and third lines have only three beats each — but with a feminine ending (an extra unstressed syllable in each):

> There *lived* a *king* in *Brit*ain,
>> And he *ruled* from *moor* to *coast*;

> He *asked* his *three* young *daugh*ters
> *Which* of them *loved* him *most*.

(This example is simply an adaptation of the "Wife at Usher's Well" — borrowing the story of King Lear.)

In a four-beat ballad line, the second and fourth beats can rhyme, as in Coleridge's "Rime of the Ancient Mariner":

> The fair breeze *blew*, the white foam *flew*,
> The furrow followed free;
> We were the *first* that ever *burst*
> Into that silent sea.

Traditional ballad subjects include murder, love, revenge, shipwrecks, and the supernatural. In fact, four centuries ago ballad hawkers were the tabloid news carriers of their day. Supermarket tabloid stories are the stuff of ballads — but without the art.

What you have to do in a ballad is combine *narrative* poetry (which tells a story) with *lyric* poetry (which sings or chants a kind of song, originally accompanied by a lyre, like the lyrics of the Greek poet Sappho). Because of the difficulty of this merging, most ballads are simple in both song and story.

1. Find a newspaper article about some violent crime. Starting with the facts presented, flesh out a list of particulars to describe the victim, the perpetrator, the scene of the crime, the motive, the background, the witnesses, the aftermath. Then put these particulars into a ballad written in the traditional form (though you should feel free to use slant rhymes if you like).

2. Retell a ghost story in ballad form.

3. Find a traditional ballad (such as "Sir Patrick Spens" or "Barbara Allen") and modernize it, changing the setting to something contemporary and adding details of modern life. Instead of Sir Patrick sailing a ship, he might pilot a Coast Guard cutter patrolling the drug routes of the Caribbean.

4. Choose a song you like that does *not* tell a story and make it into a ballad, following the song's metrical pattern, note for note, but adding a story. This exercise will force you to (1) find words and phrases to "plug into" the original's melody, and (2) be concise in telling your story.

5. Think of a familiar story and try to retell it by *singing* it. Julian Jaynes suggests this exercise in *The Origin of Consciousness in the Breakdown of the Bicameral Mind*. He points out that the two activities (singing and

talking about some subject you know) originate on different sides of the brain and are therefore hard to coordinate. He notes that the results usually sound more like an opera's recitative (the relatively unmelodic part used for "talking" and explaining) than an aria (the song). If possible, have a tape recorder running while you try this; if not, jot down what you remember "singing" immediately afterwards. Cut and trim the results into lines, rhyming if you like. Your rough notes will certainly look like a mess, but they'll give you plenty of material to fiddle with.

6. The ballad stanza also serves as the hymn stanza, often called common meter, with the same arrangement of beats (4-3-4-3) and the same rhyme scheme (though sometimes rhyming ABAB):

> When all thy mercies, O my God,
>> My rising soul surveys,
> Transported with the view, I'm lost
>> In wonder, love, and praise.
>> *—Joseph Addison (1712)*

Most of Emily Dickinson's poems were based on the hymn stanza:

> Crumbling is not an instant's Act
> A fundamental pause
> Dilapidation's processes
> Are organized Decays.
>
> 'Tis first a Cobweb on the Soul
> A Cuticle of Dust
> A Borer in the Axis
> An Elemental Rust—
>
> Ruin is formal—Devil's work
> Consecutive and slow—
> Fail in an instant, no man did
> Slipping—is Crash's law.

(Which of the longer lines—the first and third of each stanza—is shortened to three beats with a feminine ending?) Write a poem in hymn stanzas that imitates the style of Emily Dickinson—meditative, alert to unusual words and ideas. Feel free to use slant rhymes ("Room"/"Storm"); keep or omit the characteristic dashes. *Don't* tell a story.

ANSWER TO THE QUESTION IN NUMBER 6: The third line of stanza two ("A borer in the axis") lacks the customary fourth beat of the hymn or ballad stanza. It's an acceptable variation, since we really seem to *hear* it as a kind of musical rest at the end of the line.

EPIGRAMS

An *epigram* is a short poem that makes a pithy, often satirical, usually humorous point. It's the poetic equivalent of a punchline—and it needs the quickness and force of a boxer's jab or uppercut. In English, epigrams are usually rhymed and in meter (a law-abiding rhythm that follows a set pattern of accents and syllables), though they can be loose and freewheeling. The *couplet* is a favorite form for the epigram: a pair of rhymed lines in the same meter. Epigrams are especially useful for political satire and for literary or social criticism.

Examples of epigrams can be found in *The Greek Anthology* and by the Roman poet Martial, John Donne, Ben Jonson, Alexander Pope, William Blake, Robert Frost, and J.V. Cunningham. Blake's "Auguries of Innocence" is really a long string of marvelous epigrams: memorable, piercing, witty, insightful, and passionate. Here are two other epigrams by Blake:

> The Errors of a Wise Man make your Rule
> Rather than the Perfections of a Fool

> Her whole Life is an Epigram smack smooth & neatly pend
> Platted quite neat to catch applause with a sliding noose at the end

7. Write a rhymed epigram about some aspect of modern life, or about a famous person. Both your lines and your tone should be cutting, sharp, incisive. Sharpen each phrase until it stings.

8. Transform a tabloid headline into an epigram. Use the headline verbatim as a first or last line, if you like, or rephrase it if that works better.

9. Take an epigram (either an old one by a past master or one you've just written) and write a serious poem about what's underneath or behind the epigram—the real life that gets compressed out of existence in those pithy sayings. Flesh out the scene with images; reflect on the mood; enter the dream world beyond the wittiness.

(Note: Don't confuse *epigrams* with *epigraphs* (headnotes prefacing a poem) or *epitaphs* (words engraved on tombstones).)

GHAZAL

The *ghazal* comes to us from Persian, Turkish, Arabic, and other Mideastern poetry. In the originals, dating back to the eighth century, the form consists of five to twelve couplets, rhymed on the same sound throughout, using the subject of love or wine to represent mystical experience. In the final couplet, the poet "signs" his or her name.

Twentieth-century American poets have omitted the rhyme while retaining the couplet form and the approximate length. They also emphasize a disconnectedness between couplets, juxtaposing apparently unrelated observations, placing insights or images side by side without explaining their connection. These gaps can be a great source of power and mystery.

The most successful American ghazals have been collected in sequences: Adrienne Rich's "Ghazals: Homage to Ghalib," "The Blue Ghazals," and Jim Harrison's "Ghazals." This expansiveness is probably encouraged by the jumps from couplet to couplet. The more ghazals we see grouped together, the more we can make connections.

Rich models her ghazals on those of Mirza Ghalib, a nineteenth century Urdu Poet (and recommends the translations by Aijaz Ahmad). She follows "his use of a minimum five couplets ... each couplet being autonomous and independent of the others. The continuity and unity flow from the associations and images playing back and forth among the couplets in any single *ghazal*." Here is Adrienne Rich's fourth ghazal (dated 7/14/68: ii) from "Ghazals: Homage to Ghalib":

Did you think I was talking about my life?
I was trying to drive a tradition up against the wall.

The field they burned over is greener than all the rest.
You have to watch it, he said, the sparks can travel the roots.

Shot back into this earth's atmosphere
our children's children may photograph these stones.

In the red wash of the darkroom, I see myself clearly;
when the print is developed and handed about, the face is nothing to
    me.

For us the work undoes itself over and over:
the grass grows back, the dust collects, the scar breaks open.

In writing a ghazal, you have to use impulse and intuition more than rationality. It helps to make each couplet interesting and complete in itself. Fragments, glimpses, and exclamations often need no more than a couplet. And it helps to make a "jump" after each couplet, from the political to the personal, from talk to thought, from idea to image, from near to far. You can let ideas and images "carom" like a billiard ball, shooting the poem in a new, uncanny direction.

10. Find a news article that rouses your feelings. Copy down a brief quotation from the article; split the quotation into two lines. Then ask yourself what it reminds you of. Quickly jot down two lines. Keep doing this "free association" until you have seven or eight couplets. Then look over your results and see if any of the couplets seem weak, dull, or predictable. Feel free to delete, rearrange, or add new ones. You may find yourself cutting the original quotation—or moving it elsewhere in your ghazal.

11. Write a ghazal (or set of ghazals) based on the work of Adrienne Rich or Jim Harrison. Use vivid, even startling imagery. Feel free to bring in news items, political commentary, sudden exclamations, unanswered questions, new definitions of terms or phrases. Use allusions (references to other works) if you like. Address historical figures (as Rich addresses Walt Whitman, Galileo, Montaigne, and the French revolutionary Danton).

12. Write a more traditional ghazal, focusing on love or some intoxicant (real or metaphorical). Rhyme throughout, preferably on the same rhyme sound. It may help you—and the poem— if you allow yourself the freedom to use slant rhymes like wake/quick/quack/book.

HAIKU

Originally a Japanese poem of seventeen syllables in three lines, a *haiku* juxtaposes seemingly unrelated observations in order to glimpse the hidden connections between things. It relies on mood and suggestiveness. Calling it a "form" is almost an understatement, since it serves as a means of illumination, a way of thinking, in Zen Buddhism.

Here is my Americanized version of a haiku by Buson, who lived in the eighteenth century:

> Cherry blossoms drop
> in the dark Tidal Basin:
> stars on the ripples.

In the original, the cherry blossoms are falling into the water of a rice paddy, but I've changed the scene to Washington, D.C.

Technically, a haiku must refer to a season, as the one by Buson refers to spring. If it doesn't, it is really a *senryu*. But for Western poets, the distinction may not be so useful or important. We normally call a haiku any three-line poem, give or take a line, that couples insights or images together in a flash.

One approach Western poets use is to adhere to the syllable count, using five in the first line, seven in the second, and five in the third. As Etheridge Knight says in one of his haiku sequences:

> Making jazz swing in
> Seventeen syllables AIN'T
> No square poet's job.

Richard Wilbur, who uses the haiku as a stanza pattern in "Thyme Flowering Among Rocks," rhymes the first and third lines and strictly observes the syllable count of 5-7-5. James Merrill also rhymes lines one and three in the haiku within "Prose of Departure," his sequence of *haibun* (prose mixed with haiku).

Another approach aims to capture the *feel* of haiku without worrying about syllables—as long as the poem is brief, a sudden burst of recognition. According to his friend Allen Ginsberg, Jack Kerouac thought up haiku almost habitually. Here is one he composed spontaneously during his *Paris Review* interview:

> Sparrow
> with big leaf on its back—
> Windstorm

Kerouac, however, wasn't satisfied with this ("No good, won't work, I reject it") and immediately began revising it during the interview. Here's the version he finally copied into his spiral notebook:

> A sparrow
> an autumn leaf sticks to its back—
> From the wind!

Personally, I prefer the spontaneous first draft, but Kerouac asserts "haiku is best reworked and revised. . . . It has to be completely economical, no foliage and flowers and language rhythm, it has to be a simple little picture in three little lines. At least that's the way the old masters did it, spending months on three little lines and coming up, say, with:

> In the abandoned boat,
> The hail
> Bounces about.

That's Shiki." He goes on to say "You see you got to compress into three short lines a great big story. First you start with a haiku situation—so you see a leaf ... falling on the back of a sparrow during a great big October wind storm. A big leaf falls on the back of a little sparrow." Kerouac also says that in American or English we don't have to follow the seventeen-syllable meter of the Japanese.

According to Lita Hornick, Allen Ginsberg defines haiku as "first flash, second recognition, third afterthought." He also defines it as "two polarized thoughts fused by a flash of recognition," offering as his model Basho's well-known haiku about the frog jumping into pondwater. Here's my approximation of the poem, rendered in syllabic meter (5-7-5):

> In the ancient pond
> A frog leaps—and then the splash
> Of all that water.

In the original Japanese, Basho refers to the noise the frog makes leaping into the pond as a "frog-jumping-in-water-sound." But in a song entitled "Old Pond" (accompanied by his own musical setting), Ginsberg gives this haiku a fresh American twist—and quotes it all in a single, nine-syllable line:

> The old pond—a frog jumps in, kerplunk!

He also says that ideally the haiku "should contain emptiness, form and a blissful or humorous recognition of the relationship between the two." He offers as his criteria for haiku (1) "extreme compression of thought," (2) "casualness of expression," and (3) "the very subtle suggestion of the Karmic law of cause and result."

There's no reason why, in English, haiku can't be shorter or longer than three lines—as long as the effect of sudden flash, sudden illumination (what a student of mine called the "ah-ha") remains. Carolyn Kizer adds an extra line to her haiku: "I have come to prefer the four-line form which Nobuyuki Yuasa has used in translating Issa because, as he says, it comes closer to approximating the natural rhythm of English speech."

Haiku work especially well in sequences—sometimes numbered, sometimes staggered on the page, sometimes separated by space. Gary Snyder, Etheridge Knight, and William Heyen have all written haiku sequences that show vividly how to expand the form, how to Americanize it. Finally, you may want to read Basho's *Narrow Road to the Deep North* (available from Penguin and in other translations under different titles—

A Haiku Journey, Back Roads to Far Towns), a haiku narrative blending travelog and poetry.

13. Using a pocket notebook, take an excursion somewhere in your neighborhood. Look closely at the grass and the dirt and the insects crossing the pavement. Peer at the sky like radar scanning for whatever it can pick up on the horizon. Study the trees and pedestrians and dogs on leashes and stray cats. Notice the litter and the graffiti and the parked vans. Be on the lookout for anything surprising, unexpected. Jot down any impressions that give you pleasure, any ideas that may occur to you. Leave spaces between these observations. When you return home to your desk, or your sofa, or wherever you like to write, match images together, drawing from what you've gathered on your outing, adding new ones if you like. Do it quickly! Don't try to calculate the effect — use your reflexes. Arrange several of these image-pairings, these couplings of insight, into three-line units. Then put these haiku (as they have magically become) into some order.

14. Spend some time meditating. (See "Spiritual Exercises" if you need guidance.) After your mind is settled, calmed, even emptied, try writing some haiku. Allow any images that occur to you into the poems. Don't try to explain anything. Don't encapsulate your thoughts. Simply open up and welcome the flow — or the flash — of sensory impressions.

15. Write several five-syllable lines. Each one can be a name, a descriptive phrase, or an exclamation, or a brief sentence: "The red-winged blackbird," "Galls on the elm leaf," "Look at the ash heap!" Then build a haiku around each of these lines, either leading up to it or moving away from it. (In other words, this "pre-fab" line can be either the first or the third line of the poem.) Use the 5-7-5 syllable pattern. Repeat as needed.

16. Take a passage of nature or travel writing. Some authors to look into include Henry David Thoreau (*Walden* and just about everything he wrote), Herman Melville (*The Encantadas* or any of his novels of the sea), Annie Dillard (*Pilgrim at Tinker Creek*), William Least Heat Moon (*Blue Highways*), Paul Theroux, Jan Morris. Vincent Van Gogh's letters and the journals of Dorothy Wordsworth (the poet's sister) are also richly observant. Find a phrase or image that catches your attention in the passage you've chosen. Copy it in a notebook and add your own comment, or counterimage, or reaction. Mold the resulting combination into a haiku, either strictly metrical or free. Try this process several times with the same passage.

17. Search through an old journal or diary you've kept, looking for embedded haiku: descriptions or insights that possess the necessary flash of recognition. Add or subtract words and shape the material into

haiku form. Rephrase if necessary. If you can't find much in the way of images, try to recollect the place in which you originally wrote your journal entries. Put yourself back there in time. Scare up specific details that you associate with the experience.

18. Look up Wallace Stevens's "Thirteen Ways of Looking at a Blackbird" and then the title sequence of Raymond Patterson's *26 Ways of Looking at a Black Man*. Write your own poem, in short haiku-like sections, on ways of looking at something. Any subject will do! In one section, you might imagine what your subject looks like; then what it sounds like; then what it reminds you of; then what its opposite may be; then what it secretly resembles; then where it's located; then how it originated; then how it might belong in some primitive ritual; then how a vaudeville comedian might treat it; then how a scientist or historian might consider it—and so on. If you start with phrases such as "It looks like" or "It reminds me of," remove them when you revise, so that each way of looking is presented without scaffolding to prop it up. Not "It looks like a trumpet blaring out of the sand," but "A trumpet blares out of the sand." Be direct—unless it really sounds better to "explain a little." (Too much explanation, however, is tedious and insults the reader's intelligence.) Imagine yourself as different people observing different aspects of the subject. Do a little role-playing. You may focus on anything, from a "still life," such as a flower arrangement, to an object, such as a prism or a matchbox or a toy or a tool, to an animal or a building or a person. Be objective, observant, inventive. Don't be sentimental.

19. Finally, if the haiku form feels constraining, let your lines and images explode into something larger, maybe a longer poem composed in haiku stanzas. Try, perhaps, to juxtapose stray images or use the haiku "flash of recognition" in the midst of blank verse (modeled, perhaps, on William Wordsworth's *Prelude*) or long-lined free verse (like Walt Whitman's "Song of Myself").

ODE

The original *odes* were songs performed by the chorus in plays or at public festivals in ancient Greece. Pindar's odes celebrated the games at Olympia, as well as other athletic tournaments. While Pindar's odes are vigorous and rhapsodic, the odes of the Roman poet Horace are more orderly, more sedate. In English, the ode came to be used as a vehicle for meditation, often in the course of addressing and praising a person, object, or idea. Elaborately rhymed and shaped stanzas characterize the odes of Romantic poets such as Keats and Wordsworth. Odes with irregular stanzas, using lines of differing length, are called "Cowleyan" after the Metaphysical poet Abraham Cowley. In the twentieth century, Pablo Neruda wrote what he called "elemental odes," exalting common things (oil, a lemon, wine, the air, the color green, a butterfly, a chestnut on the ground) in poems with very skinny lines.

TRADITIONAL ODES

Pindaric

1. strophe (Chorus moves left)

   same stanza form, # of lines

2. antistrophe (Chorus moves right)

3. epode (Chorus stands still) — *different stanza, # of lines*

Horatian

equal stanzas, each containing:
   same number of lines
   same rhyme scheme (if any)
   lines that are equal in length or varied in a regular stanza pattern

quatrains (four-line stanzas) often used:
   first two lines often longer than last two lines
   (In Marvell's "Horatian Ode" there are two lines of
   tetrameter and then two lines of trimeter in each stanza)

Cowleyan

free and irregular in:
   rhyme pattern (if any)
   length of lines
   length and shape of stanzas

Wordsworth remarks, in a letter, that "in the transitions, and the impassioned music of the versification, would be found the principal requisites" of the ode. For the transitions, we might consider how thought moves, both flowing and flashing, leaping suddenly to something fresh and unexpected. Logic alone will not make these transitions successful; we must use intuition and imagination, plunging forward even in the dark, pausing to rest and reflect even in broad daylight.

20. Write a Pindaric ode — two stanzas identical in form, followed by one that departs from them in line lengths and number of lines. Any given stanza can have lines of different lengths, giving it a pleasantly jagged look. The easiest way to "match" stanzas one and two might be to count syllables. If you try this, you'll have a poem that sounds like free verse but is powered by exact metrical repetition and then strong, obvious variation. The look on the page will be striking: two stanzas mirroring each other, then another breaking away, an AAB structure. Remember that this three-part form represents "turn," "counterturn," and "stand." With each new stanza, you'll have to switch directions, change your focus — at least slightly.

21. Write a Horatian ode: a series of identical stanzas, possibly quatrains, possibly with the first two lines longer then the last two in each stanza (maybe two of tetrameter, two of trimeter, for example).

22. Find a translation of an actual ode by Pindar or Horace and use it as a model for your own ode. Write about a similar subject — maybe the World Series or a track meet, something athletic, if you're following Pindar — and try to copy the poet's form, using similar line-lengths, indentations, stanza units. Try *not* to ape the poet's vocabulary, but to use modern, even slangy, words you find appealing.

23. Read one of the great odes by Wordsworth or Keats and write a poem *responding* to that ode. You may choose to imitate the rhyme scheme or metrical pattern of your chosen ode, but you don't have to. Write in free verse if you like. If you're responding to Keats's "Ode to a Nightingale," remember that there aren't any nightingales in the United States — unless they're in a zoo or stuffed in a museum display case. For us, it's just a poetic species. What could we use as a substitute? A heron? A goldfinch? A red-winged blackbird? A California condor? Try to emulate the meditative mood of the ode.

24. Write an ode, in any form or freedom, that addresses something or someone. Keep in mind that this is where many a poetic "O" comes from, calling out to something beyond literal reach.

25. Choose a simple, ordinary object and write an "elemental ode" about it, using mostly short lines. If you use just a single word in any of the lines, make sure it's an *interesting* word.

PANTOUM

The *pantoum* is a Malay form. It is written in couplets and repeats whole lines in an interlocking pattern. The second and fourth lines of any stanza become the first and third lines of the stanza that follows. In the pantoum's last stanza, the first and third lines of the opening are finally repeated as the fourth and second lines. The order of those lines can be reversed, but an ideal pantoum will end with the poem's opening line — creating a kind of circle.

Pattern for repeating lines in a pantoum:

First line	a	(letters = whole lines,
Second line	b	not rhymes)
Third line	c	
Fourth line	d	
Second line	b	NOTE: Don't think, because
Fifth line	e	of this example, that pantoums
Fourth line	d	must always be three stanzas
Sixth line	f	long. They can be any length.
Fifth line	e	
Third line	c	
Sixth line	f	
First line	a	

Pantoums can expand, accordion-like, into infinitely long poems, but most are fairly short since they tax the poet's ingenuity and the reader's patience. The shortest pantoum would consist of two stanzas, since *something* must repeat and circle around. A pantoum can rhyme, but doesn't have to. If it does rhyme, the obvious scheme is the interweaving A-B-A-B.

Here is "Details," a pantoum by Judith Baumel:

A particular understanding, peculiar knowledge —
the weaver knows each string of warp;
a comfort of touch. Fingertips
sleying, drawing-in the thread,

the weaver knows each string of warp,
its path and place in the fabric.
Sleying, drawing-in the thread,
each thin piece evolves specific, separate.

Its path and place in the fabric
join with others to form the whole.

Each thin piece evolves specific, separate,
something calm and repetitive,

joins with others to form a whole
as the cook making prune jam —
something calm and repetitive —
repeats each task with regular skill.

As the cook making prune jam
pits and skins the fruit,
repeats each task with regular skill,
warm boiled fruit slips through hands.

Pits and skins. The fruit:
each reward of familiar flesh.
Warm boiled fruit slips through hands
and fingers remember

each reward of familiar flesh
for lovers in a darkened, quiet bed.
And fingers remember
how the body's map of texture changes.

For lovers in a darkened, quiet bed
each velvet hair on the low curve of back,
the body's map of texture changes
to find, perhaps, the zipper of a scar.

Each velvet hair on the low curve of back;
a comfort of touch, though fingertips
find, perhaps, the zipper of a scar,
a particular understanding, peculiar knowledge.

The pantoum is a tight, demanding form, and can easily sound stiff
and contrived. Try to phrase your lines so they can connect in different
ways. For example, "the wind in the arcade" could serve first as the
subject of a sentence, then as a direct object in the next stanza; "Light
on the windowsill" could become "flies/ Light on the windowsill" when
repeated. Try to enjamb some of the lines; if you end-stop too many of
them, the result may sound stately (if you're lucky) but will probably
sound strained. Feel free to vary the wording as lines recur — unless you
want to be strict about your repetitions for some expressive reason.

One sensible way to vary the form is to repeat (like the *sestina*) just the "end words" of each line, as in Donald Justice's "In the Attic." The result is a more natural, flowing, open poem. Of course, you might want the relentless, hypnotic, inevitable effect of a true pantoum. And it's not absolutely necessary for the pantoum to circle around and repeat lines from the first stanza. Charles Baudelaire's "Evening Harmony" (beautifully translated by Richard Howard) does not end by returning to its beginning — and it is the most celebrated pantoum ever written.

26. Write a pantoum repeating whole lines. Aim to write about 4-6 stanzas. It may help if you make the lines "open" at each end, so that they could both *initiate* and *continue* a sentence, as the need dictates.

27. Write a pantoum that repeats just end-words (or perhaps key phrases).

SAPPHICS

Very little of what the Greek poet Sappho wrote survives. We have one complete poem, the "Hymn to Aphrodite," some substantial chunks of poems, a number of phrases and brief passages quoted by grammarians, and fragments discovered on papyrus cut in strips to wrap up mummies in Egypt. The bulk of her poetry — and she ranks as the greatest lyric poet of antiquity — was suppressed and destroyed.

Yet Sappho left us, along with those radiant bits and pieces, the stanza form that bears her name. It consists of three long lines followed by a short one. The long lines each contain eleven syllables, the short one five. To be more exact, in each of the long lines the syllables are accented as follows:

STRESSED-unstressed-STRESSED-unstressed-
STRESSED-unstressed-unstressed-STRESSED-unstressed-
STRESSED-unstressed.

(It may be easier to remember this according to the traditional names for metrical feet: trochee-trochee-dactyl-trochee-trochee.) The fourth and/or eleventh syllables may also be STRESSED (making spondees instead of trochees). The short line is arranged STRESSED-unstressed-unstressed-STRESSED-unstressed (or dactyl-trochee). A teacher of mine once suggested an easy way to remember the pattern of this short sapphic line: "*Take* out the *gar*bage."

But there is a further complication. Ancient Greek is *not* accented; it is measured, instead, by the *length* of syllables, so that what we treat as an accent would be a long syllable, while our unstressed syllables would simply be short. This kind of meter is called *quantitative* (the "quantities" referring to how long it takes to utter a syllable). Even though we don't usually measure quantities in English, it can be done, and poets from the Elizabethan songwriter Thomas Campion to the Modernist expatriate Ezra Pound have experimented with it. We would distinguish, first, between long and short vowels (the dictionary helps here): "brain" would be long, while "bran" would be short. We can also consider the "weight" and "bulk" of the letters around the vowel, so that "stretch" would be long but "set" (same vowel sound) would be short.

Most poets will not want to imitate the quantitative measure of the original sapphic stanza, but I mention it because there are several *layers* of possible imitation:

1. measuring the length of syllables and the syllable count (quantitative meter);
2. measuring the stresses (or accents) and the syllable count (syllable-stress meter);
3. measuring the syllable count (syllabic meter);
4. using long and short lines of approximate length, without counting syllables or stresses (free verse).

Even loose, free verse sapphics that hint at the long-long-long-short arrangement of lines in a stanza will make us think of Sappho.

Here is an approximation of the last stanza in Sappho's "Hymn to Aphrodite," using a syllable count of 11-11-11-5 in following the sapphic form:

> Come to me, Aphrodite, and liberate
> me now from discontent. Everything I want
> and my heart dies for, deliver it to me:
>   help me, my goddess.

As this plea to the goddess of love might suggest, Sappho's great subject was love, and contemporary poems written in sapphics will often suggest love—or the absence of it. In a poem about being mugged, "Effort at Speech," William Meredith uses sapphics to underline the "hatred and guilt" that divide a black man and a white man. But we can guess that the poem originally declared itself in sapphics when Meredith pondered the mugger's actual words, "Give me your wallet." (Remember "take out the garbage"?) The form is also good for thoughtful reflection, as in John Peck's "Letting Up":

> The meander of my walking, and through it
> A sun that swings to go with me at each turn,
> And sweet fatigue that remains childlike because
>   It works at nothing.

Push aggressively enough at the stout weave
Of what is, appearances we must take as
Being at least what they seem, and you tear through,
      You come stumbling out

Where the bright warmth sealed behind late windows seems
Miniature tenderness and stale fury, seems
To dwindle with cold speed as feet find themselves
      Running now, fleeing,

Carrying a stick figure who cannot let up.
This, too, comes to me from my walking, the one
Map of it that I have, unrolling between
      One step and the next.

When the gray infantry broke through at Shiloh
They found campfires, skillets over them cooking,
Sunday breakfasts laid out, and swirls of steam still
      Coming off coffee.

Communion that seems an end, fleeting, factive,
Must begin somewhere. They stopped, ate and drank, snooped
Through tents and read letters from girls. And they were
      Lost to the advance.

Sapphics may contain humor, but they usually deal with weighty, serious matters. It is a good form for free-ranging meditation, since it can go on as long as the writer's thoughts meander, yet constantly guide the thinking by the tug of that short line. It also works well for *elegies*, poems that lament the death—and celebrate the life—of someone, as in Richard Howard's poem "For James Boatwright," subtitled "died of AIDS/ 1937-1988." Howard allows himself some metrical freedom, often dropping or adding a syllable to the long lines, following a syllable count for the short lines. But the form is poignantly appropriate—a large part of what makes the elegy so memorable.

One note of advice: Don't isolate the short line too often! Try to enjamb (let the lines spill over) *into* it, unless you want to single out a line for particular emphasis or effect.

28. Choose a contemporary topic—or recent incident—and explore it in sapphics. Follow either the syllable-stress count or the simple syllabic count. It's probably OK if some of the lines stray by a syllable either way, but keep the meter as exact as you can manage, without letting the

language become forced, awkward, or stilted (the main dangers of this form).

29. Write a love poem in sapphics (strict or free) without mentioning love.

30. Write sapphics that state what you feel or think as directly as possible. Don't adorn or embellish the lines. But also don't be mushy, sappy, or sentimental. Keep the language clipped, intense, and electric, but try to avoid exclamations.

31. Experiment with arranging long and short syllables in several lines. Try to write several lines with predominantly long syllables, then several with mainly short ones, then several that mix long and short. Read them aloud (maybe tape them) and notice how the syllable length affects the pacing of the lines. If you like any of the lines, detach them and expand them into a poem. (It need not be in sapphics.)

32. Borrow or buy a book of the poems and fragments of Sappho and some of the other Greek poets. Guy Davenport's translations in *Sappho, Alkman, Archilochos* are a good place to start. Find a fragment that interests you and write a continuation or completion of the poem. Don't feel you have to keep your poem in the ancient world, although you can if you like. Feel free to modernize what you add to the fragment.

SEQUENCES AND LONG POEMS

Sometimes a single poem isn't enough, doesn't explore the subject fully, doesn't satisfy the poet, doesn't have sufficient range or ambition. A sequence of poems is simply a string of related poems or sections or fragments, often numbered. Sonnet sequences and song cycles are familiar, but other possibilities include sequences based on calendars and days of the week, or like portrait galleries, or like chapters of a novel, or like different facets of a subject.

A long poem may range from several pages to several hundred. It can be an *epic*, like Homer's *Odyssey* and *Iliad*, Milton's *Paradise Lost*, or Ezra Pound's *Cantos*. Pound defines an epic as a "poem containing history." It can be a series of lyric stanzas, like the *Rubaiyat of Omar Khayyam* or Tennyson's "In Memoriam." It can be a hodgepodge or a straightforward narrative. It can be symphonic or like a mural. It can be a novel in verse. It can be a collage. It can be disguised as a scrapbook of clippings, or an exchange of letters, or a file of wiretap transcripts. Whatever form it takes, it has to be *long*.

Some poets, such as Poe, have disputed even the possibility of a long poem. (Poe limited poems to around a hundred lines.) Robert Frost praised William Wordsworth for writing the dull parts of *The Prelude* because they linked together the good parts. Can a long poem be consistently intense? Or does it need some subdued, relaxed stretches, some prosiness? Is there really a problem with that? Much of the answer depends on whether a story's being told or not.

Finally, most poets collect stray poems into collections that aspire to being coherent books rather than a jumble. That's perhaps another kind of sequence, the book of poems carefully arranged as a satisfying whole.

33. Write a sequence of poems on any subject, in any form you care to expand on and revel in. In length, this could be anything from three poems on. But they don't need to stand absolutely on their own. They can function as closely related sections, even fragments, pieces of the mosaic.

34. Read a long poem or epic or sequence of poems and write a brief poem about some aspect of it: a continuation of an episode, the opposite side's version of an incident, a character sketch, a monologue spoken from a hero's point of view, a description of something not described, a meditation on the theme of the original. (Look up Paul Goodman's "Wonders of *The Iliad*" — you can find it in *The Norton Introduction to Poetry*.) Enough of these responses might add up to a sequence in itself!

35. Make plans and sketches and notes for a long poem. If you were to write one, what would it be about? What would be your formal model, a poetic form like the sonnet or an analogous form from another art, such as a sonata or a triptych. How long do you think it might be? Would it be an open form into which you could pour everything imaginable — or a tight form with restricted boundaries and definite shape? You can go on to begin your projected long poem or concentrate all of your imaginings into a single short intense poem.

36. Write a "list" poem, modeled on the catalogs Walt Whitman favored. (There's a catalog of ships in *The Iliad*, and there are genealogies listed in the Bible.) Under a title that tells what you're up to (like Gary Snyder's "Things a Poet Needs to Know") you could simply make an elaborated list, without any connective words or any complete sentence. Or you can repeat the initial words in each line ("From the . . . " "From the . . . ") in Whitmanic or Biblical fashion, linking everything rhetorically. This can become a game of fill-in-the-blanks, a trivial enough pursuit, unless you do it with energy and imagination and verbal inventiveness.

SESTINA

Troubadours invented the *sestina*, a form in which six stanzas of six lines each use the same end-words in a fixed, evolving pattern. A sestina

usually concludes with a three-line *envoi* (or "send-off") using all six
end-words.

The earliest examples of the form, in Provençal, come from Arnaut
Daniel and Bertrand de Born, whose "Sestina: Altaforte" was translated
by Ezra Pound early in the twentieth century. Since then, many poets
have seized upon the form, making it one of the most popular in English.
Memorable sestinas include the two by Elizabeth Bishop ("A Miracle
for Breakfast" and "Sestina"), several by Donald Justice ("Here in Kat-
mandu," "The Metamorphosis," and "Sestina: A Dream"), and John
Ashbery ("Farm Implements and Rutabagas in a Landscape").

Here is an example from *The Whole Truth*, a sequence of twenty-four
sestinas using the Perry Mason characters, written by James Cummins:

A silent Perry remembered how it used to be: look
Hard at all the faces, figure out who's a killer.
Consider the money, that was always the best clue —
The only way you got the older ones into the game.
But, of course, money was never the real question.
The real question was, does it all end in silence?

He'd been very good at cracking someone's silence —
Watching the eyes, the critical moment when a look
Betrayed the fear he would ask the fatal question.
And he *would* ask. Without mercy. He was a killer.
He loved the chance to destroy, like flushing game
From the field of a face, each tiny twitch a clue,

Small animals of fear he tracked down, clue by clue,
Stuffing them, one by one, into the jury's silence.
It took brutality to get to this level of the game.
You had to be a hall of mirrors, give back the look
Of infinite self-loathing that spurs on the killer.
You had to be his conscience, with its one question

Pounding his brain like beaters, until that question
Drove him screaming out into the clearing of a clue,
Blinking frantically in the sun, to face his killer,
As around him the bleak farmland became the silence
Of the courtroom, his face lit up with the wild look
Of one who has outlived his usefulness in the game . . .

Perry whispered through the bars of the door, "Game?"
Outside, an intern looked up from his pad, a question

In his eyes. A nurse, marking a chart, saw his look.
"Used to be a lawyer. He's wanting his game of CLUE
In a bit. He plays a while, then lapses into silence.
He's probably hot on the trail of some crazy killer—

You know, up here." She tapped her head. "A killer?"
She nodded, twirling a finger around her ear. "Game?"
Perry heard himself say. *Does it all end in silence?*
"Game?" he repeated slyly, posing that meek question
As if trying to trick some green rookie from the ACLU.
The intern hid behind his magazine. He wouldn't look.

† † †

Questions. Shrewd looks. A fiercely guarded silence.
When it came to playing CLUE, the old bag was a killer.
"Game?" Warily, Perry tossed the dice. "Game? Game?"

The end-words are *look*, *killer*, *clue*, *game*, *question*, and *silence*. Notice how they are important words, all nouns or verbs (or both, like "look"). Some have multiple meanings—"game," for instance, which means puzzle, prey, contest, sport, and board-game at various points through the poem. The word clue becomes the game of CLUE, and then ACLU, the abbreviation for the American Civil Liberties Union. Notice how well the poem handles the prominent, noticeable repetition at the beginning of each new stanza. Notice how all six end-words are squeezed into the envoi, which is separated from the rest of the poem by a series of daggers.

You can use the accompanying chart to guide you in writing a sestina, but there's an easier way. Always base each *new* stanza on a set rearrangement of the previous stanza's end-words. Let's say our sestina contains the following end-words, in this order, in stanza one: *mountains*, *valleys*, *forests*, *music*, *morning*, and *evening* (the same end-words Sir Philip Sidney uses in his "Double Sestina"). The opening line of each new stanza must *always* use the previous stanza's *last* end-word (in this case "evening"). To get the next line's end-word, jump up to the top line of the previous stanza ("mountains"). Then drop down to the lowest remaining line ("morning"). Then up to the highest remaining line ("valleys"). Then drop down to the lowest remaining line ("music"). Then jump up to the last remaining line ("forests"). Simply repeat the process as you begin each new stanza. Remember to start with the previous stanza's *last* end-word. Then move up, down, up, down, up—like a zig-zag weaving pattern on a loom. Keep doing this until you have six stanzas. Your sixth stanza's final end-word will repeat the sestina's *first* end-word. You've gone full circle.

```
Pattern for repeating end-words in a sestina:
Stanza:      1    2    3    4    5    6
line 1       A    F    C    E    D    B
line 2       B    A    F    C    E    D
line 3       C    E    D    B    A    F
line 4       D    B    A    F    C    E
line 5       E    D    B    A    F    C
line 6       F    C    E    D    B    A
(No fixed pattern for the envoi, but it must use all six
end-words)
```

Of course, there is usually an envoi that follows, a kind of postscript in which all six end-words must recur (three at the ends of lines, three within lines). There is no real order the poet must follow here. In fact, many poets omit the envoi altogether.

A critical point occurs between stanzas, moving from one to the next without the repetition seeming awkward or too contrived. The repetition comes so suddenly, it can seem incredibly forced. You should try to maneuver the sentences so that repeating these crucial end-words seems natural, inevitable. You can do that by incorporating the end-word into the same sentence, or by asking a question, or by changing the sense of the word or its spelling ("threw" to "through," for example). You can try to disguise the repetition. Letting the sense of a line overflow, or run on, to the next one (enjambing) often helps the camouflage.

One way to vary the form is to "transform" the end-words as the poem progresses. On a simple level, this involves using puns. A more involved technique was pioneered by Donald Justice in "The Metamorphosis." Here is how his end-words evolve in undergoing their metamorphosis:

tavern	Hill	Oak	dry	Woods	went
heaven	hell	ache	draw	weeds	wind
haven	hall	oak	drew	wards	wound
having	heel	ilk	drew	woods	whined
heaving	whole	speak	dry	words	wonder
living	keyhole	like	withdraw	afterwards	unwound

(Remember that this is *not* the order in which the end-words appear!) Justice omits the envoi—enough is enough.

The sestina was originally a musical form. One of the madrigals by

Claudio Monteverdi (1567-1643) is called "Sestina — Lagrime d'amante al sepolcro dell'amata" (Tears of a lover at the tomb of the beloved). A performance by the New York Pro Musica on Odyssey Records takes over fourteen minutes, an example of how even a relatively brief poem stretches out when set to music. You might try to retain (or cultivate) a song-like, musical feel in your sestina. (See the "Music" section for some suggestions.)

It's easier to write a sestina if you dispense with meter and indulge in free verse, but some poets prefer iambic pentameter for their sestinas. Certainly meter will tighten up what can otherwise be a loose, rambling form that frequently has to lunge for an end-word. But the measuring can be casual, fairly loose, and still give the poem some steadiness. A count of syllables or accents might work well here. Rudyard Kipling wrote a kind of "prose sestina" in order to allow narrative, dialogue, and the hurly burly of daily life into the poem.

37. Make a list of (1) words that have multiple meanings, and (2) homonyms, or words that sound the same but are spelled differently. Then choose six of these words and write a sestina. Make sure you have mainly nouns and verbs, maybe adjectives, limiting the number of minor words such as prepositions and conjunctions (unless you want to repeat "or," for example, as "ore" and "oar").

38. Write a sestina using another poet's end-words, as Donald Justice wrote a "Sestina on Six Words by Weldon Kees," the end-words being *others*, *voyage*, *silence*, *away*, *burden*, and *harm*.

39. Write six lines of unrhymed iambic pentameter. Then use the end-words that have occurred in those lines to continue the poem as a sestina. Try to retain at least some loose connection to iambic pentameter.

40. Write a free-verse (unmetrical) sestina that tells a story. It's OK to vary the line lengths considerably, but don't let them run beyond the margin so they have to be indented below.

41. Write a sestina that looks at something from different angles in each stanza.

42. Write a zany, wild sestina. Draw on pop culture for your material, if you like. Make the poem absurd or serious, maybe tragi-comic, but make sure it keeps moving.

43. Take a rough draft you're unhappy with and transform it into a sestina. One way is to choose the six best lines and use them as a model stanza, supplying your set of end-words. Another way is to work repeated words into the existing fabric of the poem.

44. Write a sestina in which the end-words are hidden, buried within lines so they aren't quite as noticeable.

45. Write a sestina that constantly transforms its end-words, as in Justice's "Metamorphosis."

SONG

In their introduction to *An Elizabethan Song Book*, Chester Kallman and W.H. Auden say "The poet who would write songs is denied many poetic virtues, but he is also guarded from many poetic vices: he cannot be prolix or private or preachy or obscure." The virtues they deny the song-writer include complicated metaphors, the expression of "mixed or ambiguous feelings," and length (except in the case of "ballads and epic chants"). Songs must be brief (since the words take longer to sing than to say) and immediate (since there isn't time to figure out puzzles while the music is playing).

Although many songs are written in regular lines, the Elizabethans often preferred to arrange stanzas in irregular line lengths. Here is a song from Shakespeare's *Twelfth Night*:

	Rhyme	Syllables
Come away, come away, death,	A	7
And in sad cypress let me be laid;	B	9
Fly away, fly away, breath;	A	7
I am slain by a fair cruel maid.	B	9
My shroud of white, stuck all with yew,	C	8
O, prepare it:	D	4
My part of death, no one so true	C	8
Did share it.	D	3

Not a flower, not a flower sweet,
    On my black coffin let there be strown;
Not a friend, not a friend greet
    My poor corpse, where my bones shall be thrown.
A thousand thousand sighs to save,
    Lay me, O where
Sad true lover never find my grave,
    To weep there.

In the play, this song is sung by Feste, the fool. You can learn a great deal about songwriting by examining the two stanzas closely and noticing how Shakespeare puts the melody right in the words. You don't need the actual music to hear the song come alive. Notice the repetitions: how the "Come away, come away" pattern is repeated in the first and third lines of each stanza; how "My shroud of white" is echoed by "My part of death"; how it's a "thousand thousand" sighs. Then notice how Shakespeare varies the repetitions. The rhymes come at surprising points, especially at stanza endings, since Shakespeare lengthens and then shortens the lines dramatically. In stanza two, "Come away" is matched by "Not a flower"; though "flower" may count as a single syllable for the Elizabethans, it still *sounds* like two syllables pressed together (like two eighth notes in place of a quarter note of music). "Cruel," incidentally, counts as two syllables — and would have been spoken as two. Notice, finally, how simple the words are, how unified in mood.

It helps to have a good background in metrics and rhyming when you try your hand (and ear) at songwriting. You might want to consult the sections of this book on Meter, Iambics, Assonance, Alliteration, Rhyme, and Sound Effects. But you might also try to plunge ahead, depending on your inner understanding of what makes a good song, based on years of listening to music. You may be surprised how much you know without knowing it.

46. Listen to some songs you think especially good. Try to sample a wide range of both popular tunes and art songs. Some suggestions: spirituals, folk songs, the lute songs of John Dowland, the theater songs of Henry Purcell, the lieder of Franz Schubert, the chansons of Gabriel Fauré, the patter songs of Gilbert and Sullivan, the popular blues of Billie Holiday, the Delta blues of Robert Johnson, the Broadway numbers of Cole Porter, the country laments of Hank Williams. Write new words to one of those melodies. Follow the rise and fall of syllables, the line lengths, and the rhyme scheme as closely as possible. Try to make your words strikingly different from the original lyrics.

47. Think of a dramatic situation for a character to be in. Without having any music in mind, write a song for that character to sing. Try to imitate the irregular line lengths of the Elizabethans.

48. Write a series of lines in varying lengths, on any subject, making them as smooth and melodious as possible. You want them to be singable, so don't clog them up with tongue-twisters and mouthfuls of syllables. They should flow off the tongue easily. For example, "Among the many elements" is smooth; "A thick, black cloak conceals his sword" is not (though the sounds may be interesting and expressive in another sort of poem). Both examples contain the same number of syllables. Once you have ten or twelve of these smooth, irregular lines, choose one as the beginning of a song; as you proceed, add any of the other lines that fit.

49. Write an unrhymed song in free verse (without any meter or

repetition). What can you do that will give a free verse poem the effect of a song?

50. Many songs use *refrains*, lines that are repeated at the same spot in each stanza. In "Crazy Jane Grown Old Looks at the Dancers," by William Butler Yeats, the refrain is "*Love is like the lion's tooth*." A song can have more than one refrain, and those refrains can be varied slightly, although exact repetition has a powerful effect. The refrain can also involve a kind of "jump" from the other words of a stanza, relating to it slantwise rather than directly. The changing words might describe a place or tell a story, while the fixed refrain made a kind of aside, repeating a saying or mysterious statement. Write a song that uses a refrain.

51. Take any pop song and transform its lyrics into a real poem, either keeping the song form or dropping it. Try to improve the word choices, imagery, rhymes, and rhythms. Cut the stuff that seems like filler. Your version should be effective *on the page*, without the support of the original music.

SEE ALSO: "Ballad," "Music" (for the blues, in particular).

SONNET

We generally confine ourselves to a rigid definition of a *sonnet*: fourteen lines, iambic pentameter, following a set rhyme scheme, usually presenting a kind of argument (almost in the legal sense). But we might do well to recall that the Italian root of the word means "little song." Too often that song-like quality seeps out of the sonnet.

There are two rhyme schemes favored by most poets, the Shakespearean (or English) and the Petrarchan (or Italian), named after the two best known practitioners of the form, Shakespeare and Petrarch. Using letters to indicate where the rhymes occur, here are the two patterns:

Shakespearean		*Petrarchan*	
A		A	
B	*first*	B	
A	*quatrain*	B	
B		A	*octave*
		A	
C		B	
D	*second*	B	
C	*quatrain*	A	
D			

		C	*or*	C	*or*	C	
E		D		C		D	
F	*third*	E		D		C	*sestet*
E	*quatrain*	C		C		D	
F		D		C		C	
		E		D		D	
G	*couplet*						
G							

Fewer rhyme sounds occur in the Petrarchan pattern, making it considerably harder for a poet to handle in English. (Italian, on the other hand, is rich in true rhymes and doesn't present the same obstacle.) The Shakespearean rhyme scheme gives the poet more freedom to range widely, to veer away from the original rhymes; the Petrarchan scheme circles around the same spot, marked by those obsessive A and B rhymes. But the rhyme schemes also impose different organizations upon the sonnet: the Shakespearean scheme is basically four-part (with stanzas arranged in lines of 4-4-4-2), while the Petrarchan scheme is two-part (8-6). Naturally, the poet should not feel bound by this inherent organization. There's no reason why either pattern can't be organized as a single unit, without real divisions; or in two, three, four, five, or even more distinct parts. But historically, poets have usually followed the handy, pre-fab organization offered by the rhyme scheme.

Here is a sonnet by John Keats, "On the Grasshopper and the Cricket," written in the Petrarchan rhyme scheme:

The poetry of earth is never dead:	A
When all the birds are faint with the hot sun,	B
And hide in cooling trees, a voice will run	B
From hedge to hedge about the new-mown mead;	A
That is the Grasshopper's — he takes the lead	A
In summer luxury, — he has never done	B
With his delights; for when tired out with fun	B
He rests at ease beneath some pleasant weed.	A
The poetry of earth is ceasing never:	C
On a lone winter evening, when the frost	D
Has wrought a silence, from the stove there shrills	E
The Cricket's song, in warmth increasing ever,	C
And seems to one in drowsiness half lost,	D
The Grasshopper's among some grassy hills.	E

Another sonnet by Keats, "When I Have Fears," uses the Shakespearean rhyme scheme — but doesn't separate the concluding couplet from the rest of the poem:

When I have fears that I may cease to be	A
Before my pen has glean'd my teeming brain,	B
Before high-piled books, in charact'ry,	A
Hold like rich garners the full-ripen'd grain;	B
When I behold, upon the night's starr'd face,	C
Huge cloudy symbols of a high romance,	D
And think that I may never live to trace	C
Their shadows, with the magic hand of chance;	D
And when I feel, fair creature of an hour,	E
That I shall never look upon thee more,	F
Never have relish in the faery power	E
Of unreflecting love! — then on the shore	F
Of the wide world I stand alone, and think	G
Till Love and Fame to nothingness do sink.	G

Keats does not break either sonnet into stanza units, but he nevertheless adheres to the usual organization behind each scheme. "On the Grasshopper and the Cricket" breaks neatly into *octave* (the first eight lines) and *sestet* (the last six): the grasshopper first, then the cricket; summer first, then winter. Emphasizing this division, the lines that begin each section echo each other: "The poetry of earth is never dead" and "The poetry of earth is ceasing never." This kind of repetition is called a *rhetorical* device. "When I Have Fears" is also organized rhetorically, but according to the four-part Shakespearean pattern: (1) "When I have fears," (2) "When I behold," (3) "And when I feel," (4) "then on the shore." The first three parts are clearly laid out, allotted four lines each and separated by semicolons. But Keats starts the final part nearly half a line before the final couplet begins, interrupting that third section (which is about love, not fame) and giving the sonnet an emotional jolt. He enjambs right into the couplet, letting the words tumble into it, a wonderful effect that undercuts the form expressively.

That Shakespearean couplet presents the greatest problem of the English sonnet (as convoluted rhyming presents the greatest difficulty of the Italian form). Too often the couplet sounds tagged on, like a moral at the end of a fable, as in Shakespeare's 73rd Sonnet:

This thou perceiv'st, which makes thy love more strong:
To love that well which thou must leave ere long.

The problem is, we don't usually *want* our poems explained to us; we want to experience them, deciding for ourselves what they mean. Keats "unsettles" the form, and thereby avoids the problem lurking in that final couplet.

Although Keats wrote sonnets in both rhyme schemes, he also complained about the regimentation in his poem "On the Sonnet," whose scheme is the novel A-B-C-A-B-D-C-A-B-C-D-E-D-E. He begins, rhetorically and logically, by proposing the premise "If by dull rhymes our English must be chain'd," and concludes "So, if we may not let the Muse be free,/ She will be bound with garlands of her own."

Many sonnets follow the same kind of logical order, presenting a reasoned *argument*, making the poem a stage for ideas (or perhaps the dance of ideas). Many of Shakespeare's sonnets begin their four sections with words like "if," "when," "then," "for," and "but," words very useful in chaining together a logical or legal argument. But, more often than not, this argumentation is really, in the sonnet, a kind of wooing, the lover's plea, the rationale of seduction. And even a poem of abstract ideas must be seductive, must draw the reader in and offer a pleasure that convinces.

"But" is perhaps the key word in the annals of the sonnet, since it represents a crucial *turning* in the poem. The literary term for this turning point is the *volta*. Unless a sonnet is all of one piece, a single unit — maybe a description — it will contain some sort of turning point, perhaps several.

Just as Keats wanted to "free" the sonnet from its fetters of rhyme, other poets have to open it up or otherwise transform it. One way is to dispense with rhyme altogether. Another is to use an ad hoc rhyme scheme, or only to rhyme occasionally, or to use slant rhymes (like *sonnet* and *linnet* — or *bayonet*). Another is to make the sonnet a dialogue, or a little drama, or a story, or the description of a place, or a portrait of someone, or the facsimile of a letter. Some poets have changed the number of lines in what they call a sonnet. Norman Dubie's *Alehouse Sonnets* run fifteen lines each; John Hollander has thirteen-line sonnets in his book *Thirteens*; George Meredith uses sixteen-line sonnets in *Modern Love*. Gerard Manley Hopkins wrote "Pied Beauty" as a "curtal" (meaning short) sonnet of ten full lines and the fraction of another:

Glory be to God for dappled things —	A
For skies of couple-colour as a brinded cow;	B
For rose-moles all in stipple upon trout that swim;	C
Fresh-firecoal chestnut-falls; finches' wings;	A
Landscape plotted and pierced — fold, fallow, and plough;	B
And all trades, their gear and tackle and trim.	C
All things counter, original, spare, strange;	D

Whatever is fickle, freckled (who knows how?)   B
With swift, slow; sweet, sour; adazzle, dim;   C
He fathers-forth whose beauty is past change: D
Praise him.   C

Hopkins organizes this sonnet by *listing*. The poem is remarkable for its vivid images, inventive vocabulary, and packed rhythms. But despite all the description, it's still a sonnet that's primarily about an idea.

Since most English sonnets are written in iambic pentameter, it would be a good idea to consult the section on "Iambics," so you can learn not only the basic pattern (which is simple, an alternating of unstressed and stressed syllables—"The POeTRY of EARTH is NEVer DEAD"), but also the *variations* that make rhythm supple and subtle. (Notice, for instance, how Keats, in a regular line, gains melody by placing the weak "-try" of "poetry" in a position we expect to hear accented.) Once you've brushed up on iambics, try "scanning" the Keats poems, marking where the accents fall, noting how he departs and diverges from the regular pattern.

Keep in mind, too, that you usually don't want each line to end with a heavy pause. The effect would be like a highway littered with roadblocks; it would impede the reader's progress. Some of the lines should probably flow over to the next ones (*enjambment*, as opposed to *end-stopping*), as in these lines by Keats: "from the stove there shrills/ The cricket's song"). But the poet needs to do whatever is expressively right for the poem, so that the sonnet by Hopkins is entirely end-stopped (in fact, it's loaded with pauses *within* the lines).

In his end-note to *Notebook* (later reworked as *History*), a sequence of blank verse (that is, unrhymed) sonnets, Robert Lowell remarks that he has tried to avoid the "gigantism" of the sonnet. It is a form that lends itself to an odd kind of poetic bigness—not in length, but in its tendency to rhetorical overkill, pomposity and pretentiousness, to sermonizing on public events or philosophical profundities. But there is a place in it for imagery, understatement, craziness, and all sorts of things. In a sonnet, you not only play *with* a tradition; you also play *against* it.

Be warned, however. Once you start writing sonnets, it can be hard to stop. Something about the tidy size and the powerful wallop of the sonnet makes them addictive. Merrill Moore, who was Robert Lowell's psychiatrist, had a sonnet-writing compulsion; he wrote thousands of them. Lowell himself spent a decade working and reworking sonnets nearly to exhaustion. Because of the combination of brevity and the weightiness, the poet often feels compelled to go on, to elaborate, to explore the ideas further, in a way that he or she wouldn't if using, say, the form of the villanelle.

52. Write a perfectly regular sonnet, using either the English or Italian rhyme scheme. (If you're especially diligent, you might try both — and on the same subject.) Shape your sonnet as an argument: *If this, then that*; or *Because of x, y follows logically*; or *Although we think such and such, it is not true*. Minimize the number of metrical variations.

53. Write a sonnet that allows itself more freedom. Describe something: a person, place, or thing. Use plenty of enjambment and metrical variation. Feel free to use slant rhymes.

54. Loosen up the sonnet form, transforming it or corrupting it as much as you dare. Make the lines unequal in length, or omit the rhyming, or use a syllabic meter (counting the number of syllables per line). Write an "antisonnet" if you like.

55. Invent a form that resembles a sonnet. Maybe twelve lines. Or just the octave by itself (eight lines). Or come up with a fresh rhyme scheme.

56. Write a sonnet sequence (several sonnets that are related and form some kind of progression). If you like, write a *crown* of sonnets: seven of them, in which the last line of each one must be repeated as the first line of the next. (The crown's last line should repeat the first line of the opening sonnet.)

VILLANELLE

The *villanelle* is an intricate French form, nineteen lines in length, using two rhymed lines as refrains — and just two rhyme sounds throughout the poem. If that sounds artificial, it usually is, but many twentieth-century poets have written villanelles that are moving, meditative, or downright startling.

Here is a villanelle from Marilyn Hacker's first book, *Presentation Piece*. It is called "Ruptured Friendships, or, The High Cost of Keys":

I am obliged to repossess
some nooks and crannies of my soul.
I do not think of you the less.

Tonight's ragout would be a mess
without the red clay casserole
I am obliged to repossess.

The green chair suits my dinner dress.
The silk throw makes a pretty stole . . .
I do not think of you the less.

Six forks, two serving-spoons, and, yes,
a platter and a salad bowl
I am obliged to repossess.

Indeed, I say, more courtliness
would land me quickly on the dole.
I do not think of you the less.

Malicious mischief? I confess
the quicker I forget the role
and do not think of you, the less
I am obliged to repossess.

In the last two lines, Hacker allows herself the liberty of reversing the usual order (first then second refrain). She does this so she can repunctuate one of those key lines, transforming it from "I do not think of you the less" (end-stopped) to "and do not think of you, the less" (flowing over to the original refrain).

Since the villanelle is an unusually strict, confining form, it's not surprising that most poets try to "break the law" and see if they can get away with it. It's acceptable to rephrase or repunctuate the refrain lines as you go along. It's OK to use slant rhymes (such as lane/coin or weather/bother), although the inexactness may sound noticeably disappointing. Donald Justice has recommended omitting the fifth stanza, perhaps the fourth as well, arguing that many villanelles become too forced at that point. In his "Variations for Two Pianos," Justice includes just two lines, the refrains, in his opening stanza ("There is no music now in all Arkansas./ Higgins is gone, taking both his pianos.") and then follows it with three tercets (three-line stanzas) and the four-line conclusion. Marilyn Hacker, on the other hand, *extends* the form by adding two or three extra tercets before the conclusion, in the villanelles included in *Love, Death, and the Changing of the Seasons*. It just goes to show that you can manipulate forms as much as you like, shortening or lengthening, as long as the poem turns out well.

Most villanelles in English are written in iambic pentameter, although Hacker's poem shows that the tetrameter line works effectively. Anything shorter, however, may cramp the poet too much. (There's a challenge in that, of course.) Other means of imposing regularity — by counting syllables or accents, for example — may help, because the form thrives on steady pacing. Free verse is possible in a villanelle, but doesn't often work.

If you want to examine a very strict (but powerful) villanelle, look up Dylan Thomas's "Do Not Go Gentle into That Good Night." Even there, however, Thomas wins some variety by using "do not go gentle" both as a command and as the predicate (the verb end) of a declarative sentence: "Because their words had forked no lightning, they/ Do not go gentle into that good night."

In James Joyce's *Portrait of the Artist as a Young Man*, there is a marvelous passage in which Stephen Dedalus composes a villanelle. (His refrain lines are "Are you not weary of ardent ways" and "Tell no more of enchanted days.") Stephen devises the first three lines, in his head, before feeling "the rhythmic movement of a villanelle," an instance of how the first few lines that occur to a poet usually determine the poem's formal destiny. Of course, the poet can also decide to use the villanelle form beforehand—or recognize that a rough draft might work better in that form.

PATTERN FOR THE VILLANELLE

Rhymes	Refrains
A	1st refrain
B	
A	2nd refrain
A	
B	
A	1st refrain
A	
B	
A	2nd refrain
A	
B	
A	1st refrain
A	
B	
A	2nd refrain
A	
B	
A	1st refrain
A	2nd refrain

57. Write a villanelle in as strict a form as you possibly can. It may help to start by devising the two rhymed refrain lines. It may also help if you keep the language simple, clear, and song-like.

58. Write a talkative, gabby villanelle, using slang and the rhythms of everyday speech. Try to bring in colorful expressions and the wonderful names of mundane things (like Hacker's "casserole"). Enjamb as many lines as possible, letting them spill over into adjacent lines or stanzas. Play with the syntax (the arrangement of words) in your refrain lines. Keep the poem jumping.

59. Distort or corrupt the villanelle form, maybe shortening it (like Justice) or lengthening it (like Hacker). You might fiddle with the number of lines in individual stanzas. You might use free verse, or try omitting the rhymes. You might also try giving up the refrains, concentrating instead on the demanding rhyme scheme, without the need to repeat (or vary) whole lines.

OTHER "FIXED FORMS"

The problem with many "fixed forms" is that they are so rigid they don't give the poetic imagination much freedom or provocation. They are more for the puzzle-maker, the ingenious turner of phrases. Referring to the *ballade*, the *rondeau*, and the *triolet*, John Hollander remarks: "Some of the lyric forms from France remain a kind of metric dance, without real poetry to say but good for literary play (light verse, *vers de societê*)." (Notice the rhymes and the underlying iambic tetrameter of this passage that *looks* like prose.) If you're interested in light verse—which is outside the scope of this volume—by all means refer to Hollander's *Rhyme's Reason* or another handbook to learn how the forms go. Many people enjoy writing limericks, for example, but they generally don't need encouragement.

The most interesting of these "light" forms is the *ballade*. It consists of three eight-line stanzas, rhymed ABABACBC *throughout* (so that the first lines of each stanza will rhyme with each other), the last line of each stanza being a refrain (the same line repeated exactly—or nearly so); plus a four-line *envoi* (or "send-off"), rhymed BCBC, the last line being the refrain again. Remember that there are only three different rhyme sounds in the entire poem! The greatest ballades (such as the one whose refrain is "Where are the snows of yesteryear?") come from the medieval French poet Francois Villon. Among American poets, Marilyn Hacker has written well in the form.

60. Write a ballade on a serious subject, but keep the wording playful and inventive. You might start by thinking of a refrain that sounds good and can bear repetition.

SUMMARY OF FORMS

Repeating Forms
Villanelle (five tercets and a quatrain)
Sestina (six six-line stanzas and a tercet)
Pantoum (quatrains)
Ballade (three eight-line stanzas and a quatrain)

Stanzaic Forms
two-line stanzas (couplets)
heroic couplet (AA BB CC etc.)
ghazal (if rhymed, AA AA AA etc. from 5-12 couplets)

Three-line stanzas (tercets)
triplet (AAA BBB CCC etc.)
terza rima (ABA BCB CDC etc.)
haiku (5-7-5 syllable count)

Four-line stanzas (quatrains) (x = unrhymed)
ballad stanza (xAxA xBxB xCxC etc.)
heroic quatrain (AABB CCDD etc.)
elegiac quatrain (ABAB CDCD etc.)
In Memoriam stanza (ABBA CDDC EFFE etc.)
sapphics (11-11-11-5 syllable count)

Five-line stanzas
English quintet (ABABB) — term coined by Dacey and Jauss
Sicilian quintet (ABABA)
limerick (AABBA, stressed 3-3-2-2-3)

Six-line stanzas
quatrain + couplet (ABABCC DEDEFF, etc.)
three couplets (AABBCC DDEEFF, etc.)
alternating (ABABAB CDCDCD, etc.)

Seven-line stanza
rime royal (ABABBCC DEDEEFF etc.)

Eight-line stanza
ottava rima (ABABABCC DEDEDEFF etc.)

Nine-line stanza

Spenserian (ABABBCBCC, first eight lines pentameter, last line hexameter)

Fourteen-lines

Sonnet
English or Shakespearean (ABAB CDCD EFEF GG)
Italian or Petrarchan (ABBAABBA CDECDE)
    or (ABBAABBA CDCDCD)
    or (ABBAABBA CCDEED)
Spenserian (ABABBCBCCDCDEE)
Eugene Onegin stanza (ABABCCDDEFFEGG — iambic tetrameter)

(Note: Poets often make up a rhyme scheme for a particular poem, as Robert Frost does in "Stopping by Woods on a Snowy Evening": AABA BBCB CCDC DDDD, an interlocking pattern similar to terza rima.)

VIII. Voice

We speak of a poet finding her *voice*, a distinctive way of speaking that runs through all her poems. But that makes the long process of exploring and discovering what poems we have in us seem too willed, too determined, too calculated an approach. We want to learn simply (or complicatedly) how to say things that resonate in a poem. Some poets, in fact, discover that they speak best through the voice of another person, through monologues spoken by a character. This, then, becomes most truly the poet's own voice. In lines quoted by Richard Howard in his *Untitled Subjects*, Robert Browning says, "I'll tell my state as though 'twere none of mine." The Portuguese poet Fernando Pessoa wrote poems in the guise of several pseudonyms, all with different personalities and aesthetic views. The important thing is to get the sense of a real voice into your poems.

DIALOGUE, DRAMA, AND CONVERSATION

T.S. Eliot turned to plays because he wanted his verses *heard*, not just read silently. Of course his poetry, in particular *The Waste Land*, was already rich in voices and characters. Much of the world's greatest poetry has been written for the stage: Aeschylus and Sophocles, Shakespeare and Marlowe, Molière and Racine, Goethe and Schiller. In the twentieth century, we have Federico Garcia Lorca, Bertolt Brecht, William Butler Yeats, and Eliot making poetry into something playable.

Even if you don't want to plunge into the extra difficulties of dramatic writing, dialogue form has a nice give and take, letting you contradict and interrupt, permitting a wide variety of tones. You can often guess what the stories are that seem to hover in the echoing spaces between two voices, what they hint at but leave unsaid. In effective dialogue, two speakers rarely respond directly or attentively to the other's comments. They speak at cross-purposes usually, pursuing their own trains of thought while trying to "communicate" or feign communication for the sake of politeness. The stabs and misses and hemming and hawing and changes of subjects and sudden illuminations and misunderstandings are powerful tension builders. Dialogue thrives on conflict, clashes, and distances that can hardly be bridged.

1. Write a poem that is a dialogue, but without stage directions. One of the two voices could be indented, or underlined, or italicized, or in quotation marks, or capitalized (as in James Merrill's *Changing Light at Sandover*). The speakers can be realistic characters or "types" (male/female, east/west, young/old, good/evil, body/soul, outward life/inner life). They can be aspects of the same person. But the two voices *should* be opposed in some way. Richard Howard's *Two-Part Inventions* are dialogues, and their varied structures may suggest some fruitful approaches. He either (1) alternates voices or (2) lets one voice have its say and then the other.

2. Write a short play in verse.

3. Write a disguised dialogue. Use two warring tones or voices or themes, but don't identify them. Let them be part of the same fabric, seemingly unified.

4. Write a poem in a natural, easygoing speaking voice, making conversation and letting the poetry rise naturally from the discourse, rather than forcing it. Don't let the language get *too* loose and prosaic. It may be hard to work in metaphors or excessively "poetic" language; you want a believable, everyday voice that can make the real stuff of poetry out of the bare essentials.

5. Write a talky poem. Let it jabber, use slang, have fun with language. If a joke fits, tell it. This should be the high-voltage spiel of a real character, street-wise and quick on his or her feet, the stand-up comic as a regular guy.

DRAMATIC MONOLOGUE

Even though you write your own poems, you don't necessarily have to be the *speaker* of each one. In fact, it often improves a poem if you assume another voice, play a role, or put on a mask. Writing poems can be a kind of "method acting," in which you get under the skin of another character and talk as he or she would.

If you feel too wrapped up in yourself, too limited by personal concerns, try writing a *dramatic monologue*. In the Victorian Age, Robert Browning pioneered the form, modeling his work on the soliloquies of Elizabethan drama. Rather than present a whole play, he chose to highlight the chief dramatic moment and to confine himself to the voice of a single character in monologues like "My Last Duchess," "Andrea del Sarto," "Fra Lippo Lippi," and "Soliloquy of the Spanish Cloister." Even the titles reveal how deeply Browning drew from history and the arts in fashioning his monologues, speaking from the point of view of an Italian duke, or a Renaissance painter, or an evil monk. One thing a monologue requires is that you *know* something beyond the borders of your own life—or can imagine it fully, which amounts to the same thing.

A character in a play who delivers a soliloquy both addresses the audience (as in an aside) and talks to himself. We hear him, in effect, thinking aloud. The speaker of a dramatic monologue can do those things as well, but often he or she addresses a particular person, either another character we must imagine listening or the recipient of a letter. In Browning's "My Last Duchess," the listener is an envoy who is working out the details of a marriage between the duke and the daughter of another nobleman. We can tell, from the duke's remarks, how the envoy reacts with astonishment and horror at the end of the poem—not the duke's intention. Many of the monologues by Richard Howard, a contemporary master of the form, are framed as letters, often in the voice of a minor character who relates a story about an important historical figure, like the painter Turner.

Since the speaker of your monologue will probably not be omniscient, you can have him or her reveal things unwittingly, say things that have a different significance for the reader or for another character. This discrepancy between what the speaker *thinks* he's saying and what he *really* says is called *dramatic irony*. You can—and should—imagine the physical surroundings, even if you don't describe them, and write in a manner that sounds conversational.

The voice assumed by the poet is sometimes called a *persona*, the Greek word for "mask" (since the actors in Greek plays wore stylized masks during performances). You might think of this persona as a disguise that allows you to delve into subjects you could not explore otherwise, to free yourself to deal with difficult matters. The impersonation can be liberating.

Since the time of Browning and Tennyson, many poets have specialized in dramatic monologues. Ezra Pound called his collected shorter poems *Personae* and spoke in characters ranging from Troubadour poets to the Greek hero Odysseus. (Many of Pound's monologues are based heavily on his translations.) T.S. Eliot's *Waste Land* is really a sequence of monologues. Richard Howard has written dozens of monologues, covering much nineteenth- and twentieth-century culture, in books like *Untitled Subjects*, *Fellow Feelings*, and *No Traveller*. His *Two-Part Inventions* are "dramatic dialogues" or duets, often in letter form. Randall Jarrell, Norman Dubie, and Robert Peters have also specialized in monologues. (Peters even dresses up as the "Blood Countess" to perform one of his monologues.)

Finally, remember that there may be a different *you* writing the poem, not quite the same person who talks on the phone or commutes to work every day. Emily Dickinson said that the speaker of her poems was not herself but a "supposed person."

6. Spend some time — an hour, a day — fantasizing that you are another person. Think of what that person might do during the day, how he or she will act in various situations, what he or she would say to different people. What, for instance, would the person do if accosted by a mugger? kept waiting for service in a restaurant? lost in a strange city? reminded of an embarrassment from the distant past? pelted with drizzle? Then write a page's worth of lines in the voice of that character. Choose a form (free or metrical) that seems appropriate to the speaker.

7. Write a dramatic monologue in which the speaker is trying to reveal or explain something to another person. This speaker can be someone you know (perhaps a relative or a friend), a character from a book or a movie, a famous person from current news or history, or someone you invent. You might start by listing people you'd enjoy thinking about — and speaking through. If it helps, think of the process as a kind of ventriloquism. It's also an exercise in empathy.

8. Write from the point of view of something nonhuman: an animal (like the pig of Philip Levine's "Animals Are Passing from Our Lives"), or a plant (as in Louis Simpson's "The Redwoods"), or a building, or a chemical element, or a constellation, or whatever you can dream up. Try to imagine your way into another consciousness — even if it's an impossible one.

9. Write a dramatic monologue in the form of a letter. Have a definite speaker in mind, a particular recipient who lives in some reasonably distant place, an occasion for the letter writing, something to reveal, and something to leave unsaid (write the "secret" out in your notes but exclude it from the poem). Use as much of the format of letters as you like (return address, date, salutation, complimentary close, signature) or none of it. If it fits the speaker, include grammatical lapses or misspellings. (Ring Lardner said that, in writing his epistolary novel in the voice of a baseball player, he misspelled only shorter words, on the theory that the player would ask someone how to spell more difficult, longer ones.) In writing a monologue, it may help to begin with a prose draft, or at least some detailed notes.

10. Choose a character you want to deal with, but speak in the voice of *someone else*: a brother or sister, a friend, an enemy, a servant, a family doctor, a detective investigating that character.

11. Write a series of monologues in which different speakers tell conflicting versions of the same story. Robert Browning's *The Ring and the Book* does this to great effect.

12. Think of an emotion, such as fear, ecstasy, boredom, or nervousness, and think of a character who can embody that emotion. What you want to do is achieve some distance between yourself and a strong emotion. Put that character in a situation that forces him or her to

(1) speak directly about the emotion or (2) suppress the emotion and say something else.

13. Look through a poetry anthology and see how many dramatic monologues you can find—how many poems spoken by a character, someone clearly *not* the author. Do you get a clear picture of each speaker? Or are some of the portraits fragmentary, partial?

PERSPECTIVE AND POINT OF VIEW

Point of View represents the voice that's telling us a poem or a story, the perspective from which something is recounted. It can be first person ("I") or third person ("he" or "she"); it can be second person ("you"), although that's become a mannerism in recent years. It can be all-knowing (omniscient) or aware only of what's visible and apparent (objective). Sometimes a poem can be vastly improved by shifting the point of view. It's useful to scrutinize "Who's speaking?" and to make adjustments if something seems amiss.

Think of the journalist's "angle" on a story he or she is reporting. It's the viewpoint that makes the story interesting and fresh in our minds. The best way to revivify a tired poetic subject is to approach it from a new, even bizarre, angle, like a movie director's "camera angle." In poems, we're concerned not so much with subjects as with how we look at and consider various subjects.

These perspectives can shift during the course of a poem, switching from voice to voice, as in T.S. Eliot's *The Waste Land*. And the shifts could simply be surges in consciousness or awareness, the taking on or sloughing off of the prophet's robe or the beggar's rags. Naturally, this makes the poet's job harder and will not work or be necessary in most poems, but it *is* an option.

Time can shift as well, but you need to be careful that shifts in tense aren't taken as stupid errors. Those shifts need to have a point and to *prove* it as they move along. Sometimes it makes a poem clearer if one action is told in the present and another in the past tense to distinguish them and avoid confusion. The present tense often has more immediacy—it's happening right now!—but annoys some people who see it as another mannerism. (After all, it probably *isn't* really happening right now.)

14. Write a poem from a point of view you wouldn't normally use.

15. Think of a subject that's been nearly exhausted (the rebirth of spring, unrequited love) and view from a completely new angle. Don't be afraid to go wild. If your perspective is strange and unusual, all the better. Even the title of William Carlos Williams's "Widow's Lament in

Springtime" suggests the power of such a surprising viewpoint on a common scene.

16. Write a poem that intentionally switches voices, or shifts verb tenses, or both.

QUESTIONS

Most poems are written as a series of declarative sentences, punctuated occasionally by an exclamation. Questions, though, can be powerful intrusions. They can work dramatically well as beginnings and endings (and also for follow-up lines), but the effect shouldn't be overused.

Here are some questions used as openers:

What are we waiting for, assembled in the forum?	(Cavafy)
What shakes the eye but the invisible?	(Roethke)
Out of sight? What of that?	(Dickinson)

Here are some closings:

Was there another Troy for her to burn?	(Yeats)
Which one's the mockingbird? which one's the world?	(Jarrell)
Fled is that music: — Do I wake or sleep?	(Keats)

James Wright begins the first poem in *The Branch Will Not Break* with a question ("Po Chu-i, balding old politician,/ What's the use?") and ends with another two: "Did you find the city of isolated men beyond mountains?/ Or have you been holding the end of a frayed rope/ For a thousand years?" (In addition to being an "ancient Chinese governor," Po Chu-i was one of the best poets of his age.) In Wright's lines, the questions affect the tone of voice, giving a twist to the words; we can almost see the speaker shrugging—"What's the use?" Questions also affect the "melody" of these and any lines. Our voices waver and rise slightly in pitch to show we're asking, not telling. And since questions are simply different from declarations, we can use them for variety, punctuation, emphasis, repetition.

Richard Hugo thinks you should never answer a question you've posed in a poem, and certainly a question shouldn't lead to an obvious "yes" or "no"—unless it simply has to. If you ask something far-fetched—

"Doesn't the wind blow kisses to the past?"

—you can expect a cynical reader to answer with a big "NO." It doesn't hurt to test your questions for rhetorical silliness.

17. Make a list of questions, some you've overheard, some you've

read. Write a poem that answers one of those questions — and then, if you like, drop the originating question entirely.

18. Write a poem entirely in the form of questions. Some of them can correspond to line lengths, but some should probably run over several lines, some should take up only part of a single line. Using short or long lines will change your question poem considerably.

19. Read a poem by another poet and respond by posing a series of questions for which you don't have immediate answers.

TONE

When we say that someone "snaps" at a colleague, or "coos" at a paramour, or speaks with tongue in cheek, we're talking about *tone*. We can pick up the inflections and insinuations of a speaker's tone of voice, but in a poem we're dependent on other clues: word choice, phrasing, sentence length, rhythm. The poet must make us *hear* a voice that isn't audible.

A poem's tone is its manner of speaking, its mood. It can be neutral, of course, but often it will be colored and shaded to suggest emotions — instead of baldly stating them.

Robert Frost talks about hearing the "sound of sense" in the rhythms of "voices behind a door that cuts off the words." Here are some of the sentences he gives as examples in a letter of 1913:

> You mean to tell me you can't read?
> I said no such thing.
> Well read then.
> You're not my teacher.

He's really paying attention to the tone, the freight of human emotions carried by the rhythms. In another letter, Frost says "A good sentence does double duty: it conveys one meaning by word and syntax [and] another by the tone of voice it indicates."

One way to put a "spin" on your words is to use *irony*, saying one thing but intending another. (The Greek root of the word means "a dissembling.") It's a way to catch what Wallace Stevens calls "the beauty of innuendoes." Watch out, though, for its loutish cousin, *sarcasm*, which usually sounds too crude or obvious in a poem.

20. Choose a particular tone of voice you'd like to try out. (If you can't decide, spend some time eavesdropping in a public place like a restaurant or a ball park or a bus. Try to place the emotional shadings you hear in different voices, some pleading, some pressuring, some dis-

missive, some adoring.) *Without* settling on a subject beforehand, start "talking" in a poem and see where the talk leads you. Write as quickly as you can. Follow any interesting detours. Once you're finished, start crossing out the boring, rambling lines until you reach something interesting. That's the start of your poem. Keep revising. Add more material and shape it to make the voice come alive.

21. Sometimes a poem needs to be "toned down." Find an old poem of yours that seems excessively emotional. Rewrite it from a calmer, more detached perspective. Replace emotional "buzzwords" (like "heartache") with images and unexpected phrases. Make it more neutral and objective, showing the force of emotion by the tightness of the restraint.

22. Sometimes, on the other hand, a poem can be too bland and uninvolved. Revise an old poem that lacks spunk by emphasizing a particular tone, making it sharper. Freshening up word choices, rephrasing sentences, repeating or not repeating, and speeding up or slowing down the tempo will help mimic the sound of a real human voice.

23. Choose a scene or person or object to describe. In short bursts (only three or four lines each), talk about your subject in as many different tones of voice as you can come up with. Range all over the emotional color chart. See red, feel blue, be green with envy, or yellow with cowardice. Be funny, be serious. Be quiet, be loud. Be polite, be obscene. Talk like a cop, or a shrink, or a barfly. When you're finished, arrange the best snippets into a sequence — or a single, unified tableau of competing voices.

24. Read a variety of poems in an anthology. Sum up the *tone* of each in a word or phrase: "hardboiled," "soppy," "inquisitive," "loopy," "professorial," "legalistic," "wisecracking," "sex-crazed," and so on. Try to *hear* the inflections of a spoken voice as you silently read each poem.

25. Fill in the blank: "It's ironic that _____ ." Then write a poem about this irony. (You don't need to include the filled-in sentence.)

26. Write a poem in which you speak throughout with a second meaning in mind, an ironic edge behind your words. Think of it as speaking tongue-in-cheek. Don't start with a subject so much as an *audience* you're addressing: your boss, for example, or a politician.

UNDERSTATEMENT

It's usually more effective to suggest something in a poem than to spell it out. The poem gains intensity if the reader has to fill in spaces, make imaginative leaps. Emily Dickinson says "Tell all the Truth but tell it slant" and we ought to heed her advice, suggesting more than we state, proceeding indirectly, observing what we see from unexpected vantage points, surprising angles. The chief virtue of *understatement* is that it makes our poems more credible: we don't have to boast about emotion we may or may not actually have. And since it reduces the decibel level, we're freer to modulate the noise, raise our voices subtly or suddenly and then calm things down to the normal understated level. It's a good way to induce a kind of dreamy, trance-like state of receptiveness in the reader.

There are places for *hyperbole* (overstatement), especially in wild, rhapsodic poems — sometimes called *dithyrambs*. That overstatement can have the force of passion and urgency. But it can quickly numb the reader. The ranting becomes a drone. Even poets known for symphonic crescendi, like Whitman, must have a quieter, more delicate side. (Quiet poets, though, *don't* need to roar.) Worst of all, overstatement often sounds faked, the writer protesting too much, trying to whip up a frenzy of words to hide a vacancy of imagination. Bombast is all too easy to perpetrate.

Understatement is a holding back, a restraint, that can suggest the power *being* restrained. It is a great source of dramatic tension in a poem: what's said can hint at what's boiling under the surface. But the danger of understatement is dullness, boredom. You still have to keep things interesting.

27. Write the quietest poem you can possibly write. Goethe wrote a lyric called "Wanderer's Night Song II" that demonstrates this possibility. Here's my approximation of the poem:

Over all the peaks
Is peace.
In all the treetops
You detect
Hardly a breath.
The birds are hushed in the woods.
Just wait. Soon
Peace for you too.

("Wanderer's Night Song I," incidentally, is much louder, more rhetorical, a wonderful complement to its sequel.)

28. Write a poem about something that troubles you or moves you greatly, but try to restrain your emotions in presenting it. Try to find an "angle" from which you can launch into the subject almost stealthily. Use hints and winks, but don't blurt out how you feel.

29. Take an old poem (maybe yours, maybe something by Shelley or another Romantic poet) and tone it down, understating what's too blatant and blaring. For instance, how could you say "I fall upon the thorns of life! I bleed!" (Shelley's line) more subtly? How could you *show* the sting of wounded sensitivity?

30. Some poems, though, are cold and reptilian, rather than heroically understated, and those performances seem repulsive. (Talking about fiction, John Barth has called for "passionate virtuosity," and surely we want expertise matched by intensity.) Take a poem that seems too coldly objective and light a fire within it or under it. This doesn't mean you have to shout and shudder, but you have to indicate some *need* to say what you're saying, some underlying emotional trigger, however distanced it may seem.

IX. Sources of Inspiration

In "Digging," a poem about his father digging potatoes and his grandfather cutting turf in a peat bog, Seamus Heaney writes that *he'll* dig with a pen. For our own poems, where do we start this digging? Like Heaney, we can begin with memory. Or in dreams. Or in thinking. Or by chance. We can consult journals, if we keep them. We can borrow from other writers. We can do research. We can give our imaginations the freedom to envision preposterous things, events that never occurred, and make them seem real. Finally, we can simply start writing, digging with our pens, and see what we turn up. Sources lie all around us — and within us.

BORROWINGS

You may be surprised that poets sometimes borrow material from other writers in the course of writing poems. The key is to make it your own. In a fashion, it *is* being returned if it is imaginatively transformed, "changed, changed utterly" (in Yeats's words) — which the poet *must* do to earn clear title to the material.

Writers can be stimulated as powerfully by what they read as by their other daily experience. There is no psychological difference between real and vicarious experience; the imagination makes it one. So a poet's reading is as real and authentic (and personal) as a walk in the woods or a conversation with an ex-lover. And his or her reading is *not* like a wildlife refuge where hunting is forbidden. It is, in fact, a field of plenty.

Robert Lowell, for instance, wrote the famous opening section of "The Quaker Graveyard in Nantucket" by borrowing material from a passage in H.D. Thoreau's *Cape Cod* describing a shipwreck off the beach:

> The brig St. John, from Galway, Ireland, laden with emigrants, was wrecked on Sunday morning; it was now Tuesday morning, and the sea was still breaking violently on the rocks. There were eighteen or twenty of the same large boxes that I have mentioned (large, rough deal boxes), lying on a green hillside, a few rods from the water, and surrounded by a crowd. The bodies which had been recovered, twenty-seven or eight in all, had been collected there.

Some were rapidly nailing down the lids, which were yet loose, and peeping under the cloths,—for each body, with such rags as still adhered to it, was covered loosely with a white sheet. I witnessed no signs of grief, but there was a sober dispatch of business which was affecting. One man was seeking to identify a particular body, and one undertaker or carpenter was calling to another to know in what box a certain child was put. I saw many marble feet and matted heads as the cloths were raised, and one livid, swollen, and mangled body of a drowned girl,—who probably had intended to go out to service in some American family,—to which some rags still adhered, with a string half concealed by the flesh, about its swollen neck; the coiled-up wreck of a human hulk, gashes by the rocks or fishes, so that the bone and muscle were exposed, but quite bloodless—merely red and white,—with wide-open and staring eyes, yet lustreless, deadlights; or like the cabin windows of a stranded vessel, filled with sand. Sometimes there were two or more children, or a parent and child, in the same box, and on the lid would, perhaps, be written with red chalk, "Bridget such-a-one, and sister's child."

Lowell kept "the sea was still breaking violently," the "marble feet and matted heads," the "lustreless, deadlights," the "cabin windows on a stranded vessel, heavy with sand," and the "chalk"—though he changed it from red to yellow. Yet for all his borrowings, he makes the poem his own—blending in other vivid images, changing the context, adding allusions (to Captain Ahab of Melville's *Moby Dick*; to Poseidon, the god of the sea, the "earth-shaker"; to Orpheus, the poet of Greek myth), and clenching it all into rhymed iambic meter. Here is Part I of "The Quaker Graveyard in Nantucket":

A brackish reach of shoal off Madaket,—
The sea was still breaking violently and night
Had steamed into our North Atlantic Fleet,
When the drowned sailor clutched the drag-net. Light
Flashed from his matted head and marble feet,
He grappled at the net
With the coiled, hurdling muscles of his thighs:
The corpse was bloodless, a botch of red and whites,
Its open, staring eyes
Were lustreless dead-lights
Or cabin-windows on a stranded hulk
Heavy with sand. We weight the body, close
Its eyes and heave it seaward whence it came,

Where the heel-headed dogfish barks its nose
On Ahab's void and forehead: and the name
Is blocked in yellow chalk.
Sailors, who pitch this portent at the sea
Where dreadnaughts shall confess
Its hell-bent deity,
When you are powerless
To sand-bag this Atlantic bulwark, faced
By the earth-shaker, green, unwearied, chaste
In his steel scales: ask for no Orphean lute
To pluck life back. The guns of the steeled fleet
Recoil and then repeat
The hoarse salute.
      (*Lord Weary's Castle*, Harcourt Brace, 1946)

Similarly, Shakespeare adapted a description from Plutarch's *Parallel Lives* when composing the speech in *Antony and Cleopatra* that begins "The chair she sat on, like a burnished throne"—which T.S. Eliot parodies in *The Waste Land*.

1. Take a passage of prose by another writer and put it into lines. Omit as much of the original as you like. Feel free to shift around phrases and sentences, to add material of your own, to change words, to rearrange the results into rhyme and meter (or free verse, or whatever you prefer). Any prose passage will do—either something you've read or something you've written. Try to retain a good deal of the original diction, but compress the phrases and sentences as much as possible. Remember that you're not merely copying the original—you're remaking it into your own poem.

2. Start a poem of your own with an actual line by another poet. Or borrow a sentence from a novel, or a spoken remark by a character in a play. Or embed a line or two by another poet, as James Wright incorporates a line by Virgil ("The best days are the first to flee") in two of his poems: "The Best Days" and "The First Days" (*To a Blossoming Pear Tree*, FSG, 1977).

3. Theodore Roethke writes "I take this cadence from a man named Yeats,/ I take it and I give it back again." Borrow something (the form, tone, subject, kind of imagery, or rhyme scheme of a model poem) so you, too, can "give it back again."

4. Write a poem triggered by a newspaper article. You might want to speak from the point of view of a character involved in the story (or perhaps as an "innocent" bystander). You might want to concentrate on imagery suggested by the article. Whatever strategy you use, try to imag-

ine the scene as fully as possible, to "feel yourself into it" and report on your findings. You're not limited to journalistic style, but that may give you an idea of an angle for the poem. Ask the reporter's questions: who, what, when, where, how, and why. James Dickey's "Falling," which sprang from a *New York Times* article on a stewardess who fell from an airplane, offers a great example of the possibilities.

5. Interview someone (or several people) about some topic that interests you. Take notes or let a tape recorder run. Then write a poem that is a short "documentary," drawing on facts, quotations, or other material you've gathered. How much of the people themselves do you want to include? How much of yourself?

6. Write a poem in the form of an interview, a series of questions and answers. You can be as realistic or as fantastic as you like. Your talkers need not be human, or mortal, or tangible in any way. They can be parts of a divided self, warring angels, stars in a constellation, tortoise and hare, Abbott and Costello, Helen and Menelaos, interrogator and spy. One traditional subject for a poem is the Dialogue between Body and Soul. Use that theme if you like.

RESPONSES

In a broad sense, many poems are actually responses to what we see, what we remember, what makes us feel happy or sad or angry or embarrassed: the stimuli of our lives. But many poems begin as responses to other poems, and that's what we're going to explore here. (Your other responses will be required in nearly every section of this book—whenever you're directed to write a poem about anything.)

Christopher Marlowe's "The Passionate Shepherd" elicited responses from Sir Walter Raleigh ("The Nymph's Reply"), John Donne ("The Bait"), C. Day Lewis ("Song"), and many others, most of whom adhered to Marlowe's original form (rhymed iambic tetrameter couplets). Anthony Hecht answered Matthew Arnold's "Dover Beach" with "The Dover Bitch." It helps to consider your point of view carefully. Who's speaking? Where? When? Try switching the original point of view, unless you want the "before and after" effect of a speaker answering him- or herself. If you get stuck, either pick a different poem or try to make your response more personal, more your own.

One particular kind of response is the *parody*, usually a humorous poem, sometimes a vicious one, mimicking a well-known poem. These can be great fun to write—and an excellent way to test out your powers of criticism. W.H. Auden said that in his "dream college of bards," the only critical writing required of the student would be parodies.

Even a single parodied line can trigger a poem. Carolyn Kizer transformed Stephen Spender's "I think continually of those who were truly great" into "I think continually of those who are truly crazy" to begin the fourth section of "Running Away from Home" (from *Yin*, BOA Editions, 1984).

7. Write an "answer" to a poem (perhaps a "rebuttal" or an opposite point of view). You could, for example, agree or disagree with Allen Ginsberg's vision of his country in "America," supplying your own list of details and examples.

8. Using another poem as a model, write a poem of your own in which the point of view has shifted, perhaps to a different character, perhaps from "I" to "you" or "he" or "she." For example, you could write a dramatic monologue, responding to James Dickey's "Cherrylog Road" from the point of view of the girl in the poem.

9. Write a parody. Try to ape your chosen poet's stylistic mannerisms. You might start by jotting down a list of what some of those quirks might be.

RESEARCH

If you think of poetry as something that has to be inspired, you may be astounded that poets often engage in serious research. The problem may be your limited notions about "inspiration." A poet's reading may seem aimless, but it is really a kind of fishing; you never know when the big one may snap at your bait. *That* is what inspiration is like. If you don't have the bait, the hook, the line, the rod, the boat, the patience, and the lake, you're really waiting for a flying fish to hurl itself into your arms. Inspiration is seldom like that.

Try thinking of research as a kind of preparation. It may involve simply reading for pleasure in some area of interest. But you may want to write about the Civil War, or Joan of Arc, or the Venetian Republic, or steel mills, or organic gardening, and need detailed information to give your words authority. You may need the words themselves, the specific terminology of a subject. You may need to refresh a memory by gathering facts about a place or an activity.

Of course, you do not have to proceed like a true scholar. You can read until you hit upon the vivid details you need, or until you have a feel for the subject, or until you've made a list of curious words you want to choose from. You might immerse yourself in a subject and then *forget* the clutter of information that might get in the way of the poem. At some point, you want the imagination to "kick in." When it does, the facts you've researched will be in the back of your mind (or in your notes, if you need them), but you'll be free to transform them into something new, something "rich and strange": the poem.

10. Settle on a subject you'd like to explore. It can be something you know well, or not at all. Spend a day or two researching your subject in a library, or a historical society, or a museum. Take notes. When you think you've done enough, return home and put the notes aside. Start a poem based on what you've absorbed. Let the poem go in any direction; don't rein it in too much. Later on, when you're stuck, refer to your notes and let them propel you back into motion. Lift whole phrases, if you like, from the notes and insert them into your poem.

11. Write a poem using facts from a guidebook, a map, an encyclopedia entry, a dictionary, an almanac, a biography, a brochure, a textbook, a cookbook, or a catalog. You might want simply to fashion your poem in the form of a list, but it's usually more fruitful to find a context (a setting, scene, or situation) that can encompass the facts and particulars. John Logan's "Believe It" uses bizarre details from Ripley's Believe It or Not Museum and weaves them into a poem about the difficulties of love. Sandra McPherson's "Collapsars" (in *Radiation*) offers another approach.

JOURNALS

A journal is literally a "day book," the word deriving from the French *jour* (as in *soupe du jour*). "Diary" comes from *dies*, the Latin word for day (as in *dies irae*, "day of wrath," or *carpe diem*, "seize the day"). The connotations of these words differ somewhat, "diary" suggesting the trivial and the sentimental, "journal" suggesting a more serious notation of the day's "privileged moments." Writers and naturalists keep journals, often as repositories of observations and discoveries. Of course, diaries don't *have* to be trivial or sentimental. Anne Frank's diary is an important, compelling work.

Each passage in a journal is called an "entry," and it may be worthwhile to consider the word's implications. What you jot down in your "day book" really represents an *opening*, a means of getting into something, a way to penetrate the things around us. The casual nature of journals may make these breakthroughs possible. Entries often consist of mere sketches, or fragments, or bits of overheard conversation, or scattered details remembered from some occasion. The writing in a journal will seem fluid, not fixed, and that makes it ideal as a staging area, collection point, or gathering place where poems can originate.

What should a writer include in a journal? There are no rules. Anything that seems worth noticing and remembering belongs there. One way to proceed is to set aside a regular time each day for making entries. Just before bedtime is an obvious possibility, but early in the morning might do just as well—and may encourage you to remember and record your dreams. In Richard Howard's "1825," a dramatic monologue in the voice of Sir Walter Scott, the speaker laments:

> I have all my life regretted I did not keep
> A journal, regular to the day . . .

You can start with a date, maybe a place, and then note what you did that day, who you saw, what you thought, and so on: your remembered itinerary. So far that sounds like a diary. To make your notebook a real journal, you need to recall the specific *details*: what things looked like, what people said, how your thoughts connect to other ideas. In other words, you have to *be specific*.

You can also keep a journal without a regular schedule, scribbling down images, scraps of conversation, brief descriptions, new words, quotations from books or magazines, interesting thoughts, reminders, ideas for poems, and lists of details as the mood strikes. You can clip newspaper articles and paste or tape them in. You can comment on poems you like or dislike. You can, in fact, copy down whole poems or passages from prose works. You can write letters you never intend to mail, for your ears only, possibly to poets whose work has affected you either favorably or not.

Any kind of notebook will do. You might prefer a bound, lined composition book, or an unlined artist's sketchbook, or a dated diary, or a calendar, or a loose leaf notebook, or a yellow legal pad, or a stack of 3×5 cards, or a pocket notebook. You can use the backs of old envelopes or any sort of paper (maps, brochures, menus or napkins) if you don't like too much regimentation, if you want to keep the journal spontaneous. You can use a computer, making your entries on a word processor— although that may encourage too much rewriting and self-editing. You can use pen or pencil. You can dictate into a tape recorder. It all depends on personal whim. You might want to change your journal-keeping habits now and then, or experiment with a different way—especially if you feel hampered or blocked by your current habits.

Journals may be private, but there's usually an imaginary reader somewhere in the writer's mind. This reader may simply be an alter ego, or our idealized image of the writer, or a future version of the self. But it may be part of what we imagine as a large audience that will want to listen in, maybe the archaeologists of a distant civilization. It is often the writer's "studio," where we find sketches, blocks of marble, clay models, pictures taped to the walls, debris on the floor, tools everywhere.

These details may be picturesque in themselves (like journals), but mainly they contribute to the long process of making a work of art. In the hands of a Michelangelo, the sketches or cartoons will be artworks themselves.

Sometimes a writer is famous for casual, daily writing: Anne Frank, Samuel Pepys. Sometimes novels are written in journal form: Daniel Defoe's *Journal of a Plague Year*, Jean Paul Sartre's *Nausea*, Kenneth Patchen's *Journal of Albion Moonlight*. Sometimes journals, such as those by Henry David Thoreau and Virginia Woolf, supplement their other writings, standing beside them as almost equally important. Some journals, diaries, and notebooks worth looking into include those by May Sarton, Franz Kafka, Theodore Roethke, Anais Nin, David Ignatow, and George Seferis. W.H. Auden kept a "commonplace book" in which he copied passages and quotations he enjoyed reading. Many scientists, such as Charles Darwin, have kept journals. James Boswell, the biographer of Dr. Samuel Johnson, kept a journal that's much celebrated in its own right.

Not all writers, however, keep journals. Richard Wilbur, for example, prefers to wait for the poem to seize him, rather than to plug away at it by means of regular daily writing. For some poets, it makes sense to let poems gestate in their minds, committing words to paper only when necessary. Some poets don't need, or even want, the memory aid that a journal provides; some think it actually *dulls* the memory. A journal, by nature, is a place for false starts and dead ends; it is a maze that the writer constructs in order to escape. For its creator, of course, the maze is intricately beautiful in itself.

You don't have to keep a journal all the time. You might want to keep one for a short stretch, during a trip for example, when a travel journal can serve as a kind of extra camera. Or you might want to keep track of your dreams for a few weeks. If you do keep a daily journal, don't be surprised if there are gaps or lapses when you neglect to record your entries. You can always catch up later. A perfect attendance record is not the point.

12. Start keeping a journal, diary, or writer's notebook. Spend at least twenty or thirty minutes each day. It helps to set aside a block of time, but it also helps to carry the journal around with you and write in it at odd moments. Use your senses of sight, hearing, touch, taste, and smell to help you capture images. Be on the lookout for things that surprise you. Notice the details that give something its character: the red epaulets of the blackbird on a fence post, the damp crescent on the bill of a baseball cap. If this seems difficult, take a walk in some familiar place and tell yourself you're going to notice something new within the next

minute. Don't be surprised if you're overwhelmed with details and images. Concentrate on jotting down fragments of imagery, but also record bits of conversation you've overheard. If you find yourself stuck, comment on the weather, or the news, or what you did at work, or how you exercised or amused yourself. But reach for the exact, specific detail that describes the weather, news, work, or play. Don't just say it rained. Say *how* it rained, what it looked and felt like.

13. Use an entry in one of your journals to start a poem.

14. Take several unrelated journal entries and weave them into a single poem. (Theodore Roethke wrote some of his wilder poems this way.)

15. Look through the journal of a well-known writer. Find a passage on which you can base your own poem. Keep the original entry's flavor, if you like, or diverge from it totally.

16. Write a poem in journal form, giving dates and using fragments as necessary.

DREAMS

People have always acknowledged the importance and power of dreams. Once they were portents, warnings, sneak previews of the future. Homer distinguishes between true dreams, which enter the sleeping mind through an ivory gate, and false dreams, which enter through a gate made of horn. Freud and Jung taught us how dreams reveal the inner life of the person in symbolic form. (The two men quarreled and ended their friendship because of one of Jung's dreams that seemed threatening and hostile to Freud.)

Poems use dreams in a number of ways. They can *be* dreams that the poet attempts to transcribe, as Coleridge claimed his "Kubla Khan" sprang from an opium dream. They can be dreamlike in the way they use vivid glimpses, unexplained shifts, impossible happenings, mysterious actions. They can take place in a dreamy landscape, like Surrealist paintings. (See the section on "Thinking.") And they can draw material from dreams, as Norman Dubie does. (He feels that when he sleeps he's really hard at work on his future poems.)

One good way to remember your dreams better is to keep a "dream log," a notebook in which you record the plots and details (especially the images) of your dreams. Franz Kafka's mysterious stories owe much to the dream notebook he kept. It's a good idea to keep your notebook on a nightstand, or somewhere near where you sleep, so you can jot down your recollections before they slip away—as Gregory Orr describes the dreams of last night washing away in the sink, a "transparent rose swallowed by its stem." Making a habit of recording your dreams will actually improve your recollection of them.

Dream poems run into trouble when they seem arbitrary, contrived, or affectedly weird. (Robert Benchley has a hilarious account of a man describing a dream: "I seemed to be in a sort of big hall, only it wasn't exactly a hall either, it was more of a rink or schoolhouse. It seemed that Harry was there and all of a sudden instead of Harry it was Lindbergh. Well, so we all were going to a football game or something and I had on my old gray suit, except that it had wheels on it — ") Just because you really dreamed something, that doesn't justify slapping it into a poem. You still have to select and fit together your images carefully. Remember how boring it often is to hear someone relate a dream at the breakfast table.

Often the most tedious (and obvious) way to end a dream poem is to have the speaker wake up — or have the alarm clock screech like a jungle bird. You must have a good reason to rouse the dreamer, as Robert Lowell does in "Falling Asleep Over the Aeneid," in which nearly seventeen lines are devoted to the waking, enough room to build up a memorable scene to contrast with the dream.

17. Start keeping a record of your dreams. After a week or so, choose one of the dreams to flesh out into a full poem. Don't *say* it's a dream, but let it be odd, vivid, unsettling, even unresolved. Try to make it *feel* like a dream. Go back regularly to look for more raw material for your poems.

18. Write a poem in which you present a series of vivid, dreamlike images without any explanation of what they mean or how they connect. Choose sensory details that can suggest actions and outcomes, the way a palm tree uprooted by a hurricane might suggest mental upheaval. You can call the poem a "portrait" or a "story" if you want to give the reader a clue.

19. Write a poem in which sudden memories of a dream intrude into the speaker's everyday thoughts.

20. Write a poem that incorporates a "dream interpretation," based either on (a) Freud, Jung, or another theorist, or (b) a popular "dream guide" you can purchase in a supermarket check-out line. Talk about a dream and try to puzzle out what it means. In doing so, you don't have to minimize the imagery. Use metaphors to clarify your explanations; describe the immediate wide-awake scene as well as the dream terrain. Remember that your explanations can be contradictory, humorous, ironic, or outright wrong. If the speaker of the poem overlooks an obvious interpretation, it reveals a lot about that speaker.

21. Write a poem in which something that can't happen *does* happen. (Andrew Hudgins suggested this one.)

22. Write a poem that is mysterious, dreamlike, or centered around silence. W.S. Merwin, Louis Simpson, and James Wright demonstrate some of the possible approaches you might try out.

MEMORY

The ancient Greeks thought memory so important to the arts that they venerated the goddess of memory, Mnemosyne, as the mother of the nine Muses. Memory plays a multiple role for the poet. It supplies the kindling—and often the fuel—for the imagination. It is often the subject of poems. And it underlies the secret goal of every poem: to be memorable.

In recent years, poets have quarreled about the uses and abuses of memory. Robert Bly has observed a "war between memory and imagination," noting the problem of relying too heavily on memories, especially autobiographical trivia and family anecdotes. For some writers, to make excessive use of memories is to spend one's capital. There's only so much in anybody's account. What do you write about then?

Fortunately, it's not too hard to keep memory in its proper place—as guide, goad, trigger, storehouse. And it's worth contemplating in its own right.

23. Write a poem that recreates a memory. It may help to conjure up sense impressions of the scene: how it looked, sounded, smelled, felt, and tasted. Try to pinpoint specific, even tiny, details: *exactly* how the blade of zoysia grass felt against your cheek; *exactly* how the moonlight shattered on the lake; *exactly* how your aunt revved up her motorcycle. If there's action you want to recount, tell a story, but keep the images and specific details coming! Don't tag a "moral" onto the end. Simply create a mood that puts the reader *there*.

24. Write a poem that *questions* a recollection. Did such-and-such really happen that way? Did it actually look and feel as you remember it? Has it changed beyond recognition? Has the significance of the memory changed?

25. Write a poem that *reverses* a particular experience you remember. If it seemed happy, twist it around to sadness. If it seemed boring, make it exciting. If you won something, let yourself lose—or let someone else win. Free yourself from the literal facts. Fictionalize. Imagine what might have happened if you had taken a wrong turn on the way home, or had found your mother's lost watch, or had said "yes" instead of "forget it."

26. Write a poem about someone else's memory. Choose (1) something told by a friend or relative, or (2) something you've read. Put yourself in that person's body and imagine what the experience might have been like. Flesh out the scene with any details you can pluck out of the air.

27. Contrast a memory with something happening in the present. Describe one in detail, then the other. Or jump back and forth, from present to past to present and so on. If you like, contrast two memories. If you're ambitious, contrast *your* memory of an event with someone else's conflicting version: possibly an opportunity for a poem in dialogue form.

28. Imagine something happening in the distant future, perhaps a kind of science fiction. But present it in the form of a "memoir," as if it has already occurred and has settled into the past. When poet and novelist Denis Johnson learned that a book of his poems had been printed on paper that would last for hundreds of years, he decided that his audience would be the people of the twenty-fifth century. Place your "memoir" of the future at least 100 years from now.

29. Memorize a poem. One of the virtues of poetry is that you can practically ingest it. (Try that with *War and Peace*.) The exiled Russian poet, Irina Ratushinskaya, wrote poems with sharpened matchsticks on bars of soap when she was imprisoned. Once she had memorized a poem, she washed her hands to rub out the words. Try memorizing a poem in a form you enjoy, maybe a sonnet or a villanelle. Try memorizing something in a foreign language. Rhymed, metrical poetry may be the easiest to remember, but try learning a free verse poem by Robert Creeley or Denise Levertov or Frank O'Hara by heart.

30. Put aside the drafts of a poem you've been working on. Rebuild the poem entirely from memory—changing, cutting, and adding as you proceed. Compare versions. See if the new draft from memory has unclogged the poem and opened it up to fresh possibilities. Does it flow more smoothly?

31. Compose a poem entirely in your head, memorizing as you go. Don't set it down on paper until you have a finished draft. (You can always revise later.) Try doing this when you really don't have ready access to pen and paper: riding the bus, waiting in line, walking home. The process, of course, works better with short poems, and mnemonic devices such as rhyme and meter surely help.

32. Veer off from the set facts of a memory. Begin the poem by setting a scene as you remember it, richly detailed and evocative, but then open it up to things that *didn't* happen. Have the campfire you remember spread to the orange grove; or lose your way in an unfamiliar city; or find a rowboat under the willows and steal it for a moonlit adventure on the

lake. The familiar experience is your diving board—use it to spring into a pool of surprises. Use the memory as a booster rocket you can jettison as soon as you reach outer space; the orbit of the poem should be *far* from its launch site.

33. Write a meditation about memory itself. What is the significance of memory? How is it tricky and elusive? Why is forgetfulness important in its own right? Play with ideas, but load the poem with images, metaphors, specific details, and a wide, adventurous vocabulary.

THINKING

Thinking permeates most poems. We might, in fact, define poetry as *singing thought*. Robert Graves calls it "a way of thought—non-intellectual, anti-decorative thought at that—rather than an art." Marvin Bell observes that poetry is "*the* art of the mental," but adds that "Without a context of the physical, . . . the mental is disembodied and unconvincing." A poet thinks through a chain reaction of images, through the music of language, through associations and intuitions—sometimes even through logic and rationality, like an honest-to-goodness philosopher.

In *Poetry in the Making*, Ted Hughes discusses learning how to think. Arguing that "if we do not somehow learn it, then our minds lie in us like the fish in the pond of a man who cannot fish," he urges us to "catch those elusive or shadowy thoughts, and collect them together, and hold them still so we can get a really good look at them." He concludes by saying, "We want the progress of thoughts . . . not then concentrating on one point, but raising one point after another and concentrating on each in turn."

One particular kind of thinking is exemplified by *surrealism*. André Breton defines the term as "pure psychic automatism, by which it is intended to express, verbally, in writing, or by other means, the real process of thought." Surrealism relies on free association, dreams, and the "play of thought." It may be easier to understand it by *looking* at some surrealist paintings by Salvador Dali, Max Ernst, René Magritte, and Giorgio de Chirico. Then, if you're interested, get a copy of Michael Benedikt's anthology, *The Poetry of Surrealism* (Little, Brown, 1974). Remember, though, Wallace Stevens's remark that surrealism was like making a clam play an accordion.

34. Think your way through something—a problem or an issue or an idea—in the course of writing a poem. Collect your thoughts on the page, as chaotically as you like. Mull over it and try to view it from different angles. Feel free to change direction, interrupt yourself, quote from something you remember, give a personal example. You're placing

evidence on a courtroom bench, in effect, but you might liken it to a fisherman dumping a day's catch in a bin, watching the different shapes and colors slide together and apart.

35. Write a nonsense poem, like Lewis Carroll's "Jabberwocky." (André Breton calls Carroll a precursor of surrealism, a "surrealist in nonsense.")

36. Write a surrealist poem. Allow irrational thoughts and dream images and crazy metaphors and weird situations into the poem. Think of Dali's drawing of a woman whose torso is a chest of drawers, with an undergarment hanging out of one.

EMOTION

Many of us begin writing poems because we need an emotional outlet. That kind of writing may have therapeutic value, but a real poem has to *embody* an emotion — giving it life, articulating it in gripping words, transforming it into a vivid experience the reader can undergo — not just *express* an emotion. Wordsworth says that poetry springs from emotion "recollected in tranquility," but it takes a special effort to cultivate that tranquility, to channel our emotional flood tides.

It's all too easy to treat poetry as a stage upon which to "emote," spilling out our feelings. Sometimes a passionate outburst really does overwhelm us. But when that happens, there are *always* powerful rhythms, piercing and well-chosen words, and stunning figures of speech that carry the emotional burden. Often it helps more to *restrain* the emotions, to give the poem some tension by speaking around them. In any case, you might as well avoid concentrating on feelings, since they will work their way into your poem anyhow — if you really have them.

One particular danger is *sentimentality* — emotion that has deteriorated into cliché, automatic response, easy tears. It is falsified emotion, trumped up and padded, mushy and sloppy, too sweet for words. One writer defined sentimentality as "loving something more than God could." If you see expressions like "the joy of motherhood," "love so rare and true," or "my heart beats wildly," you're either in the presence of a sentimentalist or a conartist. If you're not sure what I mean, visit a greeting card store and examine as many "serious" cards as you can stomach. You should soon feel surfeited with all that saccharin.

Of course, it isn't emotion that is bad, but the feeble expression of it — and the fakery.

37. Although many greeting cards are written in verse, they are almost always unsatisfactory as poems: too trite, too sentimental. They have a "plug in" quality, suitable for large numbers of senders, but accom-

plished by overgeneralizing. (This is where the cliché "the lowest common denominator" comes into play.) For this exercise, find a greeting card and "translate" the message into a real poem, depending on fresh images, subtle rhythms, and a lively, specific vocabulary. For example, if the greeting card says "I love you more than words can tell,/ And that is why I wish you well," try specifying a scene, perhaps a memory ("I watched in silence as you slipped/ Your wavy hair in a barrette") or a comment ("I love the way you tilt your head,/ listening to jazz, the long waves trembling") or a speculation ("The panels open to a light/ As stunning as your eyes, but flat"). Make everything specific. Try to *suggest* the emotion without stating it directly. If you want a better sense of what I have in mind, take a look at any greeting card directed to a parent and then read Robert Hayden's poem about his father, "Those Winter Sundays." Or read Carolyn Kizer's "Great Blue Heron," which is about her mother.

38. Think about a general emotion, such as love, hate, anger, or depression, and write a poem about a specific *outburst* of that emotion (either remembered or imagined). Create the whole scene through images and action. Do not name the emotion itself anywhere in the poem.

39. Find an old poem of yours that seems too general or too sentimental in how it reveals your feelings. Make it specific, imagistic, surprising, even startling. Look especially for new words that evoke the senses.

LOVE

In Canto LXXXI, Ezra Pound says "What thou lovest well remains/ the rest is dross." That's a pretty good gauge for poetry, in that all poems are rooted in love — though not all qualify as "love poems."

The problem with love poetry is that it's often clichéd, dishonest (preferring to fake what we're *supposed* to feel), and hard to do well. Somehow a love poem must refresh, revive, reexamine, and reimagine love in its particular guises and embodiments.

Roland Barthes's marvelous book, "A Lover's Discourse: Fragments," is a good place to start this reconsideration. We might think of a love poem as, in the words of Barthes, a "site, however exiguous, of an *affirmation.*" Here are some of the section headings in the book:

"Adorable!"
To Love Love
"All the delights of the earth"
"I want to understand"
"When my finger accidentally . . . "
Events, Setbacks, Annoyances

> Inexpressible Love
> This can't go on
> The Absent One
> "I have an Other-ache"
> The Other's Body
> "Special Days"
> The Informer
> Making scenes

There are many more in the book, but we might take the hint that love is infinitely faceted, and that if we keep turning this prism to the light stunning flashes of the spectrum will burst forth, refracted, striking us with the necessary surprise of all art. Barthes draws his material from all sorts of reading and from conversations with his friends. Of course, how philosophical we can be about love is another matter. Keats says "everything that reminds me of her goes through me like a spear." One way or another, the poem has to be that kind of reminder.

40. Write a love poem that seems to be about something else. Talk *around* your strong feelings; don't declare them directly.

41. Write a poem celebrating what you love most about being alive. Be specific. Lavish images upon the poem.

42. Write a hate poem, or a curse.

43. Update a love poem you enjoy from the past. What will it take to bring it into your own world? What contemporary things and habits will militate against it?

44. Write an erotic poem, a poem about sex. It can be veiled, as long as it's not coy and cloying. Or it can be explicit and graphic. It can celebrate or bemoan. Its mood can be ecstatic, furious, bored, puzzled, embarrassed, or bawdy. It can be mysterious or "anatomically correct." It can be a fantasy or a nightmare. It might not *seem* to be about sex at all, but the words must have their own "sensual strut," as Dylan Thomas puts it. If you're feeling audacious, write a sexy poem that never mentions sex or erogenous zones.

OPPOSITES

In *The Marriage of Heaven and Hell*, William Blake says, "Without Contraries is no progression. Attraction and Repulsion, Reason and Energy, Love and Hate, are necessary to Human existence." It's easy, in writing poems, to get stuck within the limits of what's familiar and comfortable, to write the same poem over and over. In one way that's unavoidable, since we write poems out of what we are. Yet it doesn't hurt to stretch yourself (well, maybe it *does* hurt, but it's still a good idea) by looking at things from different perspectives, by questioning ourselves and our writing, by turning things upside down.

One way to open your mind to new possibilities, new insights, is to change course 180 degrees and head in the opposite direction. This may involve simply reading a different kind of poetry, maybe in a freer or tighter style than what you normally write. If you habitually cling to logic and reality, read some surrealist poetry. Try to work *against* your strengths and preferences. Sometimes that's where the real poetry resides. (Robert Bly has discussed how Carl Jung's formulation of four personality types — the intuitive and the factual, the intellectual and the emotional — applies to poets, pointing out that Frost, an intuitive poet, sought out facts and particulars, and how Robert Creeley, an intellectual poet, sought out feelings.)

Another word for opposite is *antithesis*. One sense of this term is literary: Jack Myers and Michael Simms, in *The Longman Dictionary of Poetic Terms*, define it as "a rhetorical figure that juxtaposes opposite ideas (or conclusions) of similar grammatical constructions so that a balance of tensions is achieved." Alexander Pope was a master of the device, as in the lines

'Tis more to guide, than spur the Muse's steed;
Restrain his fury, than provoke his speed
   — *"Essay on Criticism"*

(Those lines are also, incidentally, an example of the *heroic couplet* — see "Iambics.")

45. Read a poem by another poet. Then write a poem of your own that's (in some way) the *opposite* of what you've read. If the model is about a peaceful scene in the country, yours might be about a traffic jam, or a quiet winter night in a metropolis, or a range war. There are many ways to go in another direction. Follow your instincts, but be specific. Echo or undercut as much of the original poem's imagery as you like — or veer off entirely.

46. Write a poem about a "world" that seems an opposite of your own. This world could be from a different layer of society, or a different part of the globe, or a different order of reality — based on fantasy, dream, myth, heaven, hell, reincarnation, and so on.

47. Read a poem and write a companion piece, on the same subject, in a totally opposite form. If the original is in iambic pentameter, switch to short-lined free verse, perhaps. If the original rhymes, drop the rhyming. If the original is abstract, load your poem with imagery. If the original

has a sincere, gentle tone, make yours acerbic and ironic.

48. List your favorite season, color, place, relative, time of day, leisure activity, historical figure, weather, newspaper section, kind of work, mode of transportation, and type of music. Then try to list the *opposite* for each of these favorites. (You don't necessarily have to dislike them!) Write a single poem that includes or touches on several of these opposites — maybe a winter poem about a carpenter riding the subway, reading the Science supplement of the *New York Times*. Of course, you can always go on to write about *any* of these favorites or opposites, either singly or in concert.

49. Write a poem that *considers* opposites: differences between plus and minus, night and day, man and woman, east and west, anything of interest. One way to do this is to use antithesis, but you can try it in a much wilder and more experimental way. Let opposites collide.

CHANCE

Chance or luck may *always* be a part of writing. And the poet's gift may be to recognize when an accident is a lucky break, not just breakage. But some poets, inspired partly by the random methods of composers like John Cage, have used chance as a poetic technique.

For "The Assassination," a poem about the murder of Robert Kennedy, Donald Justice used chance methods, jotting words he wanted to use on file cards, shuffling them along with cards that indicated grammatical relationships, and writing his lines based on the cards he drew. It was still his choice of words (and they are appropriate to the subject, like "ballroom," "newspapers," "pulse," and "surge"), but the surprising combinations make the poem startling, eerie, dreamlike, powerful. It's a good way to deal with material that's topical, familiar to the point of cliché, and potentially sentimental and overblown.

You might seek inspiration for "random poems" in the dripped and spattered "action paintings" of Jackson Pollack, in the artworks and stunts of Dadaism (the precursor to Surrealism), in the hexagrams of the Chinese *I Ching* (where the pattern of falling sticks — or coins if you prefer — tells your fortune and offers hints to the spirit), in Tarot cards, in dice, in Scrabble pieces, in flash-cards, and so on.

Jackson MacLow, who has experimented widely and wildly with chance methods, reports: "I wrote many poems in eventual verse, the numbers of events (almost always single words in this period) in lines being determined by various chance means — dice, playing cards, random digits, the *I Ching*, &c." He says that "the number of events in a line is determined by the number of letters in the word (in the title or other 'index string') which the line spells out, & the events are words, word strings of various kinds, &/or (in a few of the poems) silences."

John Cage found the titles for his books *M* and *X* by "subjecting the twenty-six letters of the alphabet to an I Ching chance operation." He writes what he calls "mesotics": "*A given letter capitalized does not occur between it and the preceding capitalized letter.*" He adds that some mesotics "resemble waterfalls or ideograms."

Some poets have devised computer programs that work on the principle of randomness. The results usually seem silly and frivolous, although every so often there's bound to be an arresting phrase, a felicitous combination. As generators of raw material, computers might be useful, as long as a living, breathing poet can separate the grain from the chaff.

At best, chance may open up new possibilities. Freak expressions, the breaking free from habit, the serendipity of stumbling upon just the right words—all could be useful. The danger consists of turning poetry into a mere game. As Karl Shapiro says, "Poetry is never play to the poet; language is."

50. Open a book (perhaps an encyclopedia volume) to any page and start writing a poem about what you find. Anything random (such as turning on the radio) will work just as well.

51. Go outside and take a walk or a drive. Keep on going until you come upon something that strikes you as unusual or peculiar—something you don't expect. It may simply be something lying in the street or by the road, perhaps a rusted harmonica. Or it may be sheep grazing in a front yard littered with tires. When you've made your "find," return home and write a poem about it.

52. Write words that interest you on cards. They can come from anywhere: newspapers, other poems, dictionaries, conversation. Spend some time jotting them down at random. When you've got a sizable stack, shuffle the cards and draw them out, placing them in horizontal rows, two to five cards per row. (Vary the number.) These rows will be the lines of your poem, which you now write by connecting the words, filling in the spaces between to make some kind of sense. Feel free to cheat if it makes the poem better.

53. Alternately, cut up a poem that dissatisfies you—either one of your own or someone else's. Toss. Transcribe what falls to the table, rearranging as you go. Some of the lines will seem nonsensical, which may be good or bad. Some may seem like gifts. If you only like a couple of the combinations that fall into place, consider starting a new poem that uses them and jettisons the others.

IMAGINATION

In his *Biographia Literaria*, Samuel Taylor Coleridge calls imagination "the living power and prime agent of all human perception, and as a repetition in the finite mind of the eternal act of creation in the infinite *I am.*" For the poet, it is essential. Imagination can "flesh out" what's sketchy or abstract, if you're reporting on things more or less as they are, realistically. But it can also conjure up something that never was — not until your poem, at least.

Every exercise in this book requires imagination and offers you a chance to let it blossom. So turn to any page and choose one — or simply put the book aside and commune with the blank page, letting your imagination send down its roots.

X. *Things To Write About*

Although some poets strive to evade a definable subject in their poems, the easiest way to pique the reader's interest is by making your poems *about* something in particular, something interesting. Wonderful, fresh, captivating subject matter will often, in fact, make the poem. The poem simply has to set it down clearly—almost to get out of the way. And what interests us? Other people—like or unlike ourselves. Nature, the planet we live on, the animals and plants and rivers and mountain ranges and ice caps and rain forests. Places. Stories about people and creatures and the places in which they find themselves. "Human interest" explains it in part, but "Nature" would encompass more. Either, though, would be elixir to the spirit.

SUBJECTS

In "Writing Off the Subject," an essay in *The Triggering Town*, Richard Hugo notes "A poem can be said to have two subjects, the initiating or triggering subject, which starts the poem or 'causes' the poem to be written, and the real or generated subject, which the poem comes to say or mean, and which is generated or discovered in the poem during the writing." He adds that the poet "may not be aware of what the real subject is but only have some instinctive feeling that the poem is done."

Wallace Stevens once taunted Robert Frost by saying "You write on subjects." Frost retorted, "You write bric-a-brac." Covering a subject is not really the point, unless you want a poem that sounds like a term paper. It's really a question of how much you want to include or exclude, whether you want to hold things steady or let them fly. Do you think of your subject as the diving board or the pool itself? Or is it more like the air—transparent, indefinable, hovering over the familiar world? Your sense of how hard-edged a subject should be will probably vary from poem to poem.

1. Choose a subject that interests you and begin a poem about it. As soon as you feel a dropping-off of interest, switch the subject abruptly. (You can always revise for a smoother shift later, if necessary, although the sudden jump may energize the poem.) Write on that subject as long as you can keep the verbal energy from flagging. Think of it as a kind of

relay race; as soon as you've sprinted a certain distance, pass the baton. Don't, incidentally, confuse intensity with loudness and exclamations. The excitement of a poem may consist in its powers of quietness and introspection. Keep "writing off the subject," zigzagging in new directions, until you sense the poem ending.

2. Write a poem that is *not* about anything in particular. Instead of beginning with a particular topic (for example, the beauty of summer), begin with an image (such as changing a car's oil on a muggy day) and go on from there, dodging all impulses to zero in on any subject, letting your mind free-associate, jumping from the oil change to the memory of a hike around a lake, perhaps, and from that to something embarrassing, such as getting lost on the way to your senior prom. Do your best to evade an obvious subject. The point, of course, is to let the subject stay submerged, a bit mysterious, infinitely suggestive.

3. After James Dickey's first poetry collection came out, he made a list of "eighty or ninety subjects for poems" that he'd stored up in notebooks and wanted to write about. (He mentions that in *Self-Interviews*, a book of tape-recorded monologues edited by Barbara and James Reiss.) Make your own list of at least a dozen specific subjects you'd like to explore—the more specific the better. Here's a short list of Dickey titles that might indicate the breadth of his interests:

> "Dover: Believing in Kings"
> "The Lifeguard"
> "Listening to Foxhounds"
> "The Heaven of Animals"
> "In the Tree House at Night"
> "The Owl King"
> "Between Two Prisoners"
> "In the Lupanar at Pompeii"
> "The Hospital Window"

Once you've got your list, start writing. If the poem, as you write it, starts to veer away, taking a detour from your intended subject, let it. But if you manage to hold your gaze steady and keep things interesting, that's fine as well. Even if you stray from your initial subject, you can often return to it at the end—or echo it in some way.

4. Ask someone to suggest a subject to you. Regardless of how much you know about it, plunge into the subject and start swimming. Whether it's coral reefs or working on an oil rig or how coins are minted, let the subject suggest associations and likenesses as you write your poem. (Of course, you could always research the subject, but try to see how re-

sourceful you can be, how imaginative and crafty. Since it's been said that poetry is a lie that tells the truth, be a good liar. But don't falsify.)

STORIES

Stories are a wonderful way to enchant and entrance a reader. Sometimes we may feel they belong in prose, not poems, that novels let a story unfold naturally, that poems should be lyrical and song-like, but that's an unfortunate and artificial limitation. Homer is our master here, and his *Iliad* and *Odyssey* give us enduring models of how words can both sing and tell.

Narrative poems (which tell a story) are usually strengthened by the virtues we associate with lyrics: economy, word music, images, and metaphors. Similarly, good lyrics often have a secret or camouflaged plot, a suggestion of action either *in* the poem or *around* the poem (just before or just after). Lyric poems capture the moment of crisis, narrative poems the unfolding of a conflict. Lyric poems represent stasis, the "still point of the turning world" in T.S. Eliot's words, while narrative poems represent action and motion, the turning itself (just as we have plot turns and twists).

Story poems can draw on all the techniques of fiction, but must concentrate them in lines. (Prose poems that are narrative will inevitably seem like short short stories.) Plot (the thread of action that runs through the story), character, setting, scenes, dialogue, description, and exposition (the explanation of a situation) all have a place in narrative poetry. The poet will want to consider the *point of view* (who's speaking): is it subjective (I) or objective (he or she)? is it omniscient (all-knowing) or limited (giving only the observable facts)? is it spoken or thought? is it wide-awake or dreamlike? is it straightforward or stream-of-conscious? is it colloquial, perhaps in dialect, perhaps mangled or misspelled, or is it conventionally proper? The poet can use *flashbacks* (sudden shifts to events in the past) or *flashforwards* (sudden time leaps to the future). Vivid images or gestures can *foreshadow* or suggest actions to come later, like omens or portents. (The clatter of pans, for example, might foreshadow a later explosion.)

Narrative poems take some time to set forth and resolve, but they can't ramble carelessly. Even if the poet wants a strolling pace, the language must be tight, economical.

5. Tell a story as clearly and concisely as you can in a lined poem (either in meter or in free verse). Take Thomas Hardy's advice to Ezra Pound to "concentrate on subject matter." Remember that, since it's a story, you have to flesh out scenes and characters while advancing the

plot. Remember also that, since it's a poem, it must be concentrated, economical in its language. That doesn't mean your pace can't be easygoing and your tone can't be conversational; it means you have to squeeze out the prosiness, all the loose ends and extra phrases. It helps to begin a story *in medias res*, in the middle of things, with some action already in progress. If no story grabs you immediately and insists you recount it, search for narrative material by (a) recalling stories told by your parents and grandparents, (b) thinking of something embarrassing, absurd, terrifying, or peculiar that once happened to you (and if this seems elusive, try concentrating on different periods of your life—early childhood, school days, trips, work experiences—and see what you can conjure up), (c) borrowing something from a story you've read in a newspaper, magazine, or book and then adding your own details, shifting the point of view, rearranging the circumstances (a kind of jump start).

6. Write from a point of view *not* your own and tell a story, perhaps making it up as you go, inventing details, sketching characters, shifting the scene, throwing in comments, making things happen. Do this in a poem in verse, perhaps in meter. Here are some possible points of view: documentary filmmaker, detective, carpenter, trash collector, hospital volunteer, reporter, concert promoter, executive, social worker, forest ranger, psychiatrist. In effect, your poem will be a *dramatic monologue*, spoken through a character or *persona* (Greek for mask) rather than through your own voice. But for this occasion, don't emphasize the speaker's life. Simply use the viewpoint to help conjure up a story about *others*. (Notice that the suggestions I made were for occupations, not actual people, so you can slip into the role without impersonating someone real.) Don't let the reader know explicitly what your own imagined role is; simply let it help you focus on storytelling material. Start by reconstructing a scene, using your five senses, perhaps bringing in terms your "role model" might use. Think about the *objects* of your attention and the space or place where everything is occurring. If you get stuck with your story, say "But then. . . . " and see what follows. If all else fails, take a detour and make it strange.

7. Suggest a story by using nothing but images—no explicit action. Shift from image to image as a movie director would cut to different scenes. Let the story dawn upon the reader just at the end of the poem.

8. Write a story in a strict form such as a sestina or villanelle. Or write a narrative poem in heroic couplets (iambic pentameter rhymed in pairs).

Poets To Consult

Thomas Hardy, Robert Frost, George Crabbe. In recent years, a number of poets have written book-length narrative poems (or, in some case, novels in verse): Jimmy Santiago Baca, Nicholas Christopher, Brooks Haxton, and Vikram Seth, for example. Rita Dove's *Thomas and Beulah* (Carnegie-Mellon Univ., 1986), Yusef Komunyakaa's *Dien Cai Dau* (Wesleyan Univ., 1988), and Stephen Dobyns's *Cemetery Nights* (Penguin, 1987) all do interesting things with narrative.

PEOPLE

Many poems include people, but it's also possible to focus on a single person, to make a character sketch or a full-scale portrait, much as a painter or photographer would do. The poet can use the wiles of language to capture the person's speaking voice or the way he or she thinks. The portrait poem can be starkly objective or wildly subjective but should try to suggest something beyond or beneath the surface — to get at character itself.

9. Write a poem that's a portrait of someone you know, have known in the past, or have read about. Use plenty of facts and names and specific details. The portrait that emerges should practically jump out at the reader.

10. Write a caricature of someone, a grotesque distortion, perhaps with dream imagery or surrealist connections. Don't feel your caricature has to be merely satiric. It can be primitive and savage.

11. Write a self-portrait. The best preparation for this poem is to look at self-portraits by Rembrandt, Van Gogh, Durer, Picasso, and other soul-searchers. You can begin by simply looking in a mirror and studying yourself. Or you can imagine someone else viewing you, sizing you up.

OCCASIONS

Occasional poems have a bad reputation: we think of them as hack pieces that a laureate might be forced to write for the Queen's birthday — flowery, vacuous, uninspired stuff, pro forma and perfunctory. But Goethe calls occasional poems "the first and most genuine of all kinds of poetry." By *occasional* we usually mean "to celebrate or commemorate an occasion," but we could also mean "once in a while, when the mood strikes." Conviction and imagination determine whether an occasional poem matters or not. And the best occasions may not be public holidays but private moments of awareness and insight — happenings worth celebrating.

Here are some types of occasional poems:

Elegy

One of poetry's most ancient functions is to mourn the dead, to lament what has passed away. Wallace Stevens writes "Death is the mother of beauty." Shakespeare notes that what intensifies our affections is "To love that well which thou must leave ere long." A poem that laments a death (and thereby celebrates the life) is called an *elegy*. (Related terms include *dirge, eulogy, lament, requiem,* and *threnody*.)

Aubade and Nocturne

An *aubade* is a dawn or morning poem, in which the lover—Romeo, for example—bids farewell to his beloved. A *nocturne* belongs to the evening. It is really a musical form, as in the nocturnes of Chopin, but there's no reason a poet can't borrow the term. One occasion often worth celebrating is simply a particular moment in the day: dawn, midmorning, noon, late afternoon, evening, midnight. Another occasion might be the day of the week, or a birthday, or a holiday, or an anniversary, or New Year's Day, or the eve of something important, or the morning after. Poets also celebrate individual years, as in the Greek poet C.P. Cavafy's "Days of 1896," "Days of 1901," "Days of 1908," and "Days of 1909, '10, and '11"; or in James Merrill's "Days of 1964" or Gerald Stern's "Days of 1978." We celebrate—and lament—these times *because* they are passing, or have already slipped into the past. We seek to capture, or hold onto, or at least detain, something fleeting and rushing beyond our reach. That's the urge behind all occasional poems: to snatch the passing moment and make something tangible out of that evanescence.

Other Kinds of Occasional Poems

An *epithalamion* (or "epithalamium") is a poem written to celebrate a marriage, originally intended to be sung outside the bridal chamber. A *panegyric* is a poem of praise (like an "encomium" or a "paean"). *Political verse* responds to some news event or political action (or inaction), often in righteous indignation.

(Note: See also "Odes" (which often celebrate an occasion).

12. Write an elegy about someone who has died. If you didn't know the person well, be as personal as you can (the way Whitman speaks about Lincoln in "When Lilacs Last in the Dooryard Bloom'd"). If you were close to the person, try (if you can stand it) to achieve some distance and perspective. It may be wise *not* to try to "settle old scores,"

but to push aside your resentments in order to break through to some new realization.

13. You have a chance to send a brief message to someone who died before you could explain something important, or find out something only that person could reveal. Imagine that you have several minutes' worth of long distance connection to the afterlife. If you whimper and sob, the dead person will hang up. Don't be sentimental! Reach deep down to your real feelings and speak from that source.

14. Write more broadly about dying and loss. That doesn't mean you should be less exact or less specific. But cast your net wide and see what swims in. You're out to retrieve what's otherwise gone.

15. Write an elegy for yourself.

16. Write about some loss in short bursts, brief sections (perhaps numbered, perhaps separated by asterisks) that explore different facets of that loss, looking at it from different angles. You might go through the "five stages of grief" enumerated by Elisabeth Kübler-Ross: denial, anger, bargaining, depression, and acceptance. (Linda Pastan organized her poetry collection *The Five Stages of Grief* according to those categories.)

17. Resurrect something dead and gone and make it live again. Treat it as if it were still alive.

18. Write a poem about a particular time of day, or a day itself (a holiday, for example), or a special year. If you like, follow Cavafy and write your own "Days of (whatever year)." Be specific and generous with your imagery and details.

19. Write a poem celebrating — or bewailing — a marriage (or any other type of "relationship" or "love affair"). Commemorate a divorce, if you like. Nuptials and their dissolution offer rich opportunities for stories, striking details, and word music, but beware of sentimentality, sarcasm, and shrieking.

20. Write a poem of praise, a panegyric. Count your blessings, and enumerate them for the reader.

21. Write a poem responding to a current event in the news.

PLACE

Places can provide fertile ground for cultivating poems. Richard Hugo spoke of the "triggering town," a place that set poems into motion. As Shakespeare points out (or rather as Theseus points out in *A Midsummer Night's Dream*), poets must "give to airy nothing/ A local habitation and a name."

Just as a play needs a setting, the capsule drama of a poem often gains from taking place in a particular locale. It gives us map coordinates for the interplay of language. It gives the scene a sharper focus. It opens up a wealth of specific details that can ease or crowd into the poem. It offers many proper names (cities, streets, shops, rivers, hills) that can act almost as images in themselves. Frequently there is an almost mystical connection between poet and place, the sense that anywhere one has spent time will have infused the sojourner with a vivid feeling for that place, as if it glowed and resonated. These are our "holy places," wherever they might be, whatever we think about religion. Like the giant Antaeus, our strength comes from contact with the earth.

There are many poems, of course, that don't have a particular setting. Sometimes they seem to take place in the mind itself, or in an airy realm that is nowhere. But places can be extremely magnetic, whether they're faintly suggested or lavishly reproduced in miniature. They are a good point of departure for the poem, even if we leave them behind as we plunge deeper into the poem.

22. Write a poem that's set in a particular place, "grounded" in a location from the beginning. Its flights of fancy should be like a kite rising up but connected by a thread to the earth. If no place immediately springs to mind, make lists of places you've lived, places you've visited, and places you'd like to see someday. Then pick one.

23. Describe a place in great detail. Remember that one of the great ways to describe something is to show action — the way Homer describes the shield of Achilles by showing how the smith god Hephaestus makes it. Use all your senses in bringing a place (city, town, hillside, dump, truck stop, wharf, or whatever) to life.

24. Think of the most mysterious place you've ever been. Then write a poem about it, showing the mystery through images and particulars. Try to conjure up a place that's very much "your own" — not a famously mysterious place like Stonehenge or Delphi, unless you have something fresh and strange and unexpected to say about a familiar tourist stop.

25. Write a poem about going somewhere, traveling from one place to another. Or write a poem that contrasts two different places, alternately considering the virtues and vices, the plusses and minuses, of one place versus another.

26. If you have traveled, write a poem about a place you once visited, presenting the scene as vividly as you can remember it. Try not to put yourself in the poem. If you haven't traveled (or don't want to relive a trip), write about an imaginary place you'd like (or hate) to visit. You *could* combine the two approaches, writing about something imaginary in a place you've visited, perhaps an interior you weren't able to see. Concentrate on the scene. Bring it to life — without bringing yourself along as a tourist.

27. If you have snapshots of a distant place, use them as source material and inspiration for a poem.

28. Write about where you come from, your hometown, as though you were a foreign visitor. Any form, free or strict, will do, but you might consider choosing something appropriate to a particular nationality, maybe haiku for a Japanese visitor or *terza rima* for an Italian tourist.

29. In Italo Calvino's *Invisible Cities*, Marco Polo describes fantastic, preposterous cities — such as one that hangs from netting above an abyss. Make up an imaginary city and write a poem about it. Don't forget to name the place.

MODERN LIFE

We may associate poetry with nature, but much poetry lives, like many of us, in the city, whether it's Charles Baudelaire's Paris, Walt Whitman's Mannahatta, Langston Hughes's Harlem, Charles Bukowski's Los Angeles, or even Catullus's Rome. Louis Simpson has talked about a great experiment: "whether writers can live peacefully in the suburbs/ and not be bored to death." Poetry can thrive anywhere, in any surroundings. The important things are to give a sense of place, wherever it may be, and to bring as much life into the poem as possible. We *should* be able to write about the lives we really live, in suburbs or in slums, on the farm or in the office. We shouldn't delude ourselves that only the pretty has a place in poetry.

It can be hard, of course, to make city life into poetry. But, as the "Ashcan" school of painters painted the dingiest and grubbiest parts of New York City, poets like William Carlos Williams found they could depict and celebrate the city in poems like "January Morning." Ugliness could either be presented realistically or transcended. And *was* it in fact ugly?

30. Write a poem that captures the pace of urban life, using gritty (or elegant) details and possibly "street talk." If you're feeling audacious, try to write an urban *pastoral* (usually a poem of the countryside, specifically dealing with shepherds).

ANIMALS AND PLANTS

In his "Daydream College for Bards," W.H. Auden would require every student to "look after a domestic animal and cultivate a garden plot." (Count those as two bonus exercises.) Certainly an astonishing number of wonderful, memorable poems have been written about flowers and trees, both wild and tame animals. It may be easier to praise and celebrate these things that are separate from our human entanglements and yet alive.

In *Poetry in the Making*, Ted Hughes devotes a chapter to "Capturing Animals." He says, "Maybe my concern has been to capture not animals particularly and not poems, but simply things which have a vivid life of their own, outside mine." A good way to practice this escaping from the self is by looking closely at an animal, observing its habits, reading up on it maybe, trying to think and feel from *its* point of view. Ultimately we're trying to plunge deeper into the self, the real one, beneath the surface of our everyday personalities.

If you write about plants, try to avoid portraying a "still life" — the French term is *nature morte*, or "dead nature." You need the sense of plants and animals thriving, alive, unless your poem happens to deal with mortality — and even then, there should be a sense of the life that's gone. You want the poem to give you an almost palpable sensation of a living thing: the feel of a hog's bristles, the scent of honeysuckle, what Galway Kinnell calls "the rank, enduring odor of bear." It doesn't need to be pretty; it needs to leap out at the reader.

We might think of the myth of Orpheus, the poet whose singing was understood by wild beasts, which listened raptly to his performances. There's a sense of communion there, a living connection, and likewise in the story of St. Francis preaching to the animals. Many writers, of course, use animals symbolically, as in Aesop's fables and Chaucer's "Nun's Priest's Tale," which is about the rooster Chauntecleer. Since the early nineteenth century, many writers have written about wildlife more literally, although William Blake and others interested in symbolism have continued to write memorable poems that treat plants and animals as emblems, as in Blake's "The Sick Rose." Walt Whitman, who called his collected poems *Leaves of Grass*, boasted "I think I could turn and live with animals." He believed a leaf of grass was "no less than the journey-work of the stars." Marianne Moore is known for her curiosity about practically everything, in particular animals, such as "the elephants with their fog-colored skin" ("The Monkeys"). Theodore Roethke wrote a series of "greenhouse poems"; Sylvia Plath wrote numerous poems about beekeeping. Both poets have a personal stake in these subjects, since Roethke's father was a florist and Plath's father was an entomologist who specialized in bees, but they focus directly on the living things, their locations, and the activities taking place around them. Their poems are so vivid, and so obsessive, they have great resonance. We're encouraged, by those reverberations, to take the poems both literally (about the plants and animals themselves) and figuratively (about what all that blooming and buzzing might suggest). Even though we may focus on a plant or animal, we can still hint at other meanings, other significances. In many poems, of course, a plant or animal is just *part* of the story, a supporting player or a passing image.

The great danger in writing about plants or animals is sentimentality. Sometimes this is because we're just too fond of our pets or house plants. Sometimes it's because we're "faking" what a poet is supposed to feel, so we end up like the poetaster who carries a lily to proclaim his sensitivity. Most of the bad poetry about other living things comes from an insistence on the "pathetic fallacy," the idea that nature mirrors us and our feelings. The first step away from that self-indulgence should be to treat the plant or animal on its own terms, rather than imposing our own. Being objective does not rule out feelings; it's simply a necessary act of respect. This may be an ethical consideration, but it has an aesthetic point, in that good poems discover something unexpected about the familiar world; they don't rehash our personal opinions and superficial feelings.

There are several good ways to approach plants and animals. First, by direct personal observation, looking until you've discovered all you can. Second, by consulting field guides, such as the ones by Roger Tory Peterson and the Audubon Society. Third, by reading what naturalists and other writers, such as John McPhee and Annie Dillard, have written. Fourth, by joining a bird-watching club or taking a course in gardening or participating in activities of organizations like the Sierra Club and Greenpeace. Remember that one of the worst kinds of sentimentality is assuming that "nature" will always be here for us, even in our technological world. Don't treat plants and animals as scenery—among other things, it makes for bad poetry.

31. Write a poem about an animal. The point is get outside yourself and look at another creature closely. For that reason, it might be wise to avoid writing about a pet—unless you can detach yourself enough to give the animal a fresh, objective look. (That might be a good exercise in itself.) You can write from the animal's point of view, as Philip Levine adopts the outlook of a pig arriving at a slaughterhouse in "Animals Are Passing from Our Lives." You can incorporate reading about an animal, as Marianne Moore based many of her poems on articles in science and natural history magazines. You can take a field trip to the zoo and study an animal, as Rainer Maria Rilke did before writing "The Panther," in which he observes that the creature must see nothing but bars, and "behind a thousand bars, no world." You can let your imagination loose, as James Dickey does in "The Heaven of Animals." You can be humorous, celebratory, respectful, curious, precise. But try to avoid sentimentalizing the beast. Cuteness is one quality you want to avoid.

32. Write a poem about a tree or a flower. You might want to use

some action (such as climbing a maple or raking leaves) to frame this description. Be specific and use words that involve the five senses, including the hard-to-explain ones of touch, taste, and smell. Remember that Joyce Kilmer's "I think that I shall never see/ A poem as lovely as a tree" insults both poems and trees.

33. Base a poem on a wildlife documentary. You can imitate the cinematic style if you like, panning across a watering hole or depicting a gallop in slow motion, but you need not act like a camera. Do any research you feel is needed, but on the other hand feel free to open up your imagination.

34. Write a fable in verse, like those of La Fontaine but modernized, in which the animals represent some human quality. Do the results sound overly artificial? If so, try by degrees to make the poem more realistic, more specifically grounded in nature. Your proportion of "human" to "animal" will probably be weighted too heavily on "our" side at the start.

35. Begin a poem by imitating, copying, or quoting from a field guide. Go on from there, either making up a story, or filling out a scene, or simply contemplating the plant or animal you've chosen. You might jump to something that seems analogous, such as moving from a description of how a starfish devours an oyster to a speculation about the paradoxical beauty of night bombing.

36. Gerard Manley Hopkins writes "Long live the weeds, and the wilderness too!" Write about something in nature you wouldn't think worth celebrating in a poem. Find a way to praise it without irony. You might make it a wilderness poem, or a swamp poem, or a desert poem.

37. Write a poem (perhaps in long free-verse lines) that enumerates as many specific things about a plant or animal as you can summon up. (This kind of listing in a poem is called a *catalog*; much of Walt Whitman's poetry is written in this form, as is much of the Old Testament.) These details can be a mix of the scientific, the descriptive, and the fanciful. As long as they are interesting and exact, it doesn't matter. The results will be a kind of litany, a chant about a particular living thing.

38. Choose a plant or animal you'd like to write about. Make a list of the things, sayings, and ideas we conventionally associate with that plant or animal (for instance, that a rose symbolizes romantic love, that its thorns complement its beauty, that its folded petals suggest secrecy and espionage). Write a poem that gradually peels away these conventional associations to give us a fresh look at the thing itself.

39. Write a poem in which you *define* an animal or a plant. Use all your wiles and any sources you can plunder. An okapi is *what*? A trillium is *what*?

40. Write about a walk in the woods, or a hike up a mountain, or a

day in the country, or a swim in a river, or an afternoon working outside, perhaps digging weeds in a garden or picking apples—something that will let you notice a number of plants and animals in the same poem.

41. Write a poem about some other aspect of nature: looking at stars, for example, or studying rock formations.

OBJECTS

Pablo Neruda tells us "It is well, at certain hours of the day and night, to look closely at the world of objects at rest," at the "used surfaces of things, the wear that the hands give to things." Other poets have echoed this feeling. In a section of his anthology, *News of the Universe* (Sierra Club, 1980) devoted to "The Object Poem," Robert Bly writes "In the last sixty years, a wonderful new poem has appeared. It is the object poem, or thing poem." He mentions (and includes samples of) Rainer Maria Rilke's "seeing" poems—such as one about the "Palm of the Hand"—and Francis Ponge's "object" poems—such as one about an oyster and another about "The Delights of the Door." The Germans even have a word for it: *Dinggedicht*, meaning "thing-poem."

Thales, a pre-Socratic philosopher, observed "There are gods in all things." One of the poet's jobs is to find the divine in the everyday, the beauty in ordinary things, to be (as Thomas Bolt puts it) a "reporter of the unimportant."

Keep in mind, too, that a poem is also an object, something palpable, something with heft.

42. Write a poem about an ordinary household object, or a tool, or an article of clothing, or something very familiar that you take for granted. Study the object until you begin to see it freshly, differently. Look for what it resembles, what it suggests, where it came from, what it *could* be used for. If you like, make it seem strange, exotic, even bizarre.

43. Write a poem about something that really *is* unusual, weird, out of the ordinary, not part of your everyday experience. In this case, however, make it seem perfectly natural. To do this, you may have to place yourself in a different world, in the consciousness of a different person— like a Micronesian who fishes by dangling a line from a kite made of breadfruit leaves.

Poets To Consult

Pablo Neruda, Francis Ponge, Rainer Maria Rilke, Charles Simic, May Swenson

XI. Other Arts, Other Influences

Contrary to what some people think, poetry is not insulated from the rest of the world. It draws freely and copiously from other languages, other cultures; it borrows methods and material from mythology, music, painting, sculpture, photography, history, politics, science — and anything else it can absorb. Think of the arts and sciences — psychology, philosophy, anthropology, botany, zoology, astronomy, economics, sociology, chemistry, physics — and you have the stuff of poetry. But it's not confined to academic fields by any means: cooking, fishing, car repair, weaving, carpentry, and dollmaking offer as much — maybe more — to the poet in the know, alert for metaphoric connections and new ways to make poems come alive. The material always changes, of course, in the process, condensed and transformed from the merely factual or theoretical into the beautiful (however plain or hideous its details may be). The sections of this chapter give you a start, but follow your interests and your instincts in expanding the range of your poetic territory. Don't dismiss the value of anything you know that's outside the confines of literature. In fact, try to cultivate other interests. They'll give you worlds of imagery, words, facts, analogous techniques.

TRANSLATION

Robert Frost declared that "Poetry is what gets lost in translation," but those of us who aren't polyglots or great linguists depend on translations for our poetic news from other countries. And many poets have devoted much of their imaginative energy to translating, either to learn how to write, or to make a living, or to honor their poetic debts, or to perform a literary service and labor of love.

In the Foreword to his *Selected Translations:1948-1968*, W.S. Merwin says "I began translating with the idea that it could teach me something about writing poetry." His model was Ezra Pound, who translated widely from Provençal, Italian, French, Chinese, and other languages — and whose epic *Cantos* contain many translations, starting with a passage taken from a Latin version of Homer's *Odyssey*. In his Introduction to *Imitations*, Robert Lowell asserts that "poetic translation — I would call it an imitation — must be expert and inspired, and needs at least as much technique, luck and rightness of hand as an original poem." He chooses to be "reckless with literal meaning" while laboring hard to "get the tone" of the original.

The two poles of poetic translation are faithfulness and freedom. But faithful to what? The prose meaning of a poem? The meter and rhyme scheme? The tone? (According to Lowell, Boris Pasternak considered tone "everything" in a poem.) One kind of faithfulness (as in John Sinclair's translation of Dante's *Divine Comedy*) presents the original text *en face* (on a facing page) from a literal prose translation. Another kind uses free verse to convey the speaking voice of a metrical original which might sound stiff in English meter (Ezra Pound's translations of Li Po, for example). Another kind keeps the meter and possibly the rhyming, as long as the lines sound natural and close to the original (like Stephen Mitchell's translations of Rilke). But the poet can change a good deal for the sake of the *new* version, arguing that what matters is the poem that emerges. How much license can a translator take? It all depends on how much of a poet (or scoundrel) he or she is.

Although an Italian saying observes that a translator is a traitor, it is possible to capture an original not only accurately, but triumphantly. Richard's Wilbur's translations of Molière's comedies such as *Tartuffe* attest to that. They are rhymed in iambic pentameter couplets (to render the characteristic twelve-syllable lines of French); they are gracefully worded, vividly performable, and very funny. Throughout Wilbur's own volumes of poetry, translations are liberally included, very much a part of his collected poetry.

Robert Bly, who has translated many poems from Swedish, German, and Spanish, has written a book called *The Eight Stages of Translation*, in which he explains "One translates a poem in fits and starts, getting a half line here, weeks later the other half, but one senses a process." He breaks down that process into eight stages, noting that the translator usually jumps back and forth from stage to stage instead of proceeding neatly in sequence: (1) making a literal version of the poem; (2) consulting experts on meanings and usage in the original poem; (3) trying to get it into natural-sounding English; (4) putting that version "into American" to get the "spoken quality"; (5) working on the tone; (6) paying attention to sound; (7) asking "someone born into the language to go over our version . . . to find errors that have crept in"; and (8) making "final adjustments."

Bly says "No one can translate well from a poem he or she hasn't learned by heart: only by reciting it can we feel what sort of oceanic rhythm it has, which is a very different thing from analyzing the meter."

Some poets, like Robert Lowell, translate when they are "unable to do anything of [their] own." It can be a good way to keep in practice, or to scout for new material, or to rejuvenate the spirit. It can also be an outlet, a way to flee personal circumstances and limitations. In translating, after all, you form a partnership with a poet you admire. (You're always, however, the junior partner.)

One danger in working outside your own language is "translationese," a dry, flavorless, unidiomatic approximation of poetic language. Too many translations fall into this trap. You can spot them by their unnatural phrasing and their neutral quality. It's bad enough when translations lose texture and color, but sometimes poets are so influenced by this flatness that their own poems turn sickly pale. Be on the lookout.

1. If you know a foreign language, find a poem you like and translate it into English. If you don't know a foreign language well enough, try to find someone who speaks it and can act as your collaborator, supplying literal "cribs" of a chosen poem and any notes or explanations that might be necessary; then rewrite this approximation into a real poem, concentrating on word choices, rhythms, and tone in particular. If collaboration is not possible, start with a prose translation of a poem (many of the Penguin anthologies of foreign verse contain prose renderings beneath the poetic originals) and fashion it into a poem in verse. How faithfully or freely you follow (or depart from) the original depends on your own preferences. How much do you want to serve the original? How much do you want to transform it into your own poem?

2. Whether or not you know a particular foreign language, try to imitate the *sound* of a poem in that language. In their version of Catullus's poem beginning "Odi et Amo" ("I hate and I love"), Celia and Louis Zukofsky imitate the Roman poet's "quare id faciam, fortasse requiris" as "Quarry it fact I am, for that's so re queries" (when the literal meaning of the Latin is "Why that may be, perhaps you ask"). It may actually be helpful *not* to know the language! Let the sounds suggest the meaning.

3. Working from a translation, imitate the contents of the original but *change* the cultural references of the foreign country to those of your own. For instance, if the poet mentions crowds in a piazza, you might transport them to Central Park or a shopping mall. If the original mentions the Day of the Dead, you might switch it to Memorial Day—or the "Night of the Living Dead" if you want to skew the poem wildly. A game of boccie ball might become horseshoes, rice paddies might become a cranberry bog, a sari might become a tube skirt. Feel free to change idioms, word choices, names and places, but try to keep the same line lengths, the same rhythms, and (if possible or desirable) the same tone. The results should be a poem of your own, but it might be honorable to affix a "headnote" below your title (spaced down and indented), acknowledging your debt: *After Dante*, for example.

4. When T.S. Eliot was a student at Harvard, he read Dante in the

original by using a dictionary, although he didn't really know Italian. Try to read a poem that interests you *in the original*, looking up words in an English/foreign language dictionary and jotting them down. When you've finished this note-taking, reword as necessary and arrange the results into a poem.

5. Write an "imaginary translation," something that purports to be from another language, another place, another time.

MUSIC

Some critics lament (and lambaste) the flatness of much contemporary poetry. Certainly the danger of free verse is that it can deteriorate into prose. And the drawback of allowing prosiness into poems is that they may become prosaic, less fully charged. Dry, unmusical poems can be expressive, taken one by one, but when that becomes the prevailing style, something is wrong.

One way to make poems more musical is to omit the explanatory phrases that stretch out much of what passes for prose: "due to," "that should help," "of which there are." Another musical resource is the actual sound of the vowels and consonants. Paying attention to these sounds, noting the difference between "scrape" and "ring," for instance, makes an enormous difference in the poem's music. Rhythms are also crucial—how a line rises and falls, where the pauses occur, how a stanza is paced, how the sentences stretch out over a series of lines, how some of the lines run over to the next lines and others conclude with a period or other punctuation mark.

There's nothing wrong with good prose, and one of the discoveries of twentieth-century poetry is how much of the content and manner of prose can be transported into verse (both free and metrical). But too much prosiness can monotonize the language. That may even be the idea of some poets: to make the rhythms hypnotic, to seem cool, to be dry and neutral and disengaged, to be inconspicuous and unobtrusive, even to approximate a kind of perfection. Usually, however, we don't want poems that sound like business reports—although you can't rule out *any* options that might be expressive and appropriate in a particular poem.

Music, though, is more than a matter of pretty sounds and tripping rhythms. It can clash, whisper, growl, clang, storm, clatter. It can be atonal, as in Arnold Schoenberg's twelve-tone scale, or it can be random noise, as in John Cage's chance compositions. It can sound strange to foreign ears, like African thumb pianos and talking drums, or Indian sitars and tablas. We call beautiful sounds *euphonious* and harsh sounds *cacophonous*, but either can be musical under the right circumstances.

(Ezra Pound defines beauty as "aptness to purpose.") But what, if not mellifluousness, makes something musical in a poem? It can be the sound effects (pretty or not), strong rhythms, effective pauses, repetition and variation.

Plain speaking and simplicity can still be musical. Ornate language and fancy phrasing might be so cluttered and pretentious they lose all their musical interest. Poems can be thick or thin in musical texture, clotted or clear.

Poems can imitate musical forms. "January Morning," by William Carlos Williams, is subtitled a *suite*; it consists of numbered sections arranged like the dance movements of an orchestral suite. Walt Whitman modeled his long, flowing lines partly on the recitatives and arias of Italian grand opera (and partly, of course, on the Old Testament). Michael Harper uses jazz as both inspiration and subject matter in poems such as "Dear John, Dear Coltrane" and "A Love Supreme" (the title of Coltrane's four-movement masterpiece). In a note to *Mexico City Blues*, a sequence of 242 choruses, Jack Kerouac declares that he wants to write like a jazzman blowing his horn and improvising. Basil Bunting read his long poem "Briggflatts," which he called a sonata, aloud to the accompaniment of harpsichord sonatas by Domenico Scarlatti.

Traditional blues has been imitated most notably by Langston Hughes. In each three-line stanza, the first and second lines are identical, except for some slight, perhaps improvised, variations. The third line rhymes with them. Most blues lines have four or five beats, but both shorter and longer lines occur.

Even a complicated, multivoiced form like a fugue can be imitated, as in the German poet Paul Celan's "Death Fugue," which uses repetitions to depict the horrors of the Holocaust. In a fugue, the first voice plays a melody and then, a bit later, a second voice joins in by repeating the melody while the first voice plays something different to harmonize with it. Three, four, and even more voices can be added, until the melodies swirl in and out like intricate interweavings. (Listen to some fugues to get the idea — perhaps those in J.S. Bach's *Well-Tempered Clavier*.) How can poems mimic polyphonic music, when they're capable, normally, of just one sound at a time? By creating an illusion, repeating phrases in a way that makes them seem interwoven, returning to the initial theme and then varying it, the way Celan repeats the lines "Your golden hair Margarete/ Your ashen hair Shulamith."

Some poets like to play music while they write. Hart Crane found that jazz was a great stimulus to his work. Instrumental music may be less of a distraction, but maybe a piece with words could suggest possibilities, filtering in some of its phrasing to the poem in progress.

Finally, musical poems can be *about* music as well.

6. Choose a piece of music to play while you're writing. Start with any subject — the music itself or something far removed, maybe a memory or a vision — and write a poem. Keep at it until the music stops.

7. Write a poem based on a musical form. Some possibilities: a twelve-bar blues, a sonata, a symphony, an Indian raga, ragtime, a fanfare, a suite, a march, a nocturne, an operatic recitative and aria, an improvisation on a popular song (or on a favorite poem), a variation on a poetic theme, a sea shanty, an overture, an organ toccata, a fugue or a round, a tone poem. Have a musical example in mind. Decide for yourself what a poem can imitate of the musical form — a pattern of repetition, the length of its lines, the overall mood, the sound of its words.

8. Write a poem *about* a piece of music. Don't be too technical. Use metaphors to bring some visual imagery into a poem about something audible.

9. Put yourself in the position of a composer, a musical performer, or a music critic and speak in that voice. Use historical and biographical facts. Feel free to research the subject before and during the writing of your poem. (The results will be a *dramatic monologue*.)

10. Find a poem (either one you've read or one of your own) that seems flat and dry. What could make it more musical? Words with more character and sound qualities? Different, stronger rhythms? Rhyme or alliteration? Repetition? Reorganization? Go ahead and make the poem more musical, any way you can.

11. Take a poem by another writer and remove phrases from it. Arrange those phrases in a musical construction, repeating and varying as much as you like. If you repeat a phrase, you might change where the line break goes. Add lines from another poem (or an outside source like a newspaper) if you like.

12. Imitate the sound of a musical instrument without mentioning that instrument. Think of the skirl of bagpipes, the wail of a saxophone, the whine of a fiddle, the clatter of castanets. Let the instrument affect your sounds, rhythms, choice of subject, and overall mood.

13. Describe a scene as if it were really music. (James Dickey reports that someone once asked William Blake "when he looked at the sun, if he did not see a bright disk about the size of a half crown. He said, 'Oh, no, I see a multitude of the heavenly host singing and praising the Lord.'")

(Note: Also see the section on "Song.")

MYTHS AND FAIRY TALES

Try to shed the notion that myths and fairy tales aren't true. They may not be factual, but they're true in the real poetic sense: they reveal the inner life and explain the outward actions of our entire species. It's no wonder that psychologists like Sigmund Freud and Carl Jung emphasized their importance, noticed how they exemplified psychological leanings (like the Oedipus Complex) and originated from a common pool (the Collective Unconscious). Jung notes "One could almost say that if all the world's traditions were cut off at a single blow, the whole of mythology and the whole history of religion would start all over again with the next generation." He finds the mythmaking impulse in dreams, in childhood games, and in fantasizing.

The poet can act as a kind of mythmaker but can also draw from the rich storehouse of available myths. (By extension, we can include fairy tales and folk legends here — and religious stories as well.) All kinds of myths, from all over the world, could claim a rightful place in poetry, but the familiar ones, especially Greek myths, have the advantage (and disadvantage) of easy reference and a long literary pedigree: the labors of Hercules, Penelope's weaving and unweaving (designed to foil her suitors), King Midas, Dionysus, the Golden Fleece. The poet who wants to bring in Asian or native American, or African, or Polynesian myths and legends has plenty of explaining and naming to do — not necessarily a bad thing, since the relative freshness and strangeness has virtue and interest in itself. The poet who dips into Greek mythology must decant that aged wine in newly blown decanters, finding the freshness in different ways to present it.

Karl Shapiro says "The poet should read deeply in mythology, esoteric writings, scriptures, and symbolic writings. He will anyway."

14. Modernize a well-known Greek myth. Edward Field's "Icarus" (in his first book, *Stand Up, Friend, With Me*) retells the story of Icarus, the boy who flew so close to the sun that the wax holding together his wings melted from the heat — but in the poem the hero doesn't drown when he falls into the sea but emerges to live anonymously in Manhattan as "that nice Mr. Hicks." Keep the essentials of the myth but change the setting, details, and even names if necessary.

15. Imagine you're a time traveler. Visualize how the world of a myth would look and feel to the immediate listeners of the story. Write a poem as if you were living then. Describe some event that has connections with the myth, making it as realistic or fantastic as you like. Don't feel you have to do any research (although you may if you like). Put yourself there and make up whatever you need for the journey.

16. Retell a fairy tale, giving it a new twist. You might try writing from the point of view of a villain, or a victim, or a savior, or a bystander. You might try framing it as a "true confession," or a session on an analyst's couch, or a monologue in a bar, or a lament wailed under the stars.

17. Make up a new myth, maybe an urban legend, of your own and write a poem presenting it. Use plenty of images. Name names.

18. Read a poem that uses mythology, like Yeats's "Leda and the Swan," and write your own poem in reaction, looking at the myth from a different angle altogether. Keep the original poem's form, if you like, or diverge from it.

PAINTING AND SCULPTURE

In "Poems about Paintings," an essay in his collection *In Radical Pursuit*, W.D. Snodgrass writes about how he once fancied that he'd "write only poems about paintings and have life easy." It seemed a simple way to gather rich material: draw directly from books of reproductions and write about various paintings. The problem, he eventually realized, was his psyche; he couldn't find anything he was "really interested in."

Many wonderful poems have been written about paintings and sculptures, especially in the twentieth century, but we have also been flooded with uninspired poems that merely latch onto paintings like parasites. Writing about artworks should be *more* than an exercise. Start by looking closely at paintings or sculptures. Think about them. Use your imagination to "put yourself" in the scene. Ask yourself the reporter's questions: who? when? where? how? why? Read about painting and artists. Good books to start with include Robert Henri's *The Art Spirit*, Vasari's *Lives of the Great Painters*, and Mai-mai Sze's *The Way of Chinese Painting* (with selections from the *Mustard Seed Garden Manual of Painting*). Read the annotations to Joshua Reynolds' lectures by William Blake, both a great poet and a great painter. Read Michelangelo's sonnets. Read the poems of Wang Wei, one of the best poets *and* painters of the T'ang Dynasty in eighth-century China. Try your own hand at sketching, or painting, or even sculpture. One of the best ways to learn to write better poems is to practice another art or craft; the creative process will be remarkably similar — and transferable.

19. Write a poem about a painting or a sculpture. A reproduction of a work of art can be useful as a point of departure — what matters is how you take off from the picture you choose. There are many ways to proceed. Think about your point of view: who is speaking? It could be a tourist in an art museum, or a scholar investigating an earlier age, or the artist himself, or the artist's model, or a prospective buyer, or a critic, or someone from another planet, or someone *in* the scene itself, perhaps a visitor in the room that's depicted (as in W.D. Snodgrass's poem about a Vuillard painting, "The Mother and Sister of the Artist"). Your reader should *not* have to be familiar with the picture you describe; all the

information (and images) needed to understand the poem should be given within the poem. Sometimes, that background material can be tucked away in the title or in an epigraph (a short quotation or explanation). Don't feel that you're limited to mere description.

20. Imagine a painting or sculpture that doesn't actually exist. If you like, make sketches of it. Then write a poem bringing it to life through imagery, metaphor, rhythms, and/or the shape of your lines and stanzas. In this exercise, you are the painter or sculptor.

21. After spending some time looking at a painting, write a poem about what's *not* there: images beyond the frame, an incident that happened long before the scene depicted in the painting.

22. Try to capture a painting or sculpture through the rhythms of your words—without referring to the artwork in any way. For a poem based on Michelangelo's "Captives," for instance, you might want to use blocky phrases, without the action of verbs, to suggest the unfinished mass of stone; you can punctuate this blockiness with occasional outbursts, like the figures struggling to emerge from marble.

PHOTOGRAPHS

A photograph is a testament of light. We see what the light that's been filtered through a tiny opening, the camera's aperture, tells us. A series of these pictures flipped quickly before our eyes gives us the illusion of action, the cinema. Both photographs and the movies can provide wonderful inspiration for poems, immersing us in imagery, showing us things we didn't know about, and suggesting techniques, analogous ways of proceeding in our poems.

Is your poem in focus? Or is it blurry? Have you framed your subject properly? Is it too light (maybe too obvious and explained away) or too dark (maybe too private or unclear for us to "get the picture")? Does it have a good movie's "continuity"? Does it use close-ups effectively? Does it pan across a scene smoothly? Does it track action as it speeds along? Does it "cut" from scene to scene sharply and neatly, juxtaposing images or actions? Does it look at things from interesting "camera angles"? All of these questions can be helpful in sharpening the way you look at things—and the way you handle those things in your poems. (Jack Myers and Michael Simms have much useful material on cinematic techniques in *The Longman Dictionary of Poetic Terms*.)

23. Write a poem about a photograph. A snapshot from your family album or a photo in today's newspaper can be a good place to start. So can collections of photographs like *The Family of Man* or *Wisconsin Death Trip*. You might also think of Christopher Isherwood's sentence from

The Berlin Stories—"I am a camera with its shutter open, quite passive, recording, not thinking"—and treat it as your motto for this exercise. Focus! Check the light! Frame the shot! Calculate your distance!

24. Write a poem as if you were a director filming a movie. If you don't know much about filmmaking, look closely at the next movie you see and try to figure out what the director is doing. Notice especially how one scene suddenly shifts to another scene—and how you instantly fill in the gaps and adjust as you're watching. Your subject can be anything—even a movie you've just seen.

25. Write a poem from the point of view of someone *in* a photograph or a movie. What is that person like? Try to live under that person's skin through a whole poem.

HISTORY AND POLITICS

History can provide wonderful, powerful material for poetry. In "The Middle Passage," Robert Hayden makes us feel the horrors of the slave trade by presenting a panorama of scenes, a symphony of voices from nearly two centuries ago, rendered in sharp detail and mostly in blank verse. It takes, of course, some knowledge of names and places and particular details to make an historical poem interesting and believable, so you'll want to "bone up" on the past before, during, and even after you've composed your poem.

Although you seldom hear objections to the use of historical material in poems, you hear plenty about politics—which might be called history that's still up in the air. There are two widespread arguments in regard to mixing poetry and politics:

1. Good poems can't be political.
2. All poems are political.

The first is certainly fallacious. Politics harms poetry only when the poet's imagination falters and doctrine (a kind of prolonged cliché) or dogmatism (a dictatorship of the will over the imagination) takes over. We could substitute "religion" for "politics" in that sentence—something that elicits passionate devotion and adherence. There is, of course, no shortage of bad political poetry. As for the second argument, it may be that there's an underlying political slant in all poems, but it seems both tedious and tendentious to belabor the point. Poems have a right *not* to be political, even if polemicists insist that noninvolvement with issues of power and public affairs counts as a kind of involvement, a choice.

26. Write a poem that makes something historical come to life. Do whatever research or background reading you need to get a feel for the time you're writing about. Soak up the details.

27. Write a poem that reverses some historical incident. Keep your focus sharp and your details fresh.

28. Write a poem that is explicitly political—though not necessarily partisan. Don't use slogans unless there's a good *imaginative* reason for including them. (Capturing a mood, perhaps by noting the words on placards at a demonstration, might be a good reason.)

SCIENCE

In *The Double Helix*, James Watson, one of the discoverers of the structure of DNA, says that "science seldom proceeds in the straightforward logical manner imagined by outsiders. Instead, its steps forward (and sometimes backward) are often very human events in which personalities and cultural traditions play major roles." He adds that he believed "the truth, once found, would be simple as well as pretty." And indeed he was right about this molecule, the double helix that bears our genetic code. His credo could apply to poetry as well.

Although C.P. Snow, in "The Two Cultures," observed a split between scientific and literary thought, one of the poet's missions is to bridge distances—and to find a secret companionship between apparent opposites. Science provides wonderful—and underused—matter for poetic exploration.

29. Write a poem that uses scientific terms and concepts: chemical elements and apparatus, details of famous experiments, biological classifications, anatomical parts, laboratory details, the laws of physics.

30. Write a poem that imitates the "scientific method," patiently sorting through data and facts, then proposing a hypothesis to make sense of these findings. Your tone can be serious or playful, awestruck or clinical or zany. (You can emulate a mad scientist, if you like.)

XII. Finishing

There are several senses to *finishing* here. It refers to the actual ending of a given poem. It means polishing and buffing the poem, its *finish*, revising until you've got it right. It deals with wrapping up what you've been working on to make room for new work, new beginnings. Of course, you don't always know when you *are* finished. You might let a poem lie around for weeks, months, years — tinkering with it on and off — before you figure out how to make it work. The point is, the process shouldn't halt. You shouldn't be satisfied with "that tiny insane voluptuousness,/ Getting this done, finally finishing that" — Theodore Storm's words, translated by Robert Bly. In fact, as you're completing one poem, you may also be starting another, ripping apart a lax draft and rearranging it, jotting down impressions in your journal, reading a new book of poems. You can only do one thing at a time, of course, but you'll probably feel it's like juggling. The process is cyclical, and the cycles go on simultaneously, turning at different rates, beginnings and endings intermingled — a wheel in a wheel, as the spiritual puts it.

REVISION

There are two schools of thought on revision. Most poets would probably agree that writing IS rewriting and that most rough drafts need plenty of reshaping, adding and subtracting, rethinking, and nearly infinite tinkering. Some poets, however, think the first draft is the poem, period. Jack Kerouac says "First thought, best thought." Allen Ginsberg points out "Imagination is shapely" and urges poets to put enough energy and passion into the initial act of creation so that repairs are irrelevant, second thoughts nothing but timidity. Certainly John Keats's second thoughts about "La Belle Dame Sans Merci" would ruin the poem if editors ever took them seriously. (His romantic "knight-at-arms" became a "wretched wight.")

Certain short poems may land on our heads complete and unchangeable. Haiku or other poems of sudden insight may wilt under the high-intensity lamp of cogitation. Goethe apparently wrote many of his short lyrics "on the spot," during walks for instance. Robert Bly says that many of the short poems in *Silence in the Snowy Fields* are printed exactly as he first wrote them down. Seamus Heaney has spoken of "inspired quickies." Partly it depends on whether we're taking dictation from the muse (as some poets claim to hear their poems from a deep source within or, in Rilke's case, from a storm outside a castle) or whether we're on our own, struggling for every word, for every inch of line.

In fact, it doesn't much matter *how* we get our poems — as long as we don't copy them verbatim from another poet and pass them off as our own (like the "hero" in Evelyn Waugh's *The Loved One*). In "Adam's Curse," W.B. Yeats points out

> 'A line will take us hours maybe;
> Yet if it does not seem a moment's thought,
> Our stitching and unstitching has been naught.'

The important thing is for the poem itself to seem *right*, regardless of how difficult or easy the poet's labor might have been.

You can, of course, revise the poem-in-progress as you go, making alterations, backing up, crossing out, crumpling the page and starting over from a fresh angle. And you can revise as an afterthought. A poem you're wild about immediately after its birth may disappoint you the next morning, or a week later, by its obvious defects. Virgil is said to have "licked" his poems into shape, working carefully over a few lines a day.

As Thomas Hardy remarked, you don't want to revise so much that you lose the original "freshness" of the poem. But sometimes revising a poem is like administering CPR: your mouth-to-mouth resuscitation and rhythmic pressing of the heart can make the thing breathe, its heart beat more steadily. To revise means to revive.

And everyone has a system of his or her own, a personal nostrum that seems to work on an ailing patient. In his useful, cranky essay, "Nuts and Bolts," Richard Hugo says to use a #2 pencil and cross out vigorously rather than erase corrections. Robert Graves used different writing implements for drafts and revisions. Donald Justice has experimented with different colored pens to indicate different stages of revision. Robert Lowell made corrections with red ink on typescript, even minutes before walking on stage to give a poetry reading. Elizabeth Bishop left blanks in her drafts for words she couldn't get right and taped the drafts above her desk. Shelley, in the flush of inspiration, often left blanks for phrases or lines he didn't have time to mull over in the surge of writing a first draft.

In revising a poem, keep in mind that when you're unhappy with something, it's often the words *around* the trouble spot that need changing. The problem may lie in the context, as Richard Hugo has pointed out.

You usually want to inspect a poem for "prose sense," as Robert Graves points out. Ezra Pound notes that a poem must be "at least as well written as prose." Yeats thought that you should be able to *shout* the words of a poem, or at least declaim them publicly, without any strain. While looking over a rough draft, you should also check for clichés, prosy phrasing, jargon, dull expressions, unclear language, weak imagery (or a lack of it), unwanted sound effects, unfortunate repetitions (such as too many words ending in "-y" or "-ing" in close succession), unwanted grammatical errors, proofreading goofs, and other stupid mistakes. But as the Roman poet Catullus has noted, "Each has his blind spot . . . / the pack on our own back/ that we don't see." (Translated by Peter Whigham.)

It helps, in revising, to read your poem aloud — or ask someone to read it back to you. You can also change your writing tool, from pen to typewriter to pencil to word processor to tape-recorded voice. Sometimes it helps to show your new poems to another person: a fellow poet, a teacher, a classmate (or an entire class), a relative, a friend who doesn't normally read poetry, a perfect stranger. You can weigh responses and sift out the useless ones while trying to act upon the good and suggestive comments. A poetry workshop, in which members exchange and critique each other's poems, can be wonderful or terrible, exciting or boring. Many workshops pose as classes, usually for credit, but there's no reason poet friends can't band together for lively sessions of critical target practice. Ben Jonson and his fellows met in the Mermaid Tavern to talk poetry — their precedent is a good one.

Finally, you can examine revisions by other poets, Yeats for example, to see how masters have tackled the problems of revision.

1. Much writing, both verse and prose, clogs up when there are too many adjectives and adverbs. Mark Twain said that, after finishing a piece of writing, he went through each sentence and deleted *all* of the modifiers; then he went through the piece again, restoring only those adjectives and adverbs that seemed necessary. Perform the same radical surgery on one of your poems. Notice how difficult the deletions are in any poem written in meter. But also notice how many of the lines are *padded* with extra words to fill out the meter. The effect of cutting out the clutter of excess modifiers will be to clean up and sharpen the poem.

2. There is, however, an art to "piling on" the modifiers in some situations. Elizabeth Bishop is a master of the well-chosen adjective. Robert Lowell likes to set up occasional lines as a series of three adjectives, varying the number of syllables in each component: "bronzed, breezy, a shade too ruddy" in "Terminal Days at Beverly Farms." It helps if the adjectives have strong flavors, as Lowell's do. Philip Larkin's

poem celebrating the birth of a child ("Born Yesterday" in his volume *The Less Deceived*) has a memorable crescendo of *five* adjectives before the poem's last noun, culminating with an "Unemphasized, enthralled/ Catching of happiness." See if you can use words in a *series*, perhaps a string of adjectives, either in a poem you want to revise or in a brand-new one.

3. Expand a poem you're writing—either by adding to the end, or filling in the middle, or prefacing the start. Does more need to be said? Does the poem need a detour, a change of subject? Do you need to give more background information? Do you need to camouflage what you're up to? Do you need to flesh out the imagery?

4. Concentrate a poem that seems too long (perhaps the one you just expanded). Delete and combine. Rephrase. Remember that a poem that's *too* short may be undeveloped and unclear, too abrupt to register in the reader's mind—although it might also flash and click for the right reader. A poem that's too long can be redundant, meandering, bloated. Although poems should be concentrated, their scope, range, and ambition may require some length.

5. Revise a poem by rearranging stanzas or sections in a different order. Try shortening, lengthening, and/or varying the line lengths. Try tightening a poem made up of five-line stanzas (for example) into quatrains—or quatrains into tercets. Try breaking a poem that's a single block into stanzas—which can have the same number of lines or a different number in each.

6. Test a rhymed poem for its rhymes. Reject any that seem forced or clichéd (moon/spoon). Hunt for improvements. (Read the "Rhyme" section if this is news to you.) Or try to work rhymes into an unrhymed draft, making free use of slant rhymes and assonance. (It may help to keep the rhymes random, instead of trying to impose a fixed scheme or pattern—though of course *that's* another possibility.)

7. Try smoothing out a draft that seems choppy and awkward; or try roughing up a draft that seems too slick, too smooth. Most poems need some "friction," something to catch the reader's attention. But they also need to flow, to have a compelling sense of movement from start to finish. Read some poems in any anthology and try to specify which poems run smoothly and which proceed more roughly.

8. Try changing your writing tool as you plunge into a revision. If you write first drafts on a typewriter, for example, revise with a pen. Or vice versa.

9. Write a poem that corrects itself as it proceeds, quibbling about and qualifying what it says, backing up and interrupting to try to get things right, the way that Elizabeth Bishop, in "The Sandpiper," observes the bird's actions on the beach: "He runs, he runs straight through

it, watching his toes.// —Watching, rather, the spaces of sand between them."

FAILURE, IRRITATIONS, AND DIFFICULTIES

In *The Bourgeois Poet*, Karl Shapiro writes that the young poet "flunks economics, logic, history. Then he describes what it feels like to flunk economics, logic, history. After that he feels better." It helps if you can see failure as an opportunity, maybe even a gift. Whitman celebrates those who have fallen, those who have *not* won the day. Edward Hirsch, in "Song Against Natural Selection" (*For the Sleepwalkers*, Knopf, 1981), declares "The weak survive!" And we all know what Jesus teaches about the meek and the least and the last and the lowest—though you'd never know from some of the pep-talk sermons over the airwaves. It helps for a poet to be continually dissatisfied, to have enough confidence to be tough on his or her work, to feel at home with "unsuccess." One way to do this is to emulate Keats's *negative capability*, "that is, when a man is capable of being in uncertainties, mysteries, doubt, without any irritable reaching after fact and reason. . . . "

Irritations can also be useful, as goads and pinches and stings that drive us, for relief, to poetry. (Failure, of course, can be the most chafing of irritations.) Writing poetry may be a matter of finding our ease, our release, but it often dwells on what W.B. Yeats calls "The fascination of what's difficult." For the poet, failure need not be an end in itself. Allen Ginsberg talks about "a failure, big nothing—/ very satisfactory subjects for Poetry." Lucille Clifton, in "the making of poems," explains "these failures are my job."

10. Write a poem in which you attempt to do what you fear the most. (This exercise comes from Cynthia Macdonald, an especially venturesome poet whose books include *Amputations*, *Transplants*, *(W)holes*, and *Alternate Means of Transport*.)

11. Write a poem that celebrates, or at least comes to terms with, failure.

12. Write about something that seems difficult to do or to talk about, something that might be hard to explain, or painful, or embarrassing. Try not to apply the poetic "makeup" we often use to make ourselves "look better." Let the bruises and wrinkles and scars and stretch-marks show.

13. List pet peeves, things that bug you. Write about one or all of them, using imagery, sound effects, suggestive rhythms, vivid metaphors. A list structure, or something repetitive, might have the right obsessive quality. Think of it this way: If you were being tortured, what

would your tormenters do to upset and rattle you? If you were in hell, what would your punishment be?

14. Write from the viewpoint that you are nothing, empty, the least of beings. Don't dwell on this, like a moper or a whiner, but revel in it. See what floods into the poem when you squelch the ego.

15. Write the most difficult poem you can write. Then follow up by writing the easiest. To what extent is the *language* what's difficult or easy in these companion poems?

16. Find someone else's bad poem (perhaps in *The Stuffed Owl: An Anthology of Bad Verse*, edited by Wyndham Lewis and Charles Lee, Capricorn Books, 1962) and rewrite it, changing as much as you feel like changing: word choices, images, names, rhythms, phrasing. Start by making it appeal more to the senses.

17. Take two of your own "failed poems" and try combining them, keeping the good parts and deriving new energy from fusing together unrelated material. Find how they do relate. (This exercise comes from a "helpful hint" by Jon Anderson.)

MISTAKES

We all make — and love to point out in others — those significant verbal bloopers known as Freudian slips. In the process of writing, however, our inner editor is usually brutal about suppressing those telltale lapses. Sometimes they involve misspelling a word, or writing down a word you didn't intend, or saying a different word when reading the poem aloud, or stumbling over a word or phrase that's hard to say. The next time this happens, consider incorporating this "mistake" into your writing. Ask yourself *why* you stumbled or blurted. Are you evading the real right word? Are you avoiding something wild or bizarre that could wrench the poem out of your protective hands? Sometimes, it's simply a matter of rephrasing for a more euphonious sound, to eliminate the tongue twisters. But often there's a reason why things are hard to say: because they're hard to express or get out at all.

18. Elizabeth Bishop's wonderful, strange poem "The Man-Moth" is based on a newspaper misprint for "mammoth." Try to stumble across that kind of fertile error — either in a newspaper or magazine or book or conversation. Hunting deliberately for these mistakes will help scare them up. Try to recall an occasion when you, or someone else, fumbled a particular word or expression. (Children are especially adept at these felicitous verbal mishaps.) Write a poem about it.

19. Write a poem about misunderstanding an expression. (In Elizabeth Bishop's story "In the Village," the little girl thinks that a *mourning*

coat is a *morning* coat and wonders "Why, in the morning, did one put on black? How early in the morning did one begin? Before the sun came up?")

20. Write a poem in which you intentionally make mistakes: lapses in grammar, or wrong words, or stammering, or awkwardness. Make sure there's an *expressive* reason for these errors. For instance, a child, like the boy in Randall Jarrell's "The Truth," might "get everything wrong."

OMISSIONS

Poems often gain as much from what's left out as what's put in. How much can you avoid spelling out? How much can you hint at? How much can you actually do without? There are poets of inclusion, whose poems drag in wonders and debris, and there are poets of exclusion, who cut and pare and prune relentlessly and religiously. Most poets are hybrids.

In the notes to her *Complete Poems*, Marianne Moore remarks "Omissions are not accidents." She was talking about poems she had dropped, lines she had cut from surviving poems, but she makes a useful point for us. An important part of writing is *un*writing: eliminating what is false or boring or inessential.

21. In his novel *Alphabetical Africa*, Walter Abish uses only words beginning with the letter "a" in his first chapter. Here's a sample: "Abductors all agreed about abhorrent acts, about air attacks, about Alva and Alex and Allen all apart." In chapter two, he adds the letter "b," and so on in subsequent chapters until he has the entire alphabet at his disposal. Then he begins jettisoning the letters, finally returning, in his last chapter, to nothing but words beginning with "a." Choose a set of letters to use in a poem. If you play Scrabble, maybe seven would be a good number; you could draw tiles from a bag. Write a poem using only words beginning with the letters chosen or drawn at random. (Feel free to cheat a little, if you need a word like "the" or "and.") I once heard that Richard Howard assigned an exercise to type a poem using only one row of keys on a typewriter. That's another possibility.

22. Write a poem without any modifiers—no adjectives, no adverbs.

23. Write a poem without any similes, metaphors, or sensory images. Normally this is *not* what you'll probably want to do. Can you make a good poem even without those delights?

ENDINGS

The way a poem ends often makes or breaks it. Although it doesn't always need a slam-bang cymbal crash, it does need to resolve what's gone before, to resonate *beyond* the poem, and to offer the reader some discovery or realization, something gained by the poem (not, however, a moral or lesson or summary—at least not usually).

Robert Frost said "A poem begins in delight and ends in wisdom." That wisdom can be elusive, though, especially if you grasp after it. Delight can sometimes be merely frivolous, but you should trust it in poetry, plunge deeper into it, explore all its hidden passageways and mazes. Wisdom comes from the *process* of writing, not from prefabricated ideas. Insight, which is the secret goal of all good poems, comes from seeing *in* something, maybe something nebulous and undefinable, maybe something as definite as a moose. The poem is a prospector's venture, a quest (rather than an inquest), a trek of discovery. And what should be the "end of all our exploring"? In "Little Gidding," the last of his *Four Quartets*, T.S. Eliot said it was to arrive where we started, "and know the place for the first time." We are habitually as blind to what's right in front of us as we are to the invisible mysteries of the universe.

Even if we know how a story ends, we still have to discover the right words—and words inevitably remake the story. Some poets "aim" for a particular ending they know in advance, like navigators crossing volatile seas in search of a familiar harbor. But most poets begin a poem with little idea where their peregrinations will lead. That sense of adventuring through the imagination is what makes poetry writing so enjoyable—and so challenging.

Poems can end with an image, a statement, a question, a predicament, a string of fragmented words, the lilt of a song, a bit of everyday speech, a sudden recollection, a flash from the unconscious, a new possibility, or a circling back to earlier material. It needs to ring in the air; it needs an afterglow, however faint; it needs to stem the rhythmic flow without abruptness or awkwardness. T.S. Eliot ends "The Love Song of J. Alfred Prufrock" with what the Elizabethans would call "a dying fall." Sometimes a rhyme, even in an otherwise unrhymed poem, can "clinch" an ending. Sometimes the ending also concludes a long, winding sentence, or caps off a list. Sometimes short sentences, or one-word fragments, punctuate an ending effectively. The more good poems you read, the more you'll get a feel for how to resolve a poem. Everything else is just theory.

There's another "sense of an ending" as well, the letting go of the poem itself. How does the poet know when it's finished? For W.B. Yeats, it was like the click of a box being shut, once all the phrases, lines, rhymes, and stanzas were perfect. But for Paul Valery, the poem was never exactly finished: it was "abandoned." How much time should you spend with a poem? How long should you hang on to it? In "The Art of Poetry," Horace says that a poet should keep a poem nine years before publishing it: "What you have not published you will be able to destroy. The word once uncaged never comes home again." Elizabeth Bishop kept drafts of poems taped above her desk, hunting for the one right word that would fill in a last gap and thereby complete the whole poem. She would wait years, if necessary. She would withhold the poem if she couldn't find that word. Some poets return to already published poems and tinker compulsively, sometimes improving but sometimes damaging the texts. Robert Lowell was notorious for this, especially when he revised his collection *Notebook 1966-67* into *Notebook* and then into two collections, *History* and *For Lizzie and Harriet.* Yeats revised old published poems. But some poets disapprove of such tampering with the evidence. Should the poet of fifty rework (and thus censor) the work of his or her twenty-five-year-old self? Some poets, finally, write very quickly in the first place, releasing their poems almost immediately. It's hard to say which works better: letting go or sticking to it. It really depends on the poet and the particular poem.

24. Write a poem that's *about* the ending of something, a culmination, a demolition, a fading away. Maybe the tearing down of a hospital wing, or the final days of a season, or the demise of an enemy.

25. In a poem you want to revise, take an ending that "thumps" and rework it until it "eases" out of the poem, like a song fading out on a record. Or take a lackadaisical ending and give it some muscle.

26. In a poem you're unhappy with, change the ending. If you end with a statement, try capturing the same feeling with an image or gesture. Or maybe you *need* a statement if there isn't one now.

27. Extend a poem beyond its current ending.

28. End a poem *sooner* than its current ending.

29. Repeat or vary an earlier line to make an ending.

30. With a definite ending in mind (perhaps the actual wording of a last line), begin a poem in some mysterious place and try to find your way to the end.

31. Take a poem you can't seem to finish. Pull out the best line and use it to initiate a new poem.

Submitting Poems—Another Exercise

The actual mechanics of submitting poems to magazines are simple enough. Make sure your name and address appear on each page. Type your poems. Include no more than *one* poem per page, no matter how short it is. Include page numbers if a poem goes over a page in length. *Always* enclose a stamped, self-addressed envelope with sufficient postage for the return of your submissions.

Don't send dog-eared copies of poems with shoe marks where earlier editors have stomped on your work. Send fresh copies, legibly typed on bond paper that's not too thin. Editors hate "corrasable" paper, poor dot-matrix printouts, sloppy copies, anything handwritten. Some don't care for photocopies.

Should you enclose a cover letter? That depends. Will it help your submission or simply irritate the editor? Will the staff of the magazine make fun of your cover letter and pin it on a bulletin board? Do you know the editor? Has the editor asked to see more of your work? Do you have impressive credentials—publication credits, awards, teaching experience, an unusual background (time served in prison, years aboard ships, employment as an undertaker)—that may incline an editor favorably to your work? Do you need to fill in background to one of your poems? If you can be brief and professional, a cover letter probably won't hurt. Some editors appreciate the courtesy of a cover letter and take it as an indication that the poet is not mailing hundreds of photocopies of the same batch of poems all over the United States.

Multiple submission of poems has become more acceptable—as long as the editors are promptly notified when something they're considering has been taken elsewhere—but some editors can't be mollified. It's probably best to submit a given batch of poems to one magazine at a time, allowing three months before you write a query letter asking about their status. Book submissions can (and should) be multiple submitted.

Where should you send your poems? You should be familiar with the magazines to which you submit your poems. One way to find out what's available is to consult a guide to literary magazines, such as Judson Jerome's *Poet's Market* (Writer's Digest Books) and Len Fulton's *International Directory of Little Magazines* (Dustbooks). Both are updated each year. Try to read a magazine before you submit to it. You can order sample copies, or subscribe, or ask your local library to subscribe.

But the most important consideration is whether or not you feel ready to submit your poems. Are you confident enough to deal with the inevitable rejections? Will they hurt too much, or can you rebound and maybe learn something about your writing and your role as a poet? How much do you care about acceptance? Will rejection goad you to write better, or will it discourage you too much? Will *any* kind of acceptance do, or do you care passionately about where your poems will appear?

Emily Dickinson says "Publication — is the Auction of the Mind." It's hard for most of us to be so rigorous and principled. We want to share our work, circulate it as widely as possible, and crown ourselves, Napoleon-like and Keats-like, with the poet's laurel. Keats, though, felt ashamed of his audacity. If, like Shelley, we feel that poets are "the unacknowledged legislators of the world," then publication is the mandate we require.

Submitting poems takes nerve and verve. It takes an amazing amount of conceit and self-regard. We'd do well to end this consideration by mulling over Rainer Maria Rilke's advice in *Letters to a Young Poet* (translated by M.D. Herter Norton): " . . . you are disturbed when certain editors reject your efforts. Now (since you have allowed me to advise you) I beg you to give up all that. You are looking outward, and that above all you should not do now. Nobody can counsel and help you, nobody. There is only one single way. Go into yourself."

Index

Index to Exercises

Annual Market Directories
Save 15% on the following
Writer's Digest Books Annual Directories!

Maximize your chances of selling your work with these market directories that offer up-to-date listings of markets for your books, articles, stories, novels, poems, gags, photos, designs, illustrations, and more. Each listing gives contact name and address, details on the type(s) of work they're seeking, pay/royalty rates, and submission requirements, to help you target your work to the best prospects.

Artist's Market, edited by Jenny Pfalzgraf $22.95
Children's Writer's & Illustrator's Market, edited by Christine Martin (paper) $19.95
Guide to Literary Agents & Art/Photo Reps, edited by Roseann Biederman $18.95
Novel & Short Story Writer's Market, edited by Robin Gee (paper) $19.95
Mystery Writer's Marketplace and Sourcebook, edited by Donna Collingwood $17.95
Photographer's Market, edited by Michael Willins $22.95
Poet's Market, by Michael J. Bugeja and Christine Martin $19.95
Songwriter's Market, edited by Cindy Laufenburg $19.95
Writer's Market, edited by Mark Garvey $26.95
Market Guide for Young Writers, by Kathy Henderson $16.95

To receive your **15%** discount on any of the above listed Market Books, simply mention **#6299** when phoning in your order to toll-free **1-800-289-0963.**

General Writing Books
Discovering the Writer Within, by Bruce Ballenger & Barry Lane $18.95
Freeing Your Creativity, by Marshall Cook $17.95
Getting the Words Right: How to Rewrite, Edit and Revise, by Theodore A. Rees Cheney (paper) $12.95
How to Write a Book Proposal, by Michael Larsen (paper) $11.95
How to Write Fast While Writing Well, by David Fryxell $17.95
How to Write with the Skill of a Master and the Genius of a Child, by Marshall J. Cook $18.95
Knowing Where to Look: The Ultimate Guide to Research, by Lois Horowitz (paper) $19.95
On Being a Writer, edited by Bill Strickland (paper) $16.95
Research & Writing: A Complete Guide and Handbook, by Shah Malmoud (paper) $18.95
Shift Your Writing Career into High Gear, by Gene Perret $16.95
The 30-Minute Writer: How to Write and Sell Short Pieces, by Connie Emerson $17.95
30 Steps to Becoming a Writer, by Scott Edelstein $16.95
The 28 Biggest Writing Blunders, by William Noble $12.95
The 29 Most Common Writing Mistakes & How to Avoid Them, by Judy Delton (paper) $9.95
The Wordwatcher's Guide to Good Writing & Grammar, by Morton S. Freeman (paper) $15.95
The Writer's Book of Checklists, by Scott Edelstein $16.95
The Writer's Digest Guide to Manuscript Formats, by Buchman & Groves $18.95
The Writer's Essential Desk Reference, edited by Glenda Neff $19.95
Write Tight: How to Keep Your Prose Sharp, Focused and Concise, by William Brohaugh $16.95
Writing as a Road to Self-Discovery, by Barry Lane $16.95
Nonfiction Writing
How to Do Leaflets, Newsletters, & Newspapers, by Nancy Brigham (paper) $14.95
How to Write Irresistible Query Letters, by Lisa Collier Cool (paper) $10.95
The Complete Guide to Magazine Article Writing, by John M. Wilson $17.95
The Writer's Complete Guide to Conducting Interviews, by Michael Schumacher $14.95
The Writer's Digest Handbook of Magazine Article Writing, edited by Jean M. Fredette (paper) $11.95
Writing Articles From the Heart: How to Write & Sell Your Life Experiences, by Marjorie Holmes $16.95
Fiction Writing
The Art & Craft of Novel Writing, by Oakley Hall $17.95
Beginnings, Middles and Ends, by Nancy Kress $13.95
Characters & Viewpoint, by Orson Scott Card $13.95
The Complete Guide to Writing Fiction, by Barnaby Conrad $18.95
Creating Characters: How to Build Story People, by Dwight V. Swain $16.95
Creating Short Fiction, by Damon Knight (paper) $11.95
Dialogue, by Lewis Turco $13.95
Get That Novel Started! (And Keep Going 'Til You Finish), by Donna Levin $17.95
How to Write & Sell Your First Novel, by Collier & Leighton (paper) $13.95
Manuscript Submission, by Scott Edelstein $13.95
Plot, by Ansen Dibell $13.95
Practical Tips for Writing Popular Fiction, by Robyn Carr $17.95
Scene and Structure by Jack Bickham $14.95
Theme & Strategy, by Ronald B. Tobias $13.95
The 38 Most Common Fiction Writing Mistakes, by Jack M. Bickham $12.95
20 Master Plots (And How to Build Them), by Ronald B. Tobias $16.95
Writer's Digest Handbook of Novel Writing, $18.95
Writing the Novel: From Plot to Print, by Lawrence Block (paper) $11.95

Special Interest Writing Books

Armed & Dangerous: A Writer's Guide to Weapons, by Michael Newton (paper) $14.95

Cause of Death: A Writer's Guide to Death, Murder & Forensic Medicine, by Keith D. Wilson, M.D. $15.95

Children's Writer's Word Book, by Alijandra Mogliner $19.95

Comedy Writing Secrets, by Mel Helitzer (paper) $15.95

The Complete Book of Feature Writing, by Leonard Witt $18.95

Creating Poetry, by John Drury $18.95

Deadly Doses: A Writer's Guide to Poisons, by Serita Deborah Stevens with Anne Klarner (paper) $16.95

Editing Your Newsletter, by Mark Beach (paper) $18.95

Families Writing, by Peter Stillman (paper) $12.95

A Guide to Travel Writing & Photography, by Ann & Carl Purcell (paper) $22.95

How to Write & Sell Greeting Cards, Bumper Stickers, T-Shirts and Other Fun Stuff, by Molly Wigand (paper) 15.95

How to Write Horror Fiction, by William F. Nolan $15.95

How to Write Mysteries, by Shannon OCork $13.95

How to Write Romances, by Phyllis Taylor Pianka $15.95

How to Write Science Fiction & Fantasy, by Orson Scott Card $13.95

How to Write the Story of Your Life, by Frank P. Thomas (paper) $12.95

The Poet's Handbook, by Judson Jerome (paper) $12.95

Police Procedural: A Writer's Guide to the Police and How They Work, by Russell Bintliff (paper) $16.95

Powerful Business Writing, by Tom McKeown $12.95

Private Eyes: A Writer's Guide to Private Investigators, by H. Blythe, C. Sweet, & J. Landreth (paper) $15.95

Scene of the Crime: A Writer's Guide to Crime-Scene Investigation, by Anne Wingate, Ph.D. $15.95

Successful Scriptwriting, by Jurgen Wolff & Kerry Cox (paper) $14.95

The Writer's Complete Crime Reference, by Martin Roth $19.95

The Writer's Guide to Creating a Science Fiction Universe, by George Ochoa & Jeff Osier $18.95

The Writer's Guide to Everyday Life in the 1800s, by Marc McCutcheon $18.95

Writing for Children & Teenagers, 3rd Edition, by L. Wyndham & Arnold Madison (paper) $12.95

Writing Mysteries: A Handbook by the Mystery Writers of America, Edited by Sue Grafton, $18.95

The Writing Business

The Complete Guide to Self-Publishing, by Tom & Marilyn Ross (paper) $18.95

How You Can Make $25,000 a Year Writing, by Nancy Edmonds Hanson (paper) $14.95

This Business of Writing, by Gregg Levoy $19.95

To order directly from the publisher, include $3.00 postage and handling for 1 book and $1.00 for each additional book. Allow 30 days for delivery.

Writer's Digest Books
1507 Dana Avenue, Cincinnati, Ohio 45207
Credit card orders call TOLL-FREE
1-800-289-0963
Stock is limited on some titles; prices subject to change without notice.

Write to this same address for information on *Writer's Digest* magazine, *Story* magazine, Writer's Digest Book Club, Writer's Digest School, and Writer's Digest Criticism Service.